1999

Managing Financial Resources in Sport and Leisure Service Organizations

Russell E. Brayley and Daniel D. McLean

Sagamore Publishing

Champaign, IL 61820
www.sagamorepub.com

ISBN: 1-57167-454-3

Library of Congress Catalog Card Number: 99-65696

Cover Design: Jennie Scott

Interior Design: Janet Wahlfeldt

Cover Photos: Courtesy of Jennie Scott

Copy Editor: David Hamburg

Sagamore Publishing, Inc.
P.O. Box 647
Champaign, IL 61824-0647
Web Site: http//www.sagamorepub.com

Dedication

To Our Families

Renée, Doug, Austin, Erika, Natalie

• Russell Brayley

JoAnn, Donna, Jennifer, Suzanne, Timothy, Sally, Michael, and Kristine

• Daniel McLean

Table of Contents

PREFACE   xii

SECTION A—Concepts and Practices of Financial Management   1

Chapter

1. Economic Principles   **3**

    Introduction   3

    Supply and Demand   4

    Estimating Supply and Demand   7

    Inflation   14

    Interest   14

    Future Value   15

    Present Value   17

    Depreciation   18

    Economic Impacts   21

    Summary   24

2. Financial Management in Public, Private Not-for-profit, and Commercial Sport and Leisure Organizations   **27**

    Introduction   27

    Public Enterprises   27

       Legislative/Legal Parameters   28

       Social Roles/Expectations   28

       Market Management Techniques   28

       Indicators of Success   29

       Financial Management Opportunities and Challenges   29

       Other   29

    Private Non-Profit Enterprises   30

       Legislative/Legal Parameters   30

Social Roles/Expectations   31

Market Management Techniques   31

Indicators of Success   31

Financial Management Opportunities and Challenges   31

Other   32

Commercial Enterprises   32

Legislative/Legal Parameters   32

Social Roles/Expectations   32

Market Management Techniques   33

Indicators of Success   33

Financial Management Opportunities and Challenges   33

Competition and Cooperation   34

Summary   35

3. Organization   **37**

Introduction   37

Financial Responsibility   38

Financial Functions of the Organization   38

Organizational Structures   39

Director of Finance   39

Controller (also called "Comptroller")   39

Treasurer   39

Assessor   39

Purchasing Agent   39

Auditor   40

Organization for Financial Management in the Public Sector   40

Organization for Financial Management in the Private Nonprofit
 and Commercial Sectors   42

Politics and the Financial Management Organization   42

Summary   43

SECTION B—Revenue Management   45

4. Income Sources   **47**

  Introduction   47

  Types of Income Sources   47

  Compulsory Income Sources   48

      Types of State and Municipal Taxes   49

          Real Property Taxes   49

          Other Types of Taxes   52

      Other Sources of Compulsory Income   53

          Special Assessments, Dedication Ordinances and
          Regulations   53

          Licenses and Permits   54

          Federal Government Sources   54

  Gratuitous Income   55

  Earned Income   56

  Investment Income   58

  Contractual Receipts   58

  Partnerships and Collaborations   59

  Revenue Structure Plan   60

  Summary   62

5. Pricing   **63**

  Introduction   63

  Purposes of Pricing   63

      Pricing to Recover Costs   63

      Pricing to Create New Resources (Added Value Pricing)   64

      Pricing to Establish Value   64

      Pricing to Influence Behavior   64

      Pricing to Promote Efficiency   65

      Pricing to Promote Equity   66

The Appropriateness and Feasibility of Pricing   66

The Nature of Price   67

    Monetary Price   67

    Opportunity Price   68

    Psychological Price   68

    Effort Price   68

    Approaches to Establishing Price   69

        Calculating Costs for Unit Pricing   70

        Subsidization and Unit Pricing   72

        Other Considerations in Establishing Price   74

            Willingness to Pay / The Going Rate   74

            Sensitivity to Changes in Price   76

            Adjusting Prices   78

    Summary   80

6. Grantseeking   **81**

Introduction   81

Why Pursue Grants?   81

The Grantmaking Environment   82

The Grantseeking Process   84

    Step 1: Identifying a Potential Idea   84

    Step 2: Discovery, Selection, and Contact with a Granting Agency 85

        Searching for Grantmakers   86

        Selecting a Grantmaker   88

        Contacting the Grantmaker   88

        Securing Grant Guidelines   90

    Step 3: Preparation of the Grant Proposal   90

        Cover Letter   91

        Executive Summary   91

        Statement of Need   92

        Project Description   93

Organizational Information 95

Budget 95

Evaluation Process 96

Commitment and Capability 97

Step 4: Submission of Grant Proposal 97

Step 5: Grantmaker's Decision 97

Step 6: Grant Administration 98

Summary 99

7. Philanthropy and Fundraising **101**

Introduction 101

Philanthropy 101

Why Fundraising is Important 102

The Role of Fund Development 103

Why People Give 104

Charitable Organizations 105

Fund Development 106

Fundraising Sources 108

Goal Setting, Relationships, and the Gift Pyramid 110

Goal Setting 111

The Gift Pyramid 112

Fundraising Strategies 113

Annual Campaigns 113

Planned Giving 114

Special Events 117

Support Organizations 117

Summary 118

SECTION C—Expenditure Management   121

8. Accounting / Reporting   **123**

Introduction   123

Stock and Flow   124

     The Balance Sheet   124

     The Income Statement   126

Internal Control   127

     Petty Cash   129

Reporting   130

     The Budget Statement   130

     Project / Event Report   132

Summary   133

9. Budget Preparation   **135**

Introduction   135

Budget Processes   135

     What is a budget?   135

     The Budget Cycle   136

         Budget Preparation Cycle   137

Funds   140

Budget Presentation Format   143

Budget Preparation Activities   143

     The Relationship of Strategic Planning to Budget Preparation   149

     Budget Preparation Philosophies   149

     Preparing the Departmental Work plan   150

     Estimating Personnel Service Requirements   151

     Staffing Issues   152

     Determining Salary Costs   153

     Contractual Service Requirements   156

     Materials, Supplies, and Equipment Costs   157

Reviewing Budget Estimates at the Department Level 158

Preparing a Simple Activity Budget 158

Summary 162

10. Budget Formats **163**

Introduction 163

Budget Formats 163

Object Classification / Line Item Budget 163

Program Budget 169

Performance Budget 172

Running Budget 176

Zero Based Budgeting 178

Advantages and Disadvantages of Zero-Based Budgeting 181

Modified Zero Based Budgeting 182

Budget Presentation 182

Summary 183

SECTION D—Long-Term Financial Planning 185

11. Business Planning **187**

Introduction 187

Format of the Business Plan 188

Title Page 188

Front Matter 189

Executive Summary 189

The Enterprise 190

The Industry 190

Product/Service Offering 191

Market Analysis 192

Market Plan 192

Development Plan 193

Production/Operations Plan 193

Management team   194

Financial Plan   195

    Current Financial Statements   195

    Financial Projections (for new enterprises)   195

    Ratio Analysis   196

  Appendices   201

Summary   202

12. Capital Budgeting   **203**

Introduction   203

Capital Budgeting in the Public Sector   203

  The Capital Budgeting Process   204

Capital Improvement Revenue Sources   209

  Bonds   211

  Other Capital Improvement Revenue Sources   214

Capital Budgeting in the Commercial Sector   217

  Decision Processes   217

  Income Sources for Commercial Capital Projects   220

Summary   220

Index   **223**

Preface

Effective managers in sport and leisure service organizations are required to have a wide variety of skills and a good understanding of all of the resources that they manage. Not only should they be competent as personnel managers, but they also need to know how to manage their physical facilities. In addition, they need to be effective in their management of time, for time is one resource that cannot be renewed. Good managers also need to know how to use their financial resources effectively.

Throughout the history of our profession, there have never been times of such great prosperity that decisions could be made or practices maintained without consideration of their financial implications. Certainly, there have been situations where financial constraints have been minimal, but even then, some measure of financial accountability has been required of those who receive and spend an organization's money.

Similarly, there has never been a time of such flexibility that some degree of planning was not required of resource managers. In fact, experience has shown that a lack of planning reduces flexibility, as choices are replaced by externally controlled consequences. Budgeting and long-term financial planning are areas of understanding and skill that every sport and leisure service manager must develop and magnify.

This book has been written with the needs of the sport and leisure service manager in mind. It has been written by two people who have worked in a variety of sport and leisure settings in several different parts of the United States and Canada and who have discovered that there is no place to hide from the opportunity or responsibility to know about budgets, finance, and fiscal management. It has been written for the mathematically challenged, for the preprofessional, for the professional who received on-the-job training, and for the professional who is keenly interested in and dedicated to continuous improvement.

Readers will learn important principles of economics and finance. They will also learn the skills necessary to prepare, present, and manage budgets, as well as generate revenues for capital development and day-to-day operations. Discussions include examples from the "real world" and offer illustrations to facilitate the learning of some of the more complex or technical points.

Section A

Concepts and Practices of Financial Management

The first three chapters of this book lay the foundation for detailed discussions of the most important aspects of managing financial resources in sport and leisure service organizations. Although we could have provided the reader with a thorough introduction to and exploration of the principles of economics as a preface to an examination of the structural or technical aspects of financial management, we have chosen to highlight and discuss in Chapter 1 only those basic economic principles of most immediate concern to managers in the field. Later in this section, the reader will also be introduced to the sport and leisure service delivery system. Chapter 2 compares and contrasts the public, private, nonprofit, and commercial sectors with respect to financial management problems, opportunities, structures, and issues. Chapter 3 describes typical approaches to organization for financial management and outlines the responsibilities and activities of different financial officers that might be included in the management or support teams of the sport and leisure service enterprise.

Chapter 1

Economic Principles

Introduction

An effective sports and leisure service manager is not only capable of establishing, directing, and implementing procedures of sound financial management, but he is also aware of the basic economic and accounting principles that relate to those procedures. This first chapter introduces some elementary economic concepts that are particularly relevant to financial management in sports and leisure service organizations. It should be noted that this is a very basic discussion of a few key principles and in no way is meant to supplant the valuable learning that can be gained from a full course of studies in economics.

While financial management and accounting require development of technical proficiency, we gain from their parent discipline an understanding of the human element of resource allocation. Economics is a social science which contains specific assumptions about the way people behave as they allocate available resources for the purpose of realizing their wants and needs. Economics involves the measurement and quantification of observed or expected relationships and transactions between economic agents. Individuals, families, teams, government departments, and not-for-profit and business organizations are all examples of economic agents.

When, for example, an event manager predicts the attendance at a championship baseball game for which the admission price is $8.00, he applies his understanding of the economic principles of supply and demand. If a public recreation administrator is trying to decide whether investing today in a particular recreation facility or piece of equipment will provide the future returns that she feels are appropriate, she will need to apply her understanding of the economic concepts of inflation, interest, and future values. Furthermore, accounting for the changing value of facilities or equipment over time requires a manager to understand the notion of depreciation, and articulating the benefits of a sports or leisure program or enterprise will require an understanding of multipliers, leakage, and interindustry purchasing as they relate to economic impact assessment.

These key economic principles are important to the effective management of programs, events, and facilities. Among other benefits to be gained from studying economics and understanding these few principles is an increased ability to recognize and measure the probable financial outcomes of decisions that might be made with respect to product development, pricing, and promotion. Exploring and understanding these principles can help managers of leisure and sport services to see the full effect and impact of specific financial decisions and thereby enhance their ability to meet successfully their respective financial objectives.

Supply and Demand

The terms supply and demand have more precise meanings than are suggested in their everyday use. In casual conversation, for example, reference is made to the supply of gasoline, and an opinion might be expressed that, after learning about the huge oil reserves in the Persian Gulf, there is a large supply of gasoline—certainly enough to meet the public demand. More correctly, the assertion is that there is a large stock of gasoline—enough to meet current needs. The difference between stock and supply is subtle, but important. Stock refers to the quantity of a product or resource that exists. Supply refers to the quantity of a product or resource that the owner is willing to offer or make available at a given price. Oil-producing nations with large petroleum reserves have extensive stock, but may have a very small supply when the price being offered is only 10 cents per barrel. Without any change in the stock of oil, the supply would increase significantly if the price rose to $25 per barrel. Similarly, there is a very small supply of excellent basketball players who will play for a professional team when offered a salary of $50 per year. The supply will, however, increase considerably when the annual salary offer goes to $50 million. In this illustration, the number of excellent basketball players did not increase, but the supply for the professional league did. The relationship between quantity made available and the price offered is graphically represented in Figure 1.1 and is referred to as the supply curve.

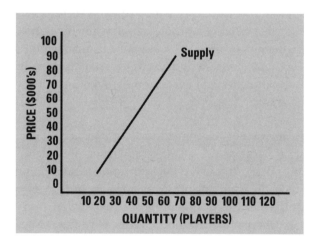

Figure 1.1. The supply curve for athletes in a professional sport.

From the data presented in Figure 1.1, it appears that there are only about 25 excellent basketball players who are willing to play for a professional team for $20,000 per year. There are, of course, many more equally talented players, but they probably will choose to pursue more lucrative careers for which their college education has prepared them. When the invitation to join the team comes with a $40,000 salary offer, there are many more (about 40) players willing to consider the opportunity. Teams that offer $90,000 per year find an even greater number (approximately 70) of excellent players from whom to recruit. The supply curve illustrates the human behavior expected in situations of exchange. The supply curve shows how the quantities that are available increase and decrease in relation to the prices offered for the product or resource.

In discussing demand, it is common to refer to the amount wanted or needed. The more traveling a team wants to do, the more it wants gasoline for its bus. However, the precise meaning of demand is the amount of a product or resource wanted at a given price. When the consumer price of gasoline is 30 cents per gallon, the team is more inclined to travel, and the quantity of gasoline wanted is greater than when the price is $2.40 per gallon. Similarly, if would-be professional athletes are demanding annual salaries of $20 million to play, the number of teams and the number of player positions will be less than if players can be contracted for $50,000 per year. The relationship between quantity wanted and the price of the resource is graphically represented in Figure 1.2 and is referred to as the demand curve.

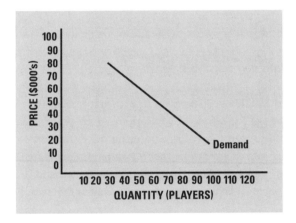

Figure 1.2. The demand curve for athletes in a professional sport.

Using the demand curve represented in Figure 1.2, it is observed that when players demand $80,000 salaries, the league is only interested in or able to acquire approximately 25 players. If the salaries are only $20,000, perhaps smaller markets can afford to have teams, team rosters can be expanded, and more players (approximately 100) will be needed. As the price goes down, the demand goes up.

The supply and demand curves shown in Figures 1.1 and 1.2, respectively, appear to be straight lines rather than arc-like curves. The extent of curvature will vary according to the nature of the resource and the behavior of the market. A straight line may, in fact, be the best representation of the price/quantity relationship and is, for convenience and simplicity, used in our discussion of supply and demand. All curves shown in Figure 1.3 can be accurate reflections of either supply or demand.

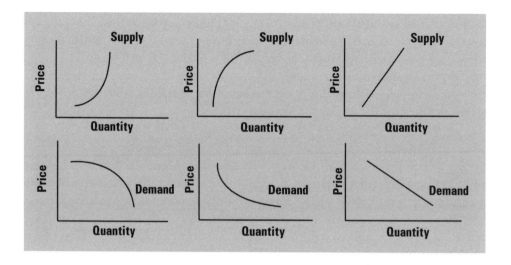

Figure 1.3. Examples of supply and demand curves.

It might also be observed, when comparing the above supply and demand curves, that the supply and demand curves slope in opposing directions. Supply curves have a positive slope. That is, they show that the quantity made available increases when the price offered increases. Conversely, demand curves have a negative slope. This means that increases in price are associated with decreases in the quantity wanted.

If the supply curve and the demand curve for a particular product or service are both drawn on the same field, they will intersect at some point. This point is called the equilibrium point. At the equilibrium point, the corresponding price motivates the supplier to make available the same quantity of a resource that is wanted by the consumers at that price. At any price above the equilibrium point, there is insufficient demand (i.e., too much supply). At any price below the equilibrium point, there is inadequate supply (i.e., too much demand).

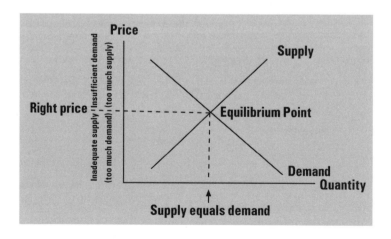

Figure 1.4. The supply/demand equilibrium point.

Supply and demand curves are constructed using data that describe the availability of and the want for resources at different prices. They are the result of experimentation, simulation, and observation of behaviors in similar exchange situations. In the following example, some very simple data will be used to illustrate three different approaches to the estimation of supply and/or demand.

Estimating Supply and Demand

Data:

A marina developer calculated that appropriate revenues could be generated if he offered 20 boat slips for $10 each. If, somehow, his customers could be convinced to pay $90 for a slip, the developer could build a larger facility and realize appropriate revenues by offering 73 boat slips. After studying marina operations at another waterfront in the area, he found that one which charged only $20 was able to attract 100 customers, and another which charged $80 attracted only 25 boat owners. These data are summarized in Table 1.1.

Price	Supply	Demand
$90	73	
$80		25
$40	?	?
$20		100
$10	20	

Table 1.1. Summary of supply and demand data for proposed marina.

Problems:

- How many boat slips should he build if he decides to charge $40 per slip?

- How many customers would want his $40 boat slips?

- At what price will the supply of boat slips equal the demand?

- How many boat slips should he build in order to take full advantage of the demand without creating more capacity than is necessary?

There are three approaches to solving these problems: (1) visual graphing, (2) algebraic graphing, and (3) algebra. These approaches are explained in the following examples:

i. Visual Graphing

Using graph paper, plot the known data points and draw the supply and demand curves (Figure 1.5). For a given price, find its intercept on the supply or demand curve and identify the corresponding points on the horizontal axis representing units of supply/demand. For example, at $40, it appears that the supply will be about 40 units and the demand will be for about 75 units.

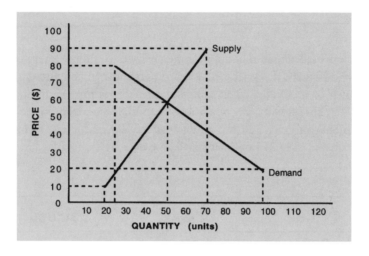

Figure 1.5. Supply/demand curve graph.

It also appears that the equilibrium point (where the supply and demand curves intersect) is somewhere around the $60 mark, with supply and demand at that price being approximately 50 units.

ii. Algebraic Graphing

Plot the data with reasonable accuracy, but not necessarily with exactness.

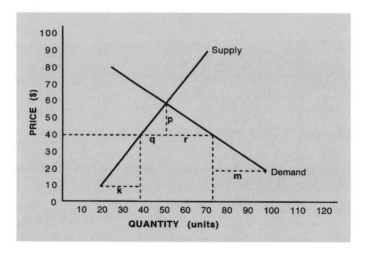

Figure 1.6. Reference algebraic graphing solution.

First calculate the slopes of the supply and demand curves (note: means "change in").

$$\text{Slope = Rise/Run}$$

$$\text{Slope (supply)} = \Delta\text{price}/ \Delta\text{quantity}$$

$$= (90\text{-}10) / (73\text{-}20)$$
$$= 1.5$$

$$\text{Slope (demand)} = \Delta\text{price}/ \Delta\text{quantity}$$

$$= (80\text{-}20) / (25\text{-}100)$$
$$= \text{-}0.8$$

Next, calculate the supply at the given price of $40. For the supply curve, find the known coordinates of any point on the line. For example, use $10 and 20 units and a slope of 1.5.

At $40, the supply is (20 + k). Since the price increases from $10 to $40, Δprice = 30 and Δquantity = k.

$$\text{Slope (supply)} = \Delta\text{price} / \Delta\text{quantity}$$

$$1.5 = 30 / k$$

$$k = 20$$

Look again at the reference graph (Figure 1.6). The information needed to calculate the distance of line q + r is now available.

$$\text{q+r = the demand at \$40 - the supply at \$40}$$

$$\text{q+r} = 75\text{-}40 = 35$$

Using the slope information, it is also known that r = p / -0.8, and q = p/1.5. Therefore:

$$(p / \text{-}0.8) + (p / 1.5) = 35$$

$$p = 18.3$$

The price at equilibrium is $40 + p which equals $58.30.

To estimate the quantity at equilibrium, use the calculated value of p and the slope information to calculate either q or r.

r = p / slope(demand)   or   q = p / slope(supply)

r = 18.3 / -0.8   q = 18.3 / 1.5

r = -22.8   q = 12.2

The quantity supplied and demanded at equilibrium is:

75 - 22.8 = 52.2 units   or   40 + 12.2 = 52.2 units

iii. Algebra

Use the formula for calculating any point on a straight line. In this case, the straight lines are slopes.

y=ax+b

where: y is a given price

x is the quantity supplied or demanded at that price

a is the slope of the supply or demand curve

b is a constant

First calculate the slopes of the supply and demand curves:

Slope (supply) = Δprice / Δquality

=(90-10) / (73-20)

=1.5

Slope (demand) = Δprice / Δquality

=(80-20) / (25-100)

= -0.8

Next, calculate the constants for both the supply and demand curves:

For the supply curve, use the known coordinates of any point on the line. For example, use $10 and 20 units and a slope of 1.5. Thus:

$$10 = 1.5 (20) + b$$

$$b = -20$$

Likewise, for the demand curve, use the known coordinates of any point on the line. For example, use $20 and 100 units and a slope of -0.9. Thus:

$$20 = -0.8 (100) + b$$

$$b = 100$$

To estimate the supply and demand when the price is $40, simply use 40 as the value for y, use the same values for the slope and the constant, and solve for x.

(ignore the minus sign)

Supply	Demand
$y = 1.5x - 20$	$y = -0.8x + 100$
$40 = 1.5x - 20$	$40 = -0.8x + 100$
$x = 40$ units	$x = -75$ units

Therefore, if the price is set at $40, the supply will be 40 units, but the demand will be for 75 units. It would be useful to find a price where the supply meets the demand and to know what that supply/demand quantity will be.

With slopes and constants already established, x (the quantity at equilibrium) can be calculated by equating y (price), even though its value is not yet known.

If y(supply) = y(demand), then

$$1.5x - 20 = -0.8x + 100.$$

$$x = 52 \text{ (the quantity supplied/demanded at the equilibrium point)}$$

To calculate the price at equilibrium, substitute the calculated value for x in either of the equations for supply or demand.

Supply: $y = 1.5 (52) - 20$ Demand: $y = -0.8 (52) + 100$

$y = \$58$ $y = \$58$

It has now been determined that, at a price of $58, the supply and demand will both be 52 units.

It is important to note that supply and demand curves are not fixed for eternity. Rather, they reflect the behavior of a certain market or industry at a particular time. Either curve or both curves may change in response to common circumstances or conditions. For example, the pattern of demand for spectator seating at a high school football game may move to the right (i.e., more will be demanded at a given price) if it begins to be apparent that the team has a good chance of qualifying for the state championship for the first time in 25 years. Likewise, the curve can move to the left (i.e., less will be demanded at a given price) if the football team consistently loses by 30 or more points to competitors who play their second string for three quarters of the game. Such movements in patterns of demand do not necessarily change the supply curve, but they will likely affect stock. Refer to the new equilibrium point shown in Figure 1.7 and notice how the number of seats that can be sold and the price at which they can be sold increase solely as a result of change in demand.

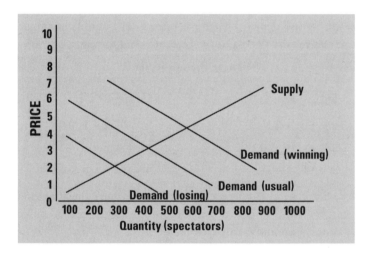

Figure 1.7. Illustration of shifts in the demand curve.

Not only can shifts in demand occur, but also attitudes about and opportunities for supply can change. For example, a Boy Scout camp may, because of surplus capacity and a generous operating grant, be able to substantially reduce individual participation fees for the usual number of campers. This price reduction also means that the camp administrators will be under pressure to serve more campers because of the increased demand at those lower prices. Figure 1.8 illustrates the impacts of changes in supply conditions.

There are many conditions that can influence shifts in supply and demand curves. Generally, they relate to capacity and production opportunity, or to consumer need and sentiment. Some of the most common influences of supply and demand for leisure and sport services are identified in Table 1.2.

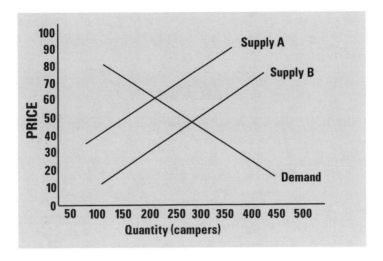

Figure 1.8. Illustration of shifts in the supply curve.

Condition	Influence
Increased ability to offer services due to: —new or expanded facilities —new or expanded staff —new equipment —staff with new skills/certification	Move supply curve to the right.
Reduced capacity of physical plant	Move supply curve to the left.
Realization of greater efficiency due to economies of scale.	Move supply curve to the right.
Revised operational mandate or mission.	Move supply curve in either direction.
Change in market need / problem resolution.	Move demand curve to left if problem resolved or need reduced. New problems or needs move demand curve to the right.
Change in market resources.	Move demand curve to the right if time, money, transportation, etc., more available. Move demand curve to left if constraints increased.
Panic / Perception of scarcity.	Move demand curve to right.
Competition	Move demand curve to the left.

Table 1.2. Common influences on supply and demand for leisure and sport services.

Managers of leisure and sport services who understand the economic principles of supply and demand are well equipped to deal with the relative uncertainties of forecasting revenues and anticipating expenses. They are better able to apply the art of anticipating human behavior in exchange situations to the technical process of budgeting and other aspects of financial management.

Inflation

In discussing the principles of supply and demand, it is evident that decisions with regard to the offering of or desire for stock reflect the natural desire of both producers and consumers to maximize their returns. Consumers want as much as they can get for the least amount of money, while suppliers want as much money as they can get for the least amount of stock depletion. Human nature is such that, in a free market economy, this valued drive for maximization results in a gradual increase in the price of goods and services. This phenomenon is called inflation. The impact of inflation is the erosion of the purchasing power of financial resources that do not grow at least at the rate of inflation. The challenge to the leisure and sport service manager is to protect vital resources from the eroding effects of inflation.

Interest

Regardless of the source of money that a leisure or sport organization acquires and uses in its operation, interest will play a significant role in financial decisions. If the financial resources used by the organization come from lenders or investors, then interest will be paid to them in addition to the original amount borrowed or invested. If the funds used come from internal reserves, then their use will reduce the interest that could have been earned by those reserves. The impact of interest should not be ignored. In fact, this point is emphasized in the unofficial definition: "Interest—those who understand it, get it; those who don't, pay it."

Interest is the time value of money. It represents what it costs an economic agent to consume immediately by using funds that it does not have. It represents what an economic agent receives for postponing consumption by lending or investing funds that it does have. Interest is typically expressed as a percentage of an original amount (called principal) that is paid by a borrower or earned by a lender on a per annum basis. For example, 7% interest on a principal of $2,000 would oblige a borrower to pay the lender the original $2,000 plus $140 interest after one year. The lender may extend the loan period for one more year, after which the borrower would repay the $2,000, plus another $140 (if interest was also paid after the first year). In this case, the time value of the money was $280. If the borrower did not make the $140 interest payment after the first year, that amount would be considered as an additional loan and be added to the principal to be repaid after the second year. After the second year, the borrower would, in addition to the $2,140 principal, pay an interest charge of $149.80 (7% of $2,140). The total time value of the money when the interest is compounded (i.e., carried over and included in the principal) was $140.00 + $149.80 = $289.80.

Future Value

Unless the owner of money hides it in a sock or under the mattress, that money will be invested and thereby has the potential to grow or increase in value over time. Such is the effect of interest. However, the effect of inflation is the erosion of the purchasing power of money over time. Obviously, it is hoped that the rate of growth will be greater than the rate of inflation. The financial manager works to protect the purchasing power of the leisure and sport organization's money. In other words, the financial manager's first goal is to ensure that the future value of a sum is sufficient to overcome the impact of inflation. Earlier in this chapter, it was shown how a sum of money increases in value over time, thanks to interest. The *future value* of an investment can be calculated as follows:

If interest is paid each year for a given number of years, the future value (F) of an original sum is $P+n$ (Pi), where P = the principal (the original amount invested), n = the term (number of years until repayment of the principal), and i = the interest rate. After 2 years, the value of $2,000 earning 7% paid annually is:

$$F = P+n \ (Pi)$$

$$2000 + 2(2000 \times .07) = \$2,280.$$

If the interest is compounded, the future value of the original sum is calculated using a more complicated formula:

$$F = P(1+ i)^n$$

Fortunately, table values can be used to avoid calculation of $(1+i)^n$. Interest Table A (which can be found at the end of this chapter and is excerpted here in Table 1.3) provides interest factors (T_A) to be substituted in a restated formula for the future value of a sum with interest compounded. The restated formula is $F = PT_A$.

Attendance at amusement parks is growing as rides are becoming more innovative.

n\i	6%	7%	8%	9%	10%	12%	15%
1	1.060	1.070	1.080	1.090	1.100	1.120	1.150
2	1.124	1.145	1.166	1.188	1.210	1.254	1.323
3	1.191	1.225	1.260	1.295	1.331	1.405	1.521
4	1.262	1.311	1.360	1.412	1.464	1.574	1.749
5	1.338	1.403	1.469	1.539	1.611	1.762	2.011
6	1.419	1.501	1.587	1.677	1.772	1.974	2.313
7	1.504	1.606	1.714	1.828	1.949	2.211	2.660
8	1.594	1.718	1.851	1.993	2.172	2.476	3.059
9	1.689	1.838	1.999	2.172	2.358	2.773	3.518
10	1.791	1.967	2.159	2.367	2.594	3.106	4.046
15	2.397	2.759	3.172	3.642	4.177	5.474	8.137
20	3.207	3.870	4.661	5.604	6.728	9.646	16.367
25	4.292	5.427	6.848	8.623	10.835	17.000	32.919

Table 1.3. Excerpt from Interest Table A $(1 + i)^n$.

Note that the product of P (the original $2,000 investment) and TA (the table value for n = 2 years and i = 7%) is 2000 x 1.145 = $2,290. This outcome is essentially the same as was earlier determined to be the future value of the sum after 2 years earning 7% interest.

The foregoing discussion of future values helps the leisure and sport organization to determine the future value of resources that it currently has and is willing to invest. For example, an agency that plans to fund a future building project by setting aside (investing) $10,000 at the beginning of each year for the next five years is able to calculate the expected balance of that earmarked account at the end of the five-year period.

Assuming a stable interest rate of 8% for 5 years, the future value of the first amount invested (F_1) will be:

$$F_1 = P(T_A) = 10,000(1.469) = \$14,690$$

To this amount, add the future value of the next $10,000 installment (F2) invested at 8% for 4 years:

$$F_2 = P(T_A) = 10,000(1.360) = \underline{\$13,600}$$

Continue calculating the future values for the remaining installments (while paying attention to the fact that the TA value should reflect the declining *n* [years of investment]). Sum the future values to determine the money that will be available for the project after 5 years.

$$F_1 = P\ (T_A) = 10{,}000\ (1.469) = \$14{,}690$$

$$F_2 = P\ (T_A) = 10{,}000\ (1.360) = \$13{,}600$$

$$F_3 = P\ (T_A) = 10{,}000\ (1.260) = \$12{,}600$$

$$F_4 = P\ (T_A) = 10{,}000\ (1.166) = \$11{,}660$$

$$F_5 = P\ (T_A) = 10{,}000\ (1.080) = \underline{\$10{,}080}$$

Total $62,630

By setting aside $10,000 per year for the next five years, the organization will have $62,630 for its building project.

Present Value

The calculation of future values requires knowledge of a beginning amount (principal), a term of investment, and the applicable interest rate. There are, however, situations wherein the financial manager has a target future value but needs to know how much to invest at a given rate for a specified term to achieve that target. In a sense, the manager needs to reverse the procedure for determining future value in order to calculate a *present value*.

For illustrative purposes, assume that an athletic team has been invited to travel to and participate in a prestigious tournament in just a little more than two years from now. The team's manager has worked with a transportation agency, hotels, and others to secure a firm price for services needed at the time of the event. The estimated team expenses to be paid at the time of the trip total $40,000. Team members are required to have 50 percent of the trip funds deposited in the team's interest-bearing account two years before the event. The remainder is payable at the end of the two years, just prior to departure. How much money has to be deposited now? The amount of $20,000 comes to mind quickly, but, after considering what was just discussed about future values, it becomes evident that all that is needed is an amount that in two years will have become $20,000. The question is actually "What is the present value of the future sum of $20,000?" Using, for example, 6% as the interest rate, the present value can be calculated in the following manner:

$$P = F[1/(1+i)^n]\ = 20{,}000\ [1/(1+.06)^2] = 20{,}000\ (0.890)\ = \ \$17{,}800$$

The team needs to deposit only $17,800 now and $20,000 later to have the full $40,000 at the time of the trip.

Once again, a formula has been introduced that may look a bit intimidating. Fortunately, there is another table that eliminates the need for cumbersome calculations. Interest Table B (which can be found at the end of this chapter and is excerpted here in Table 1.4) provides values from the solution of $[1/(1+i)^n]$ when calculating present values.

n\i	6%	7%	8%	9%	10%	12%	15%
1	0.943	0.935	0.926	0.917	0.909	0.893	0.870
2	0.890	0.873	0.857	0.842	0.826	0.797	0.756
3	0.840	0.816	0.794	0.772	0.751	0.712	0.658
4	0.792	0.763	0.735	0.708	0.683	0.636	0.572
5	0.747	0.713	0.681	0.650	0.621	0.567	0.497
6	0.705	0.666	0.630	0.596	0.564	0.507	0.432
7	0.665	0.623	0.583	0.547	0.513	0.452	0.376
8	0.627	0.582	0.540	0.502	0.467	0.404	0.327
9	0.592	0.544	0.500	0.460	0.424	0.361	0.284
10	0.558	0.508	0.463	0.422	0.386	0.322	0.247
15	0.417	0.362	0.315	0.275	0.239	0.183	0.123
20	0.312	0.258	0.215	0.252	0.149	0.104	0.061
25	0.233	0.184	0.146	0.116	0.092	0.059	0.030

Table 1.4. Excerpt from Interest Table B $1/(1 + i)^n$.

In the previous illustration, solution of the formula $[1/(1+i)^n]$ generated an interest factor of 0.890. The Table B value corresponding to $i = .06$ and $n = 2$ also generates the interest factor of 0.890. The formula for calculating present value can, therefore, also be expressed as

$$P = F(T_B).$$

Depreciation

Physical assets used by sports and leisure organizations do have a finite life span. With the exception of land, assets such as buildings and equipment eventually wear out or become obsolete because of market or technological developments. The loss of or reduced productivity of these resources is recognized and quantified as *depreciation*. In accounting, depreciation is considered as an expense, but not in the same way as is the cash outlay for the purchase of production supplies or services. The precise accounting procedure for dealing with depreciation is discussed in Chapter 8. At this point, the techniques for calculating depreciation will be presented.

One way of calculating depreciation is to divide the original value (sometimes referred to as the starting book value) of an asset by its expected life span. For example, a $6,000 electronic notice board at a community center may have a five-year life span, after which any repairs needed would be too expensive or may be impossible because of changing technology. Table 1.5 illustrates the steady reduction in value of the bulletin board during the five years. This is called *straight line depreciation*. Note that the bulletin board has no book value or salvage value at the end of its life span.

Period	Starting Book Value	Depreciation Amount	Remaining Book Value
Year 1	$6,000	$1,200	$4,800
Year 2	$4,800	$1,200	$3,600
Year 3	$3,600	$1,200	$2,400
Year 4	$2,400	$1,200	$1,200
Year 5	$1,200	$1,200	$0

Table 1.5. Annual starting values, depreciation, and remaining book values after straight line depreciation.

Not all assets depreciate to zero value at the end of their projected life spans. Furthermore, only some will depreciate at a constant rate, as was expressed in the preceding example of straight-line depreciation. In reality, many assets will decrease in value more at the beginning of their use than later on, and many will outlast projected life spans, as well as maintain some salvage value, even when obsolete or nonfunctional. *Declining balance depreciation* reflects these realities. With declining balance depreciation, a depreciation rate is set for an asset based on industry standards. This rate affects both the amount of annual depreciation and the salvage value.

To calculate first-year depreciation and remaining book value (salvage value), divide the starting book value of the asset by its life span, and then multiply that number by the appropriate depreciation rate. Expressed as a formula:

(Starting Book Value/Life Span) x Depreciation Rate = Depreciation

For example, a $6,000 pitching machine with a 5-year life span and 150% depreciation rate would depreciate ($6,000/5) x 1.5 = $1,800 in the first year and have a remaining book value of $6,000 – $1,800 = $4,200. After the second year, it will have depreciated ($4,200/5) x 1.5 = $1,260 and have a remaining book value of $4,200 – $1,260 = $2,940. As shown in Table 1.6, the final year's depreciation will be much lower (only $432), and there will be a salvage value of $1,009.

Period	Starting Book Value	Depreciation Amount	Remaining Book Value
Year 1	$6,000	$1,800	$4,200
Year 2	$4,200	$1,260	$2,940
Year 3	$2,940	$882	$2,058
Year 4	$2,058	$617	$1,441
Year 5	$1,441	$432	$1,009

Table 1.6. Annual starting values, depreciation, and remaining book values after declining balance depreciation (150%).

An important advantage of declining balance depreciation is the tax shelter it offers to profits generated early in an enterprise. Since depreciation is considered an expense, the taxable profits are reduced, but not the cash that is generated from operations. These cash reserves are more critical in the early stages of an enterprise than later, when the depreciation amount is reduced.

Table 1.7 provides a comparison of the depreciation amounts and remaining book values of a $6,000 asset that is straight-line depreciated, and declining-balance depreciated at 150 percent and 200 percent. The choice of depreciation method and seemingly small differences in depreciation rates clearly have significant impacts on how the sports or leisure service organization accounts for the mortality of its physical resources.

Period	Straight Line	150%	200%
Year 1	$1,200	$1,800	$2,400
Year 2	$1,200	$1,260	$1,440
Year 3	$1,200	$882	$864
Year 4	$1,200	$617	$518
Year 5	$1,200	$432	$311
Total Depreciation	$6,000	$3,991	$5,533
Remaining Book Value	$0	$1,009	$467

Table 1.7. Comparison of depreciation amounts and remaining book values for straight line declining balance (150%) and declining balance (200%) depreciation of a $6,000 asset.

Large crowds are drawn to some parks, requiring significant
additional funding in order to maintain the area.

Economic Impacts

A common strategy for winning support for a major recreation or sport development project
is the declaration of economic benefits that will be realized in the community by virtue of
that particular project. A city council considering the construction of a major sports stadium might be influenced by the promise of hundreds of new jobs in the community and
millions of dollars of additional sales, household income, and tax revenues. Because of the
influence that such promises may have, it is important for the sport and leisure service
manager to understand the basics of economic impact analysis and be able to critically
evaluate such considerations.

A simple illustration will lay the foundation for this discussion. Assume that Maurice visits
the small town of Bloomville and spends $100 on crafts made and sold locally by Jean. Jean
needs a new display case, so she hires Stefan to build one for her. She pays Stefan $80 and
spends the remaining $20 at Virginia's produce stand at the Farmer's Market. Stefan pays
$35 for materials bought in Indianapolis, spends $30 on computer software from a mail-
order company in St. Louis, and buys $15 worth of produce from Virginia. Virginia pays
$35 to her lawyer, Susan, who hires Rufus to tend her garden while she attends a profes-
sional meeting in Orlando. Rufus is paid $20, while the remaining $15 of Susan's income
goes towards her trip. Rufus spends his $20 on garden tools manufactured in Seattle by
Ethel & Pen Tool Co. Figure 1.9 diagrams this series of transactions.

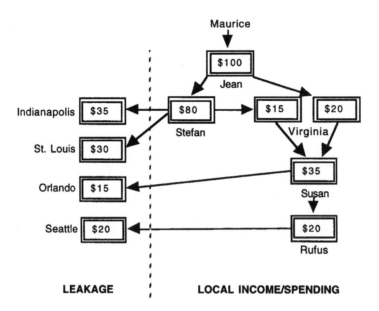

Figure 1.9. Transaction series showing local re-spending and leakage.

Note that, in the above scenario, money was introduced into the Bloomville economy by Maurice and was re-spent by several people. Some of the money was spent on locally produced goods and services and some was spent outside the community. Eventually, all the money introduced by Maurice was sent to Indianapolis ($35), St. Louis ($30), Orlando ($15), and Seattle ($20). The exogenous funds had circulated within the economy and then leaked out through outside spending. However, Maurice's $100 did result in $270 of spending (economic activity) in the community. Its direct impact was multiplied 2.7 times, and it contributed to the employment income of five people in Bloomville.

Economic impact assessment measures the amount of local re-spending of money that comes into the economy because of a particular event or project. It results in a description of the local income, local sales, and local tax revenues generated by exogenous funds. It results in quantification of the employment created by new income, sales, and tax revenues. Figure 1.10 details the flow of dollars from nonlocal sources as they move through the local economy and affect government, industry, and household spending activity.

The direct effect of money spent on a major sports or leisure project is the local purchasing and employment required for that project. The indirect effect is the local purchasing and employment that results from direct sales and employment income. Induced effects result from third and subsequent rounds of economic activity having their genesis in the project.

Economic impact studies are occasionally conducted to provide justification for a "dream" project. Such studies must be viewed with a critical eye, as the results may reflect more of a political will than an economic reality. When evaluating the results of an economic impact study, the sports and leisure service manager should consider the following:

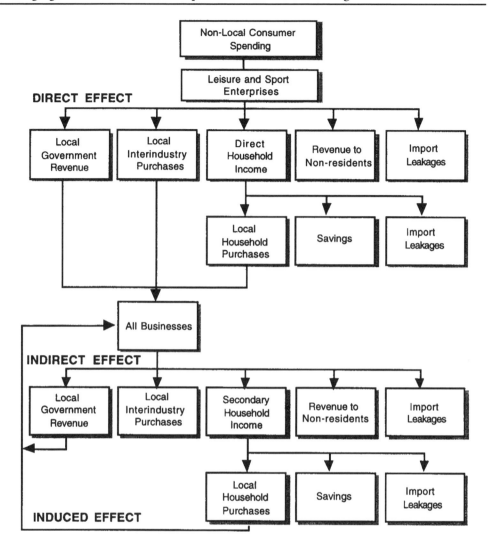

Figure 1.10. Flow of exogenous funds through the local economy
(adapted from Loftus and Var, 1985).

- Does the study focus on the impact of money coming from outside the community? This is an important distinction, because the impact of spending local funds is, in most respects, independent of the project. In fact, a project that only stimulates spending of local money may create more import leakage than it does new sales, income, and employment.

- Are the multipliers that are used truly reflective of economic conditions within the community? Extreme caution should be exercised when applying a sales, income, or employment multiplier that was computed for another community that may have a more diverse economic base or may be less subject to seasonal constraints and market fluctuations. While it may be convenient or less expensive, a "borrowed" multiplier just may not fit.

- Are projections of direct spending based on solid market research or on unsubstantiated optimism? Investment decisions that would require an economic impact analysis are much too important to make on the basis of unreliable or biased information.

Summary

As an introduction to the economic principles that underlie the successful management of financial resources in the sport and leisure service organization, this chapter has emphasized the need to develop an understanding and working knowledge of the concepts of supply and demand. Additionally, attention has been devoted to the impact of interest on decisions about present or future use of money. The concepts of depreciation and economic impact assessment were also introduced. The economic principles presented help the financial manager to understand how individuals and society work; that is, they provide insights into basic human behavior. Furthermore, the technical aspects of the discussion also serve as a review of the basic mathematical skills that are needed for procedures discussed later in this book. An understanding of basic economics is important to the development of skills and the strengthening of the decision-making ability of financial managers in sport and leisure service organizations.

n/i	2%	3%	4%	5%	6%	7%	8%	9%	10%	12%	15%
1	1.020	1.030	1.040	1.050	1.060	1.070	1.080	1.090	1.100	1.120	1.150
2	1.040	1.061	1.082	1.103	1.124	1.145	1.166	1.188	1.210	1.254	1.323
3	1.061	1.093	1.125	1.158	1.191	1.225	1.260	1.295	1.331	1.405	1.521
4	1.082	1.126	1.170	1.216	1.262	1.311	1.360	1.412	1.464	1.574	1.749
5	1.104	1.159	1.217	1.276	1.338	1.403	1.469	1.539	1.611	1.762	2.011
6	1.126	1.194	1.265	1.340	1.419	1.501	1.587	1.677	1.772	1.974	2.313
7	1.149	1.230	1.316	1.407	1.504	1.606	1.714	1.828	1.949	2.211	2.660
8	1.172	1.267	1.369	1.477	1.594	1.718	1.851	1.993	2.144	2.476	3.059
9	1.195	1.305	1.423	1.551	1.689	1.838	1.999	2.172	2.358	2.773	3.518
10	1.219	1.344	1.480	1.629	1.791	1.967	2.159	2.367	2.594	3.106	4.046
11	1.243	1.384	1.539	1.710	1.898	2.105	2.332	2.580	2.853	3.479	4.652
12	1.268	1.426	1.601	1.796	2.012	2.252	2.518	2.813	3.138	3.896	5.350
13	1.294	1.469	1.665	1.886	2.133	2.410	2.720	3.066	3.452	4.363	6.153
14	1.319	1.513	1.732	1.980	2.261	2.579	2.937	3.342	3.797	4.887	7.076
15	1.346	1.558	1.801	2.079	2.397	2.759	3.172	3.642	4.177	5.474	8.137
16	1.373	1.605	1.873	2.183	2.540	2.952	3.426	3.970	4.595	6.130	9.358
17	1.400	1.653	1.948	2.292	2.693	3.159	3.700	4.328	5.054	6.866	10.761
18	1.428	1.702	2.026	2.407	2.854	3.380	3.996	4.717	5.560	7.690	12.375
19	1.457	1.754	2.107	2.527	3.026	3.617	4.316	5.142	6.116	8.613	14.232
20	1.486	1.806	2.191	2.653	3.207	3.870	4.661	5.604	6.727	9.646	16.367
21	1.516	1.860	2.279	2.786	3.400	4.141	5.034	6.109	7.400	10.804	18.822
22	1.546	1.916	2.370	2.925	3.604	4.430	5.437	6.659	8.140	12.100	21.645
23	1.577	1.974	2.465	3.072	3.820	4.741	5.871	7.258	8.954	13.552	24.891
24	1.608	2.033	2.563	3.225	4.049	5.072	6.341	7.911	9.850	15.179	28.625
25	1.641	2.094	2.666	3.386	4.292	5.427	6.848	8.623	10.835	17.000	32.919

Interest Table A $(1 + i)^n$

n/i	2%	3%	4%	5%	6%	7%	8%	9%	10%	12%	15%
1	0.980	0.971	0.962	0.952	0.943	0.935	0.926	0.917	0.909	0.893	0.870
2	0.961	0.943	0.925	0.907	0.890	0.873	0.857	0.842	0.826	0.797	0.756
3	0.942	0.915	0.889	0.864	0.840	0.816	0.794	0.772	0.751	0.712	0.658
4	0.924	0.888	0.855	0.823	0.792	0.763	0.735	0.708	0.683	0.636	0.572
5	0.906	0.863	0.822	0.784	0.747	0.713	0.681	0.650	0.621	0.567	0.497
6	0.888	0.837	0.790	0.746	0.705	0.666	0.630	0.596	0.564	0.507	0.432
7	0.871	0.813	0.760	0.711	0.665	0.623	0.583	0.547	0.513	0.452	0.376
8	0.853	0.789	0.731	0.677	0.627	0.582	0.540	0.502	0.467	0.404	0.327
9	0.3837	0.766	0.703	0.645	0.592	0.544	0.500	0.460	0.424	0.361	0.284
10	0.820	0.744	0.676	0.614	0.558	0.508	0.463	0.422	0.386	0.322	0.247
11	0.804	0.722	0.650	0.585	0.527	0.475	0.429	0.388	0.350	0.287	0.215
12	0.788	0.701	0.625	0.557	0.497	0.444	0.397	0.356	0.319	0.257	0.187
13	0.773	0.681	0.601	0.530	0.469	0.415	0.368	0.326	0.290	0.229	0.163
14	0.758	0.661	0.577	0.505	0.442	0.388	0.340	0.299	0.263	0.205	0.141
15	0.743	0.642	0.555	0.481	0.417	0.362	0.315	0.275	0.239	0.183	0.123
16	0.728	0.623	0.534	0.458	0.394	0.339	0.292	0.252	0.218	0.163	0.107
17	0.714	0.605	0.513	0.436	0.371	0.317	0.270	0.231	0.198	0.146	0.093
18	0.700	0.587	0.494	0.416	0.350	0.296	0.250	0.212	0.180	0.130	0.081
19	0.686	0.570	0.475	0.396	0.331	0.277	0.232	0.194	0.164	0.116	0.070
20	0.673	0.554	0.456	0.377	0.312	0.258	0.215	0.178	0.149	0.104	0.061
21	0.660	0.538	0.439	0.359	0.294	0.242	0.199	0.164	0.135	0.093	0.053
22	0.647	0.522	0.422	0.342	0.278	0.226	0.184	0.150	0.123	0.083	0.046
23	0.634	0.507	0.406	0.326	0.262	0.211	0.170	0.138	0.112	0.074	0.040
24	0.622	0.492	0.390	0.310	0.247	0.197	0.158	0.126	0.102	0.066	0.035
25	0.610	0.478	0.375	0.295	0.233	0.184	0.146	0.116	0.092	0.059	0.030

Interest Table B $(1 + i)^n$

Chapter 2

Financial Management in Public, Private Nonprofit, and Commercial Sport and Leisure Organizations

Introduction

Approaches to the management of financial resources in sport and leisure service organizations vary greatly, depending on the mandate and goals of the organizations, as well as the political environments in which they operate. However, almost every sport or leisure service organization can be classified as either *a public, private nonprofit, or commercial* enterprise, and each type of organization has unique and uniquely common features which relate directly to financial management and budgeting.

This brief chapter examines the finance-related differences between the three types of sport and leisure enterprises and explores related legislative/legal parameters, social roles/expectations, market management techniques, indicators of success, and particular financial management opportunities and challenges. A concluding discussion focuses on competition and cooperation between sport and leisure service organizations of different types.

In devoting this discussion to the unique characteristics and differences among public, private nonprofit, and commercial sport and leisure service organizations, there is a danger that their many important similarities will be ignored. Such is not the intent of this chapter. Although it is important to understand the differences, it is just as important to acknowledge the common principles, practices, structures, and competencies associated with financial management. Those similarities will receive ample attention in subsequent chapters.

Public Enterprises

A sport and leisure service enterprise operating in the public sector generally has a broad mandate to provide services that directly or indirectly benefit an entire community. The organization is usually an arm of government (e.g., a municipal recreation department or a public educational institution) that is charged with enhancing the quality of life of its patrons by providing enriching experiences and remedying social problems. The "public" nature of the organization is not only emphasized in its nondiscriminatory offering and delivery of services, but also in the nondiscriminatory way in which its operating funds are expropriated. Public sport and leisure service organizations receive their base financial resources from the public through taxation. They may also charge fees and receive gratuitous income from private sources; but the foundation of their support is the ability of government to meet its operational goals by taxing its constituents.

Legislative/Legal Parameters

In order for the governing body of a public leisure service organization to compel its constituents to contribute funds to support the operation of that organization, it must first win a legal right to levy taxes and to use those taxes for such purposes. The U.S. Constitution sets the legal parameters for the federal government to collect and use public funds for sport and leisure services. The federal system also provides for the establishment and public funding of state and local governments and government programs. State governments must have their own constitutional provisions for taxation and public funding of sport and leisure services. Local (i.e., municipal) governments, on the other hand, may extend public financial support to sport and leisure services only if the state government already has enacted appropriate enabling legislation.

Social Roles/Expectations

Public leisure service organizations exist for the purpose of meeting social needs. The taxpaying public expects sport and leisure service organizations to be engaged in enterprises and programs that use public funds for the common good and community betterment. Within the community, there is general acceptance and tolerance of certain services receiving tax subsidies, and many low-cost or free (i.e., completely subsidized) services (e.g., neighborhood parks) are expected, demanded, and even required as basic elements of social order and as important tools in social engineering.

Market Management Techniques

Modern practices of sport and leisure service organizations include market segmentation and target marketing. Public organizations use "need" rather than "profit potential" as the primary segmentation criterion in their marketing efforts. Products, prices, and promotional strategies are established in consideration of the desire to appeal to as many as possible in the community who need the service. Distribution considerations also reflect the priority of the public sector organization to ensure service delivery to as broad a market as possible. For example, when faced with a new private or commercial sector competitor, a public agency may choose to withdraw from the marketplace—not because it is unable to compete, but because the competitor has demonstrated that it can meet the same needs without tax support and, perhaps, with greater efficiency. The marketing objective of the public sport and leisure service organization is either to provide the benefit or to accommodate its provision by another appropriate supplier.

Indicators of Success

Financial managers in the public sector measure their success by comparing their achievements to their goals. That is also true of financial managers in the private nonprofit and commercial sectors, but the goals of the latter organizations are more precisely associated with financial returns on financial investments. Public financial managers focus on achieving targeted levels of revenue and expenditure and on the social benefit realized by those expenditures.

Financial Management Opportunities and Challenges

Public sport and leisure service organizations enjoy several opportunities that are unique to their sector. One opportunity is that of tax exemption. By convention, no government may charge taxes to a government at another level, which means that the local public agency has greater purchasing power due to being exempt from state or federal sales taxes. Another opportunity lies in the ability of the public institution to borrow money for capital projects. The government is a low-risk borrower, primarily because it can use its taxing power and its access to the taxable wealth of the community as collateral. A third opportunity enjoyed by the public sector is the goodwill and altruistic behavior of people in the community. Actively encouraged and supported volunteer programs provide human resources without the loss of the sport and leisure service organization's financial resources.

A challenge experienced by financial managers in the public sector is the scrutiny of and accountability to the public and to other legislative/regulatory bodies. True to the democratic ideal, citizens voice their views about how their taxes are being used, and there is always someone who was not elected who is certain that he or she could do a better job. The close scrutiny of financial management also comes from other formal organizations or agencies whose job it is to ensure that the public treasury is being properly managed. This close scrutiny is usually facilitated by seemingly countless forms and reports which the financial manager must take time to complete. A second challenge is in the form of changing political winds. Financial management in the public sector requires sensitivity to the political environment, and changes in political priorities may require readjustment of financial plans or management structures.

Other

Two other aspects of financial management in the public sector require a brief mention before looking at financial management in the private nonprofit sector. One aspect concerns the advantage that comes to the public sport or leisure service organization by virtue of its taxing authority—an advantage over competitors or would-be competitors that cannot compete because they must raise capital funds at market prices *and* pay taxes to their competitor, the public agency. In many cases, the charge of unfair competition leveled at the public sector may be well deserved. The second aspect concerns the belief in the private sector that, because of the seemingly unchecked taxing power of government, the public sport and leisure service organization has "deep pockets." Therefore, the reasoning goes, only public agencies can or should be expected to raise the capital necessary to build and maintain such major facilities as a 100,000-seat sports stadium or domed arena. Financial managers in the public sector are, however, quite aware of the limitations of public tolerance for taxation and have shortened their reach into the taxpayers' pockets. Sometimes this restraint has been self-imposed, and sometimes it has resulted from public pressure and sentiment, such as that expressed in several landmark propositions passed by voters in recent years.

Private Nonprofit Enterprises

The private nonprofit sector is composed of organizations that provide sport and leisure services without the direct support of public funds and without the requirement to generate increased personal wealth for any owners or investors. These organizations are private in the sense that they are not owned or directed by government. They are nonprofit in the sense that they must generate income to at least cover their expenses, yet do not generate profits for the purpose of making anybody richer. They may make a profit from certain enterprises, but overall profit is not the goal, and any profits that are realized are used to maintain or enhance the viability of the organization. Private nonprofit sport and leisure service organizations exist to meet the service needs of selected consumers in situations where the public sector is either unwilling or unable to function, and where commercial organizations are also either unwilling or unable to conduct business. Well-known examples of private nonprofit sport and leisure service organizations include the YMCA, local church groups, community sport and athletic associations, recreation clubs, Boys and Girls Clubs, Boy Scouts of America, and Girl Scouts.

Private nonprofit organizations receive financial resources from membership fees, fundraising projects, donations, grants, and user fees. Their need for money from such sources is reduced considerably by the ability of private nonprofit organizations to attract and keep committed volunteers. After religious organizations (which also offer many recreational programs), community sport and leisure organizations receive the greatest share of volunteer support in the United States and Canada.

Legislative/Legal Parameters

Private nonprofit organizations are permitted to operate because of several important laws that free them from some of the restrictive controls that otherwise encumber public and commercial operations. For example, private nonprofit sport and leisure service organizations enjoy a tax-free status. Additionally, the U.S. Postal Service and most commercial retailers and service suppliers offer specially reduced rates for nonprofit organizations. Federal and state income tax laws also encourage individuals and corporations to donate to charitable nonprofit organizations by recognizing tax deductions or offering tax credits according to the amounts donated. In order for a donor to apply for such a tax benefit, the donation must go to an organization that is registered with the Internal Revenue Service as a 501(c3) Charitable Organization. Other state and federal tax law provisions also exist to support the valued work of private nonprofit organizations.

In addition to filing with the IRS, all private nonprofit sport and leisure service organizations need to be properly constituted and registered as corporate entities. This registration may need to be with local, state, and/or federal agencies that regulate the operations of commercial and nonprofit organizations.

Social Roles/Expectations

Like public agencies, private nonprofit sport and leisure service organizations exist to meet social needs. However, they are more selective in the needs that they try to meet. Usually, a private nonprofit organization is identified with a single "cause" or specific interest, such as helping at-risk youth, strengthening families, promoting mass involvement in camping, developing coaching skills for basketball, or promoting literacy.

Market Management Techniques

The relatively narrow focus of the nonprofit organization tends to restrict the scope of its market and dictate the techniques it must use to effectively and appropriately manage the consumption process. The identity of the client base is readily established by the needs or the shared interactions of the people with the target needs. Pricing decisions reflect the requirement to break even or generate modest profits when additional money is needed for other service activities of the organization. Service allocation for private nonprofit sport and leisure service organizations is based primarily on need, with little regard for merit or profit potential.

Indicators of Success

Financial managers in the private nonprofit sector measure their success by comparing their achievements to their goals. That is also true of financial managers in the public and commercial sectors; however, the goals of the public organizations are not at all associated with financial returns on financial investments, and the overarching goal of commercial sector organizations is to make as much money as possible for the owner(s). Private nonprofit financial managers focus on achieving social benefits while generating enough revenue and other resources (e.g., volunteers) to stay in operation and continue benefiting their specialized markets.

Financial Management Opportunities and Challenges

Public sympathy and affection are two important advantages enjoyed by organizations in the private nonprofit sector. This factor is particularly helpful both in fundraising efforts and the recruitment of volunteers. Tax breaks and discounts also provide opportunities for private nonprofit sport and leisure service organizations to get the most out of their financial resources.

One challenge that smaller private nonprofit organizations have is the lack of staff (or at least highly qualified staff) that can manage the financial resources in a consistent, accurate, and timely manner. Reliance on volunteers for financial management functions can, occasionally, have disastrous results for the organization. Another challenge is the relative risk associated with extending credit to an enterprise that depends so much on the popularity of its cause and the generosity of its supporters. Credit is based on confidence, and confidence is something that most small nonprofit organizations enjoy from conservative lenders. A third significant financial management challenge is that of protecting the financial resources of the organization from short-term governing bodies that do not always act with long-term wisdom. Many nonprofit sport and leisure service organizations have failed or struggled because a new board of directors decided to use their carefully developed cash reserves for an immediate program expansion or initiative that did not result in sustained or enhanced financial strength.

Other

Financial management in the private nonprofit sector requires many of the same skills and involves many of the same activities as those in the public sector. Sports and leisure in the private nonprofit sector is likely to continue as a strong and viable part of community life. It will, however, need more sophistication in the management of its financial resources as every aspect of operating in a modern society becomes more complex.

Commercial Enterprises

Sport and leisure service enterprises operating in the commercial sector are distinguished from the others previously discussed by their profit motivation. It is important to note that "profit motivation," rather than "profit generation," is given as the defining characteristic. Commercial sport and leisure enterprises may not always produce profits (especially in the early stages of development or during off-seasons), but the commercial enterprise will only stay in business if, over a reasonable period of time, an expected return on the investment is eventually realized. These organizations do not exist out of a need for a particular type of service. They exist because satisfying the need for a particular type of service is profitable.

Commercial sector organizations do not receive tax revenues—they pay taxes. Commercial sector organizations do not typically receive operating grants or other forms of gratuitous income—they are called upon to make donations. Commercial sector organizations do not use volunteers—they support them. Because the commercial sector exists to benefit certain individuals (investors), it does not have access to the major revenue sources utilized by public and private nonprofit agencies. Commercial sport and leisure businesses must cover most or all of their costs of operating by charging fees, selling goods and services, and making other types of investments. Examples of commercial sector sport and leisure service organizations include professional sports teams, resorts, amusement parks, meeting management companies, bowling centers, movie theaters, outdoor outfitters, travel managers.

Legislative/Legal Parameters

There are many laws aimed at supporting and regulating commercial activity. Profit-motivated sport and leisure service organizations are subject to those laws that apply their particular situations. The application of some laws will vary depending upon whether the sport or leisure business is set up as a corporation, syndicate, or partnership or is individually owned.

Social Roles/Expectations

The primary social role or social expectation of the commercial sport and leisure enterprise is to contribute to the economic well-being of the community. Proposals for new commercial enterprises often highlight community benefits such as diversity in leisure options, opportunities for social interaction, promotion of health, development of community pride, and educational enrichment, but the benefit that is most eagerly sought is described in terms of jobs created, household income produced, sales activity, and tax revenue generated. Of course, there is the basic expectation that the enterprise will be consistent with community social standards, but the economic impact of the venture is regarded with the most interest and concern.

Market Management Techniques

Market management in commercial sport and leisure services is designed to do one thing: tap consumer spending power. Therefore, the only market that is of interest is the market that can pay enough and is willing to pay enough to help the organization realize its financial goals.

Responsiveness to market conditions is a key to success in commercial enterprises, and this responsiveness is often reflected in pricing strategies and in the use of advertising as a major promotional tool. Pricing strategies in the commercial sector focus on the total bottom line. That is, variation in pricing is frequently used to attract consumers by responding to price sensitivity on certain elements of the total service package. In a movie theater, for example, the admission price may be reduced to a point where it barely covers the costs of providing the cinematic opportunity, and yet, the price of the popcorn may be kept at a level which consumers can accept and which makes the whole moviegoing event (movie + snacks) profitable for the theater operator. The commercial sector is usually more responsive and more flexible in pricing than organizations in the public and private nonprofit sectors. For similar reasons, the commercial sector is also more inclined than other types of organizations to use advertising (both institutional and product) to promote desired consumer responses.

Indicators of Success

Financial managers in the commercial sector measure their success by comparing their achievements to their goals. Unlike their counterparts in the public and private nonprofit sectors, managers of commercial enterprises set goals that focus on the financial growth of the enterprise and on the return on the investment made therein. The balance sheet and the income statement serve as the primary evaluation documents rather than participant evaluation surveys. There is concern for the quality of consumers' experience, but only so far as it affects the financial bottom line. The commercial sport and leisure service organization also measures its success by comparing its financial ratios with standards established for the industry. Financial ratios are discussed further in Chapter 11.

Financial Management Opportunities and Challenges

Commercial sport and leisure service organizations enjoy several opportunities that are somewhat unique to this sector. Because they are profit motivated, they are not required to prop up socially beneficial but financially ineffective programs and services and can, as a result, concentrate on maximizing the utility of their assets. They can more easily identify and avoid products that do not meet their standards of success. The entrepreneurial spirit has free reign in the commercial sport and leisure business environment and managers find excitement in the many opportunities to move resources from areas of low productivity to initiatives that offer greater results.

Challenges associated with financial management in the commercial sport and leisure service organization include developing the knowledge and skill competencies required in order to be effective. Foremost among the skill requirements are investment management, bookkeeping, and financial forecasting. Effective financial managers continually add to their store of management abilities by reading and studying, attending conferences and workshops, and furthering their formal education in this discipline.

Although public, private nonprofit, and commercial sport and leisure service organizations are alike in many ways, there are important differences among the three sectors with respect to financial management goals and practices. The foregoing discussion of differences is summarized in Table 2.1.

Area of contrast	Public	Private Nonprofit	Commercial
Ownership	Usually government	Private organization	Private corporation
Legal Authority	Through enabling legislation	Through enabling legislation and designation of tax status.	Through incorporation (state and federal government recognition, control, and protection)
Mandate	Serve social welfare needs of all citizens	Serve specific social welfare needs or leisure interests of a specific population.	Realize maximum return on investment through service to most profitable market.
Source of Funds	Taxes, grants, donations, earned income	Grants, memberships, donations, fundraising activities, earned income	Investors, creditors, earned income
Market Management	Market limited to geographic/political constituency. Market segmented on basis of need. Might not compete.	Market defined by particular need.	Market composed of those who can pay. Defined by merit.
Success Indicators	Social change	Social change. Financial viability.	Profitability. Growth. Return on investment.
Opportunities	Tax exemption. Volunteers. Bulk purchasing and discounts.	Tax exemption. Volunteers. Public concern.	Entrepreneurship. Support for eliminating financially unsuccessful products.
Challenges	Public accountability and scrutiny. Changing political directions.	Relative uncertainty. Reliance on gratuitous income and volunteers. Limited, qualified staff. Inconsistent leadership.	Developing and maintaining skills.

Table 2.1. A summary of finance-related similarities and differences among public, private nonprofit, and commercial sport and leisure service organizations.

Competition and Cooperation

Although there are important differences among sport and leisure service organizations operating in the public, private nonprofit, and commercial sectors, this does not mean that these sectors never relate to each other. In one respect, they may be competitors trying to serve the same markets, provide the same kinds of services, or compete in other ways. In another respect, they may be cooperating in enterprises and activities that provide mutual benefits. It would not be unusual, for example, to see similar aquatics programs offered to a community by the YMCA, the local college, and the city recreation department. In this case, the three agencies (representing public and private nonprofit sectors) are competing directly for customers. On the other hand, the city and the YMCA may also have an agreement that youth soccer leagues will be offered exclusively by the YMCA, while the city recreation department will offer all softball and baseball programs in the community. Furthermore, a commercial local sport management firm might be contracted by both agencies to train and manage the officials and the umpires for both the soccer and baseball leagues.

Competition among public, private nonprofit, and commercial agencies provides a number of benefits. They include the following:

- Greater choice for consumers (e.g., variety in program features, scheduling, location, price)

- Greater attention to high-quality service (necessary for maintaining competitive advantage)

- Greater ability to respond to increasing demand

- Greater opportunity to focus on specific market segments (i.e., establish a market niche)

Cooperation among public, private nonprofit, and commercial sport and leisure service agencies also provides some benefits. They include the following:

- Operational efficiency (by reducing duplication of physical and human resources)

- Synergism (i.e., the total benefit of agencies working together can be greater than the sum of the benefits provided by each alone)

- A coordinated approach to the delivery of sport and leisure services in the community (ensuring that a full range of needs and interests are considered)

- Conversion of competitive energy to service energy

Summary

The delivery of sport and leisure service in the community is achieved through a system which includes organizations operating in the public, private nonprofit, and commercial sectors. Public agencies have a clear social mandate and are supported by public funds, especially tax revenues. Private nonprofit agencies do not receive tax dollars to fund their operations, but rather seek funding through donations and enterprise activities. They may, through service fees and other fundraising activities, generate profits; but those profits are used to maintain the organization and sustain other nonprofitable activities or services. Commercial sport and leisure service organizations are motivated by profit and an expected return on investment. All business activities in the commercial sport and leisure organization are ultimately expected to generate a profit. Although the three sectors differ in other ways, those differences do not deny them the opportunities for direct competition and cooperation in service delivery.

Chapter 3

Organization

Introduction

Effective management of financial resources in the sport and leisure service organization requires the assumption and recognition of responsibility, as well as the deliberate assignment of authority and duties to the appropriate departments, offices, and individuals. Those who are responsible for the financial well-being of the organization are the financial *decision makers*. They are the ones who are the sources of authority, and they are the ones who are ultimately held accountable for the consequences of their decisions. Those to whom they delegate authority may make financial decisions within the parameters of their stewardships, but they typically function with limited responsibility as financial *administrators*. Financial administrators are those in the organization who are authorized to implement financial policies and follow established financial management procedures. They have specific duties and authority and are responsible not for the financial well-being of the organization, but rather for how they perform their duties and exercise their authority.

This brief chapter examines the elements of organizational structures that are designed to facilitate the integrated efforts of financial decision makers, financial administrators, and program/facility managers in sport and leisure service agencies. It also describes the roles of the different types of financial managers in a variety of settings, including public agencies operating at all three levels of government; private nonprofit agencies with local, regional, and national programs; and commercial sport and recreation enterprises of different sizes.

Distinctions between the financial management roles of individuals or units within the organization are most evident on the vertical dimension of the organizational chart. Specifically, those who occupy positions at the top of the organizational chart are the financial decision makers, while those at the bottom of the chart are, in varying degrees, the financial administrators. For example, the owner of an indoor sports complex in a responsive market will, as the financial decision maker, establish policies about such things as cost recovery targets, free services, employee compensation, etc. However, the implementation of those policies is left to her financial administrators: program managers (who set prices and incur program costs), cashiers (who collect admission fees or check passes), and clerical staff (who handle the payroll).

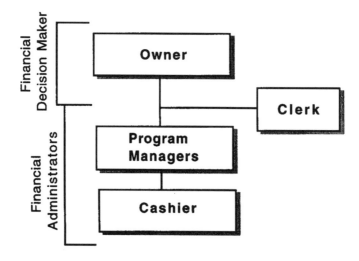

Figure 3.1. Financial management roles within the organizational structure.

Financial Responsibility

In the preceding example, the owner is *responsible* for her decisions, regardless of the outcomes. If she sets the cost recovery target too low, authorizes too many free passes, or pays her staff too well, then she may not make a profit. On the other hand, if she has instituted sound policies on cost recovery, complementary services, and employee compensation, then she is likely to enjoy a suitable return on her investment. The owner is responsible for either outcome.

In order to realize her financial goals, the sports complex owner will delegate authority and prescribe duties to her staff. The likelihood of her realizing a profit is dependent on her staff exercising that authority and performing their duties the way she expects. If they exceed the limits of their authority or fail to do their duty, the staff are responsible for those offenses only; however, the owner is still responsible for the resulting profit or loss. In financial management, as in any other area of management, authority can be delegated, but responsibility cannot.

Financial Functions of the Organization

Sport and leisure service organizations facilitate two primary financial functions: controlling and acquiring. *Controlling* is an internally oriented function that involves recording, monitoring, and managing the financial consequences of past and current activities. *Acquiring* is an externally oriented function that deals with securing financial resources required to meet current and future needs. The organizational chart of a sport and leisure service agency will usually reflect these two functions in the identification of a *controller* and a *treasurer*. In large organizations, there may be many people working in both a controller's office and a treasurer's office; in smaller organizations, the two functions may be handled by the same person. Furthermore, that single controller/treasurer may also have other nonfinancial duties. Although desirable in certain situations, there is usually no requirement that a crowd of financial managers be included in the organizational structure. These two primary functions should, however, be addressed therein.

Organizational Structures

Other than the two officers mentioned above, financial management divisions of large sport and leisure service organizations may include other personnel with specialized duties. The duties of the most common financial management positions are briefly described below:

Director of Finance

The duties of the director of finance include supervising and coordinating the activities of the Department of Finance. The director of finance serves as a financial adviser to decision-making bodies within the organization and often serves as the chief budget officer.

Controller (also called "Comptroller")

The controller's duties include describing (by using generally accepted accounting principles [GAAP]) the financial events that have occurred within a certain period of time. The controller develops and maintains a management information system and prepares financial forecasts for use by financial decision makers. Additional duties include pre-auditing purchase orders, handling receipts and disbursements, and issuing all payments and invoices. The controller may also be charged with maintaining inventory records.

Treasurer

The duties of the treasurer focus on the acquisition of funds needed for the operation of the sport and leisure service organization. Private funds may come from a variety of sources, thus requiring the treasurer in the private or commercial setting to maintain and nurture relationships with lenders, stockholders, security markets, and regulatory agencies. In contrast, the treasurer in a public agency works primarily with tax collection and fund generation through special assessments. In addition to collecting all revenues, the treasurer plans cash flow, invests available funds, and recommends pricing policies/strategies that will help to achieve funding objectives.

Assessor

Public sport and leisure service organizations receive much of their funding from tax revenues. Property taxes are collected according to assessed property values, and the establishment of those values is the duty of the assessor. Working closely with the treasurer, the assessor applies relevant state laws, studies property values, and assesses property for taxation purposes.

Purchasing Agent

The duties of the purchasing agent go well beyond processing paperwork for ordering materials, supplies, and equipment. An effective purchasing agent establishes standards for regularly purchased items and prepares specifications for each item to be purchased. By maintaining relationships with vendors and suppliers, the purchasing agent can economize on certain bulk or special-order purchases, as well as advise program managers on new services or materials that are available. The purchasing agent purchases all materials, supplies, and equipment for the organization and then receives and inspects them to ensure that specifications have been met. Significant monetary savings can also be realized through the purchasing agent's maintaining of warehouse storage and commodity distribution systems.

Auditor

Though not incorporated in the finance department, the auditor has a position of great importance to the financial well-being of the organization. The task of the auditor is to periodically provide an independent, objective evaluation of financial management systems and practices. The independent auditor serves as a check on executive officials by determining whether any errors (unintentional misstatements) have been made or whether there are irregularities (deliberate misstatements or unauthorized/illegal depletion of financial resources).

The auditor thoroughly reviews procedures and statements to determine and report whether

- the financial statements present fairly the organization's financial position;
- the financial statements accurately present (in accordance with GAAP) the results of agency operations;
- the financial activities of the organization are in compliance with local, state/provincial, and federal laws and regulations;
- the organization has established an adequate system of internal accounting and control;
- there are questionable expenditures;
- there is evidence of waste, abuse, or fraud.

Since the finance department is the primary administrative body (and subject to input by executive officials), it would be unwise for the auditor's position to be too closely associated with that department. To avoid the appearance of the finance department checking up on itself, auditors are usually directly accountable to the chief executive officer or directing authority (board of directors, city council, etc.) and may not even be an employee of the agency. Many large and small sport and leisure service organizations contract with or retain an independent accounting firm to serve as their auditor. In a few local governments, the audit function is carried out by an independently elected auditor or controller.

Organization for Financial Management in the Public Sector

Figure 3.2 presents a basic organizational chart for a local government (e.g., a city, county, or town). Detailed in the chart are the relationships of the independent auditor to the elected governing body, and the Department of Finance to the institutional hierarchy and other civic departments. This model also represents the general structure of state/provincial and federal governments in the United States and Canada. Note that the responsibility and full authority to manage public finances is vested in the elected governing body. In a representative democracy, this authority comes from the people, and it is to them that the elected body is accountable.

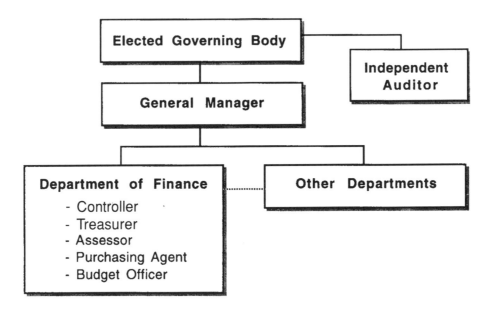

Figure 3.2.   Basic organizational chart emphasizing financial management unit.

Figure 3.2 shows an independent auditor who reports to the financial decision-making body. It is a standard practice and often a legal requirement for local, state/provincial, and federal governments to have auditors who submit public reports of their reviews to their respective legislatures. As much as possible, these auditors operate independently and without regard to personal or partisan politics.

Also shown in this basic organizational chart is the position of general manager. The general manager is the senior civil servant to whom all department heads report and through whom government policies are articulated. The director of finance reports to the general manager, thus making the latter an important figure in the financial management system. That importance is underscored by the dual role that the general manager, at times, appears to play. This top official is effectively both a financial decision maker and a financial administrator. Technically, financial decision making or policy setting does not exist at the level of the general manager; still, however, it must be recognized that this person is in a position to provide selective information that leads the elected body to make certain decisions. Thus he or she has *effective* decision-making power without having *formal* decision-making authority. The general manager is also the top financial administrator in the government and oversees the work of the director of finance. In this oversight role, the general manager interprets the policy decisions of the elected governing body and, thereby, has further opportunity to broadly influence financial management in the organization.

The organizational chart in Figure 3.2 uses a dotted line to represent the relationship between the Department of Finance and the other governmental departments. The dotted line indicates that one department does not take direction from the other(s), but rather, departments must communicate and work together to ensure proper management of financial resources. In reality, the Department of Finance is a support unit to the other program-based departments, yet it does maintain control over most procedures pertaining to budget implementation. In some organizations, financial administrators working within program-based departments actually report both to the program department head and to the Department of Finance. This matrix structure can be an efficient way to manage financial functions with a degree of consistency, as well as avoid duplication which occurs when other departments feel the need to keep their own financial records and develop their own financial management information systems.

Organization for Financial Management in the Private Nonprofit and Commercial Sectors

Whether large, small, private nonprofit, or commercial, most nonpublic organizations will have a similar basic structure to the government organization typified in Figure 3.2. Instead of from an elected governing body, the private nonprofit agency will receive policies and directives from an appointed board of directors. In the commercial sector, the decision-making body will be the owner(s) or board that represents the shareholders.

The value of an independent auditor is just as great for nonpublic organizations as it is for public entities. The independent auditor position is frequently mandated by the organization's charter or by law. Some small private nonprofit sport and leisure service agencies rely on local volunteers to conduct their financial audits, while major commercial enterprises may have large in-house auditing departments.

As in the public agency, the day-to-day management of the private nonprofit or commercial organization is entrusted to the general manager. The title used for this top management position varies, but the most common alternatives are "chief executive officer" or "president."

Finally, the finance division is also an important part of private nonprofit and commercial sport and leisure service organizations. In these nonpublic settings, the finance division continues to fulfill the basic functions of acquiring funds and controlling internal financial activities while relating in a supportive way to the organization's program-based departments.

Politics and the Financial Management Organization

Managers of public sport and leisure service organizations are generally quick to point out that there is no work environment where politics so much influences day-to-day management as it does in government agencies. Private nonprofit managers would likely disagree and describe the many frustrations that they experience in their own politically sensitive positions. Further claims to the title of "Most Political Organization" could also be made by managers of commercial sport and leisure service organizations who feel that too much of their time and energy is spent on keeping the owners happy rather than doing the job properly.

A reality of management life is the constant exposure to and influence of corporate politics: It is a part of public service management. It is a part of management in the private nonprofit sector. It is a part of how the commercial sport and leisure service organization operates. It is natural, and it is not necessarily bad.

Financial decision makers are usually in such a position because their political viewpoint is consistent with that of the power base (i.e., the voters or the shareholders). It is believed that the management philosophy of the financial decision maker will lead to desired results, and the decision maker is, therefore, empowered to establish fiscal policies for the organization. Financial administrators are expected to reflect that management philosophy in their implementation of the fiscal policies. In reality, it is just as important for the financial administrator to be responsive to the political context as it is to be efficient and effective in performing the technical finance functions of the organization. To underscore the importance of this responsiveness, most financial administrators serve "at the pleasure of the board," and their job security depends on how well they reflect political ideologies and achieve desired results.

In some public organizations, however, there is a stated need for and interest in achieving nonpartisan, technical competence in financial management. In other words, the voters want to be sure that their tax dollars are managed by the most competent financial administrator, regardless of political party affiliation. In such cases, the organizational structure may include a variety of autonomous or semiautonomous elected fiscal agencies (ranging from boards of tax appeal to boards of assessors) and elected officers such as controllers, treasurers, and assessors. However, the more integrated financial system and organizational structure, with the general manager as the chief steward and distributor of authority, is most common in the public sector and almost universal in the private nonprofit and commercial sectors.

Summary

The many aspects of financial management in the sport and leisure service organization can most effectively and efficiently be addressed through an organizational structure that clearly defines the lines of authority and differentiates between financial decision-making bodies and financial administrators. Financial officers develop systems and apply standard procedures to monitor, control, and report on the financial position, activities, and future of the organization. They also implement policies that generate required financial resources, as well as relate to program-based departments. The general organization for financial management varies little between public, private nonprofit, and commercial agencies and maintains the same basic elements in both small and large enterprises. Inherent in any organization is politics, and the responsiveness to the political environment and awareness of administrative systems of the organization are critical to the success of the financial manager.

Section B

Revenue Management

The next four chapters of this book examine the need and opportunities for revenues to be used in support of the sport and leisure service enterprise. Revenue management is a crucial skill to develop because, without the acquisition and management of revenues, there can be no expenditures and therefore no activity. Chapter 4 identifies major sources of income for organizations in the public, private nonprofit, and commercial sectors. It provides a detailed discussion of compulsory income and introduces other sources, including earned income. Pricing is an important consideration in the generation of earned income and is the topic of Chapter 5. Pricing principles and strategies are presented, and the impacts of price and price adjustment on consumer behavior are described. Gratuitous income is discussed in Chapter 6, and the process of grantseeking is carefully detailed. Because grants are usually awarded by foundations or other philanthropic organizations, this section concludes with an exploration of philanthropy and fundraising in Chapter 7. Thanks to a firm foundation in the principles and practices of revenue management, the financial manager will then be prepared to focus on expenditure management through budget development and administration, and through accounting and reporting.

Chapter 4

Income Sources

Introduction

Income is essential to all sport, commercial, and public leisure service organizations. Without income, they would not be able to function. Regardless of whether it is a private fitness center, a nonprofit sports stadium, or a state park system, each uses similar, and yet different, sources of income. The different types of leisure service organizations rely on different types of income in different ways, and in some cases, their sources of income will be unique. Initially, this chapter will discuss the types of income common to the three sectors: commercial, private nonprofit, and public. Governments have different ways to secure income, and the methods of achieving it may vary on a state-by-state level. This uniqueness of government sources will receive particular attention.

Types of Income Sources

There are multiple sources of income available to any organization. In this section, five of the most common types of income will be discussed. They are compulsory income, gratuitous income, earned income, investment income, and contractual receipts. While these are the most commonly accepted terms, not all organizations use them. For example, the National Association of State Park Directors, a nonprofit organization, uses revenues appropriated, revenues unappropriated, general funds, dedicated funds, and federal funds to describe sources of income for the various state park systems. The meanings are similar, but this example of a different classification system emphasizes the point that while there is a general acceptance among terms, they are neither universally used nor necessarily understood. Table 4.1 illustrates the five most common sources of income for leisure service organizations and identifies the level of importance each of these has to the three sectors. Table 4.1 depicts the uniqueness of compulsory income to the public sector, the importance of earned income, and the varying levels of utilization of the remaining income sources to all three sectors.

Compulsory income consists of funds secured by government organizations that are generated through taxes, licensing, or some other sort of government-instituted income source that requires all or specific individuals or organizations within a legislative jurisdiction to contribute. *Gratuitous income* is received without expectation of a return. Sources for gratuitous income include grants, bequests, gifts, and blind and open sponsorships. In each case, the giver typically does not receive a direct benefit or compensation for the gift. Much of what is discussed in Chapters 6 (Grantseeking) and 7 (Philanthropy and Fundraising) is included as gratuitous income.

Sector / Income	Compulsory Income	Gratuitous Income	Earned Income	Investment Income	Contractual Receipts
Commercial Sector	None	Minimal - more often provide this type to other sectors	Major source of income for operations	Key source of income for some businesses	Can be a major source of income, depending upon scope or business
Nonprofit Sector	May have some impact when tied to public funding, but limited	Essential and major source of income	Essential and a major source of income	Limited, based on organization and availability of fiscal resources	Growing importance
Public Sector	Essential source of income	Growing importance as income source	Essential source of income	Limited source of income, but frequently used	Growing source of income among some agencies

Table 4.1. Income sources and their level of importance to the three sectors.

Earned income consists of cash resources generated from fees and charges instituted by the leisure service organization. These can include program fees, charges for use of areas and facilities, income from sales of supplies, equipment, gift shops, entrance fees, admission fees, rental fees, and user fees. Fiscal investments that earn interest are also considered earned income. *Investment income* includes new money generated from investment interests, dividends, and capital appreciation. Investment income is the result of investing a fixed amount of dollars (principal) in such a way as to generate new money (interest). The interest becomes the investment income available to sport and leisure service organizations.

Contractual receipts are revenues generated from legal agreements with private and nonprofit organizations. Agreements can include the management of resources, rental of facilities, rental of equipment, management of special operations such as golf courses or marinas, concession operations, tennis centers, zoos, stadiums, gift shops, or other types of enterprises. They can also include those arrangements that are generally referred to as *privatization,* a practice which has become popular in recent years.

Compulsory Income Sources

Compulsory income includes cash and noncash sources collected through the taxing and regulatory powers at different government levels as prescribed by state and federal law. Government sources of income have changed dramatically for leisure service organizations since 1978, when California voters passed Proposition 13 (a landmark initiative which cut property taxes by almost 50 percent). Prior to that, public agencies had gained the vast majority of their income from the general fund, which was primarily supported through property tax revenues. Since 1978, governments all across the United States have responded to voter demands for lower taxes with sometimes massive tax cuts. In some cases these have been prompted by voter-initiated propositions, as in California, Oregon, and Massachusetts. In other states, the legislatures responded to what they saw as a growing trend and to the pressures of their constituencies. Even the federal government has not been immune to the trend, as the president and Congress have sometimes competed with each other over who could appear to cut taxes more. The declining availability of general fund monies has required that public leisure service organizations at all levels rethink how they gather sources of income and use that income.

Taxes continue to represent the largest single source of income to government. There are several different types of taxes, including real property tax, personal property tax, excise tax, use tax, income tax, local option tax, special assessment tax, and impact tax. Each has a specific purpose and is discussed in the next two sections.

Types of State and Municipal Taxes

Real Property Taxes

Real property taxes are assessed in all 50 states and their subordinate jurisdictions (counties, cities, municipalities, etc.). Jurisdictions can set the tax at the local level in compliance with state law. Real property is defined as land and whatever is developed or erected or growing on the land. This includes subsurface features such as oil or mineral deposits. Tax assessors (see Chapter 3) are appointed at the local level and have primary responsibility for determining the value of the property.

In 1957, real property taxes represented 69 percent of the total local government tax base. By 1992, property taxes had shrunk to 33 percent of the tax base. Other types of taxes increased over the same period and became a larger part of the mix of revenues available to leisure service organizations. In spite of the recent changes in compulsory income sources, property taxes remain the single largest source of revenue for local government. Table 4.2 depicts the various sources of revenue available to local governments between 1980 and 1995, as reported by the U.S. Census Bureau. It can be seen that, while property taxes as a source of revenue declined over the period, total taxes paid increased by almost 300 percent. Because this table represents both state and local governments, not all results can be universally applied.

Revenue Source	1980		1990		1995	
	Amount ($)	Percent Distribution	Amount	Percent Distribution	Amount	Percent Distribution
General Revenue Total	299,293	100.0%	712,700	100.00%	940,733	100.00%
Taxes	223,463	74.7%	502,619	70.50%	660,557	70.20%
° Property	68,499	22.9%	155,613	21.80%	203,451	21.60%
° Sales and Gross Receipts	79,927	26.7%	177,885	25.00%	237,268	25.20%
° Individual Income	42,080	14.1%	105,640	14.80%	137,931	14.70%
° Corporate Income	13,321	4.5%	23,566	3.30%	31,406	3.30%
° Other	19,636	6.6%	38,915	5.50%	50,521	5.40%
Charges and Miscellaneous	75,830	25.3%	211,081	29.60%	280,156	29.80%

Table 4.2. Percentage of state and local government revenue from own sources, comparative years (in billions of dollars).

Source: 1998 Statistical Abstract of the United States, U.S. Census Bureau

Municipal governments are allowed to establish different tax rates for different classifications of property. Decisions about the levels at which different properties are taxed are made by the local legislative body. Personal homes, undeveloped land, businesses, and farm property are typically taxed at different levels. Permanent tax-exempt status may be granted to certain types of land uses, such as that involving governments, school districts, and religious and charitable organizations. A *tax abatement,* which is an exemption from paying taxes, can be granted to an organization for a specified period of time. Tax abatements are generally granted, as an incentive, to firms considering moving to a particular region.

Determining the value of real property is based on an estimation of its *taxable worth* or *assessed value.* Assessed value is different from market value. In most states, assessed value is much lower than *fair market value.* Fair market value is that at which a home may be valued for sale, whereas its assessed value for taxation purposes may be as much as 30 percent to 50 percent lower. For example, a home with a fair market value of $240,000, which is assessed at 50 percent of the fair market value, would have an assessed value of $120,000.

Each potential jurisdiction with real property taxing powers has a *tax base.* The tax base is the total assessed value of all taxable property in a community. Assessed values of communities will differ considerably and are difficult to compare within a state and almost impossible for comparison between states.

Tax rates are based on revenue needs of the government. In other words, a government determines it needs $4 million to operate on in the upcoming fiscal year. This decision is made after the public agency has completed its budgeting process and identified what portion of its operating budget needs to come from real property taxes. The tax rates are determined by dividing the property tax requirements by the assessed valuation. Assessed valuation, however, does not include all real property within the jurisdiction because some organizations or groups have a tax abatement. When the tax abatement property is removed from the assessed value, what remains is a *net assessed value.* The example below shows how net assessed value is determined.

Net Assessed Valuation Example	
Total assessed valuation of community	$100,000,000
Tax exempt property	- $10,500,000
Net assessed valuation	$89,500,000

Tax rates are assessed on the basis of net assessed valuation. If the community used in the above example determines that it requires $15 million from taxes to operate, the following formula is used:

Tax Rule Formula

Required Taxes / Net Assessed Valuation = Tax Rate

Tax Rate Example

$15,000,000 / $89,500,000 = .167

There are three ways in which tax rates are expressed: (1) as a percent of the value of property, (2) as a mill rate, or (3) as mills. The preceding example would be expressed in the three alternatives as shown below:

Tax Rate Expressions
% Tax Rate... 16.7%
Mill Rate 0.167
Mills... 167

The relationship between % Tax Rate and the Mill Rate is obvious. The 16.7 percent means 16.7 per hundred, which is 16.7/10, which equals .167. A mill, on the other hand, is equal to 1/1000 of the assessed property value. Figure 4.1 shows the conversion factors for the three expressions.

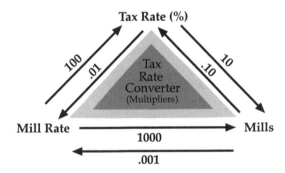

Figure 4.1. Conversion factors for three expressions of the tax rate.

Knowing the tax rate, the owner of property can calculate the property tax that is owed. For example, the owner of a $240,000 home assessed at 50 percent will have the tax rate applied to the assessed value of $120,000. If he is required to pay 10 mills to the city, he will pay 10 one-thousandths of $120,000.

Property Owner's Tax Calculation
Example 1: % Tax Rate
Tax Rate x Assessed Value = property tax
1% x $120,000 = $1,200
Example 2: Mill Rate
Mill Rate x (Assessed Value / 100) = property tax
0.01 x 120,000 = $1,200
Example 3: Mills
10 x (Assessed Value/1000) + property tax
10 x 120 = $1,200

The property tax system is based on the idea that the more a person owns, the more that person should pay. The methods of tax calculation, shown on the previous page, follow the principle that a property owner should contribute the same portion of the total tax revenues as he or she owns of the total assessed property in the community.

Other Types of Taxes

Personal property taxes were allowed in 41 states in 1997. Taxing of personal property occurs in three common forms: (1) household tangible property (e.g., automobiles, recreational vehicles, and sports transportation devices); (2) business tangible property (e.g., inventory, business fixtures, furniture, equipment, and machinery); and (3) intangibles (e.g., stocks and bonds). In most states, individuals declare the value of their personal property to tax assessors.

Sales tax is administered at the state level, but there may be provisions for a local sales tax. State sales tax rates vary from 3 percent to 7 percent. In some states, a portion of the tax may be reserved for state and local park and recreation functions. For example, Missouri voters supported the allocation of one-tenth of each cent collected through the state sales tax for operation of their state park system. Eighty-five percent of Missouri's state park system's operating expenses are now covered by the dedicated sales tax. Sales tax is applied to a broad range of goods and is determined by state legislatures. Only four states (Delaware, Montana, New Hampshire, and Oregon) do not have a state sales tax.

A *use tax* is imposed in some states on individuals who purchase items outside of their state of residence and who do not pay any state sales tax on those otherwise taxable items. The use tax is designed to replace uncollected sales taxes for items purchased outside of the taxing jurisdiction. Use tax is gaining popularity in some jurisdictions.

Excise tax is imposed on the sale of specific goods such as gasoline, cigarettes, and alcoholic beverages and specific functions such as hotels and motels (sometimes called a lodging tax), restaurants, and auto rental. These taxes may be levied at the state or local level. Excise taxes, which are authorized at the state level and collected at either the state or local level, are never popular with those who have to pay, but are also often controversial in the circles of those whose agencies might benefit from them. The hotel/motel/restaurant excise taxes are sometimes known as *local option taxes.* Owners of lodging establishments and others involved in the tourism industry often oppose such taxes because they are believed to be detrimental to tourism and business. Because of this ongoing debate about the appropriateness of excise taxes, many state legislative assemblies require local option taxes to be approved by the electorate at the local level.

Income taxes are administered at the municipal, state, and federal levels. There are two types of income taxes—personal and corporate. Personal income taxes are present in 43 states. Personal income taxes are typically levied on people who resided in the state and/or earned income in the state. Corporate income taxes are prescribed by state law and administered at the state and/or the municipal level.

Local option taxes are applied at the local level, but legislatively enabled at the state level. One of the most popular local option taxes is a local sales tax that is added to the state sales tax. In 1997, local option sales taxes accounted for about 10 percent of all local government revenue. There is enabling legislation for local option taxes in 40 states (local option taxes are not authorized in Connecticut, Maine, Massachusetts, Rhode Island, Maryland, New Jersey, Kentucky, Mississippi, West Virginia, and Hawaii). Supporters of local option sales taxes argue that the taxes allow local governments (city and county) to diversify their revenue bases. They also argue that this form of taxation allows geographically large areas to provide programs and services from local funds rather than tapping state resources. Local hotel/motel taxes are also a very common form of the local option tax. These taxes were initially focused on convention and travel destination localities, but have become much more widespread. Local option taxes are used for a broad variety of purposes. In some cases, the enabling legislation can be very specific about the use of these taxes, while in other instances, the legislation can be very vague.

Other Sources of Compulsory Income

Special Assessments, Dedication Ordinances, and Regulations

Special assessment taxes are enabled at the state level and administered at that level or lower. Most often, however, they are administered at the local level. These types of taxes focus on a specific geographical area, such as the downtown or a specific neighborhood. Consequently, the taxes collected may be spent only in the source neighborhood. They may be used for improvements in a particular area, for land purchases, or for salaries to maintain an area. The introduction and elimination of special assessment taxes are generally agreed to by those who will be taxed.

Dedication ordinances and regulations are available to local governments and are typically instituted by county and city councils within guidelines established by state legislatures. These sometimes result in cash income to public agencies. When dedication ordinances and regulations were initiated, they required developers of neighborhoods to set aside a portion of the land for park and recreation use. While this was commendable, all too often, the land set aside was not acceptable for park and recreation use, but was land the developer could not use. Local governments quickly began to look at alternatives to land dedication. In some instances, they tightened up local ordinances and became more specific in the type of land they deemed acceptable. In other instances, they began to accept money in lieu of land dedication. The money generally had to be used to improve or add to existing property or to purchase new property for parks and recreation. One common use was to purchase greenbelts that linked the community and its parks together.

The imposition of *impact taxes* is another method of recovering development costs, and it is one that has been around for over 30 years. The idea behind impact taxes is to require developers and new home owners to help pay for public improvements required as a result of the construction process. It has been argued that existing city residents should not have to pay for the development of new home and commercial sites, but that the cost should be borne, in part, by those who will benefit most directly from the development. Impact taxes are most likely to be used for infrastructure costs such as streets, utilities, schools, and other essential services. Leisure service organizations have successfully argued in a number of communities that they are an essential service.

**Impact fees and other taxes and fees can be one-time sources
of income to offset new construction.**

Licenses and Permits

Licenses and permits are a relatively small source of income for leisure service organizations. A *license* is an authorization to act or to engage in an activity. Probably the most common license is the driver's license. Licenses in leisure service organizations are frequently granted for the distribution or sale of a particular product. The New York State Park system, for example, entered into a license agreement with a soft drink company, thereby granting exclusive rights to the sale of its products in the park system.

A *permit* is an authorization for a person to engage in a particular activity—not necessarily recreational—or to use a facility or equipment. A common permit is a building permit issued by a local jurisdiction. In leisure service organizations, a permit might be issued for the serving and consumption of alcoholic beverages at a public facility, for the rental of a facility, or for the use of a significant natural recreation resource. Usually, permits are good for a shorter period of time than a license.

Federal Government Sources

The federal government has long been a source of revenue for state and local governments. Monies collected by the federal government and redistributed to state governments are called *transfer payments.* In 1980, the federal government made transfer payments worth $83 billion. By 1990, that amount had risen to $137 billion, and in 1995, it was $229 billion. By far the greatest share of transfer payment money has been used for public welfare, but other programs, such as highways, education, health and hospitals, and housing and community development have also received significant amounts. Historically, leisure service organizations have been well served by transfer payments and federal government programs. However, federal government fiscal support for state and local leisure service organizations has been on the decline in recent years. For example, state parks received $15 million in 1997 from federal sources, but that is a major reduction from the $630 million they received just two decades earlier.

Some of the legislation and programs through which the federal government transfers funds to the states and local jurisdictions include the Land and Water Conservation Fund, the National Recreational Trails Act, the National Highway System, Intermodal Surface Transportation Efficiency Act of 1992 (ISTEA), highway safety programs, scenic highway programs, and metropolitan planning. Each program has provided varying levels of funding to leisure service organizations. The *Land and Water Conservation Act* (LWCF) has been in place for more than 30 years. During its early years, it provided significant levels of revenue to state and local governments. Beginning in the mid-1980s, levels of funding declined to the point where it now provides little to no funding at the state and local levels. The *National Recreation Trails Act* has received limited funding since 1993. It is set up so that 30 percent of the funds go to motorized trails, 30 percent to nonmotorized trails, and 40 percent to multipurpose trails. The money can be spent on maintenance, as well as construction of trails. The *National Highway System* provides a potential source of money for trail development next to any National Highway System highway (excluding the interstate system). The ISTEA has been the steadiest source of income for leisure service organizations in local government in recent years. As with other transportation sources, ISTEA focuses wholly on trail development and maintenance.

The growth of water-play devices has increased revenue at aquatic centers dramatically.

Gratuitous Income

Gratuitous income receives significant attention in Chapters 6 and 7. Grants are an important source of potential income for sports and leisure service organizations. In 1996, $13.8 billion in grants were awarded from public and private grant sources. It is estimated that leisure service organizations received $552 million of those grants.

Fundraising is an organized process of seeking out gifts to support leisure service organization and capital improvements. The growth of fundraising and support organizations for sport and leisure service organizations has been dramatic over the last 10 years. Examples could include a community park and recreation agency that creates its own foundation or a sports promotion corporation that is supported by a companion foundation or a corporation that creates its own freestanding foundations for distributing wealth. In 1997, individuals, bequests, and foundations gave over $143 billion, and of that total, individuals were responsbile for $110 billion, or 70 percent, of all giving. Grantseeking and fundraising are intertwined; leisure service organizations look to both of them as increasing sources of income structure.

Earned Income

Earned income consists of cash resources generated from fees, as well as charges assessed by the sport and leisure service organization. Types of fees can include program fees; charges for use of equipment, areas, and facilities; income from sales of supplies; gift shop revenues; entrance fees; admission fees; rental fees; and user fees. Fiscal investments that earn interest are also considered earned income. In recent years, the greatest growth in revenues for sport and leisure service organizations has been from earned income. To illustrate, the City of Sunnyvale, California, has specifically designated earned income as a key revenue source for its parks and recreation department. For many sports organizations, earned income is the primary source of operational funds. The emphasis upon earned income has helped to reshape leisure service organization management over the last 20 years. As a result of this emphasis, management has become more entrepreneurial and business focused.

Earned income comes primarily from fees and charges. The Government Finance Officers' Association, suggesting a technical difference between fees and charges, agrees that in most cases, the terms "fees" and "charges" are used interchangeably. A fee may be imposed as a result of a public need to regulate activities, safety, or other protective measures. Fees constitute the purchase of a privilege or an authorization and are applied to services rendered, such as an inspection or the issuance of a building permit. In leisure service organizations, the term "fees" has come to be associated with the delivery of programs and services.

Examples of major classifications of earned income include entrance and admission fees, rental fees, user or program fees, sales revenue, and special fees. *Entrance and admission fees* are charged for entrance to any public or private sports or leisure facility, movie theater, art museum, children's museum, monument, historical building, etc. Income from fees may be used to cover the cost of operations, but in some cases, it may be intended to also provide additional revenue for such needs as debt retirement and capital improvement funding.

Rental fees are charged for the exclusive use of a tangible property such as a Santa suit, park pavilion, sports equipment, sports complex, picnic equipment, game equipment, public address system, stroller, lawn chairs, paddle boats, coin telescopes, cabin, lodge, resort room, horse, camping equipment, bicycle, toilets, and golf clubs. The list is as long as one's imagination. Revenue from rental fees may be used to recover the cost of the purchase and replacement of the rental item(s), storage and handling, or maintenance and cleaning. Sport and leisure service organizations may also use rental fees to offset operational costs in other areas, provide renters with additional recreation opportunities, and/or contribute to profits.

User and program fees are defined as charges made for the use of a facility or for participation in an activity, program, or service. The fee may be used for reimbursement of the cost of capital development, debt retirement, maintenance operations, operations of the facility or program, and capital improvements. User and program fees could be charged for almost any type of program offering, such as figure skating classes, pottery classes, modern dance classes, tie-dyeing classes, child care, etc. The 75-page brochure for one service organization that serves a community of 150,000 included (for a three-month period) over 900 programs with fees attached to them. In this instance, fees were differentiated between residents and nonresidents, with the latter paying a premium fee. User fees can also be charged for the use of facilities and may be compared with rental fees in some ways. However, in this instance, exclusive use of a tangible property may not be present. For example, the curling club may operate the curling facility two evenings a week while under contract with the sport and leisure service organization. The participants pay a club membership fee to the club and a program fee to the sport and leisure service organization that owns the facility. This is a common arrangement. Some state parks operate railroad concessions and provide train rides. The cost of operation of the railroad is covered partially or wholly in the user fee.

Sales revenue comes from the sale of goods and services through gift shops, stores, concessions, restaurants, and similar types of operations. Concession operations are becoming a major source of income for sport and leisure service organizations. The major national parks produce significant amounts of revenue from sales of goods such as groceries and fuel, mostly through contractual arrangements. Sales activities are almost always implemented in conjunction with some other service operated by the sport and leisure service organization. In a fitness center, for example, there may be a pro shop, a snack bar, and a full-service restaurant. In Tacoma, Washington, the city parks and recreation department contracts with an outside organization to operate a full-service restaurant on the waterfront. Many golf courses have pro shops and restaurants as part of their operations. Museums have gift shops, restaurants, snack bars, and other revenue-generating amenities. State

State resort parks provide opportunities for users to experience state parks who do not choose to camp and provide the agency with earned income.

and national parks may accommodate grocery stores, gas stations, motels, and lodges. The purpose of sales activity is to provide a service to the user and to generate revenue for the organization.

Special fees are generally charged for providing some extraordinary service to consumers. In many cases, special fees might also be included in one of the previously identified fee types. Examples include lights for tennis courts, park ranger security for special events, and use of portable stages, sound equipment, and the like. In some communities, a fee is charged for night use of facilities. This charge is made by some sport and leisure service organizations for night softball, and teams are charged a fee to recover the cost of the utilities, maintenance, and replacement of the lights. Other examples include fees charged for special camps (basketball, baseball, cheerleading, computer, etc.), equipment storage, and reservation privileges.

Investment Income

Investment income represents those funds that are generated from the investment of existing funds in different types of money markets. All public agencies, nonprofits, and commercial enterprises are allowed to invest either all or portions of their existing funds in various investment income opportunities. Some of the most common are municipal and corporate bonds, money market certificates, stock transactions, and mutual funds. The investment of such monies is almost always made in consultation with an investment professional who has expertise in the public, nonprofit, or commercial sector. In some instances, especially with public agencies, the investment is for short periods of time (less than six months). Even investments over such a short period of time allow the organization to realize additional income for its operations. Investment income reduces the need for other types of income, especially income from property taxes. Such investments are usually made in opportunities that are "safe," in the sense that they are less strongly affected by major downturns or upturns in the stock market. Nonprofits may use investment income as a major source of revenue for their operations. Many state park and recreation associations and universities have made investments in mutual funds, bonds, or other sources and then use the annual interest income to fund scholarships and other operations.

Contractual Receipts

Contractual receipts are revenue generated from legal agreements with other related organizations. Income-generating agreements can be entered into for the management of resources, rental of facilities, rental of equipment, management of special operations such as golf courses, marinas, food concessions, tennis centers, zoos, stadiums, or gift shops. They can also include those varied operations collectively referred to as subjects of *privatization*— a concept which has become popular in the management of sport and leisure service organizations.

A *contract* is a term that describes a unit of trading for a financial or commodity future. Contract management requires proficiency in a set of business and fiscal management skills from both the contractor and the owner. In the early years of contract management, it was not uncommon for a public agency to unwisely "give away" any potential for revenue from the contract and then provide little oversight to contract compliance. In response, one city eventually canceled the private contract for its golf course operations after the facility regularly posted losses of over $500,000. The city managers determined they could no longer justify using tax dollars to support golf operations with major losses. In the first year after canceling the contract, the city discovered that the driving ranges had revenues of over $250,000 and expenses of only $40,000. Under the previous contract, all of the driving-range profits had been going to the golf pro. In this case, the golf pro had not done anything wrong, but the city had written a rather one-sided contract and had also failed to manage it carefully. Good contract management requires time and expertise.

Partnerships and Collaborations

Partnerships and collaborations are becoming a more common approach to generating income for sport and leisure service organizations. The terms partnership and collaboration are frequently used interchangeably; however, they have very different meanings. *Partnerships* are formed through agreements between two or more parties with an interest in satisfying a mutual need that is common to those organizations. A partnership may be for a fixed or indeterminate length of time. The key to success in a partnership is for all organizations to clearly understand and easily identify their needs. By contrast, in *collaborative* arrangements, different organizations may work together to achieve a common goal, but they do not entirely share the same vision, resources, or risks. The foundation of collaborations is the hope that, by working together, several organizations will have a better opportunity to resolve an issue than would a single organization. Sport and leisure service organizations use both partnerships and collaborations, but partnerships are more likely to produce income.

A partnership results from a formal or informal agreement between two or more organizations to work together to provide a service or to fund a project. Partnerships can include any combination of public, nonprofit, and commercial organizations. For example, a partnership may involve cosponsorship of a 5K run by the public Parks and Recreation Department, the YMCA, a women's shelter, a local bank, a sporting goods dealer, and the local hospital. The Parks and Recreation Department plans and jointly conducts the event with the YMCA; the hospital's marketing department develops brochures, logos, T-shirt designs, and the like; the bank and sporting goods store provide the awards to the runners and help pay for advertising costs; and the women's shelter receives the bulk of the revenues earmarked for its operations. Each of the organizations involved receives some benefit from a partnership. In this fictional case, the Parks and Recreation Department, the YMCA, the hospital, the sporting goods store, and the bank all received recognition for their efforts. The Parks and Recreation Department and the YMCA were perceived as meeting their mission to serve the community. The bank, the hospital, and the sporting goods store succeeded in enhancing and reinforcing their image as socially responsible entities. The women's shelter received financial support, additional legitimization as a social service agency, and a positive image boost. Each participant received support, recognition, and a feeling of contribution that it might not have been able to secure independently.

Partnering is about working towards common goals and outcomes. It brings to the table unique resources from each organization that may be unavailable to the other organizations. It reinforces the assertion that "the whole is greater than the parts" and shows that, by working together, all participants in a partnership can expect to receive a positive return on their investment. It need not be a fiscal return, but it could be an intangible benefit such as image, goodwill, legitimization, etc.

Further examples of partnerships and the benefits of partnership can be found in numerous communities such as Indianapolis, Indiana, and Naperville, Illinois. The Indianapolis Parks and Recreation Department worked with neighborhood community groups to formalize their involvement and leadership in local parks. Both community groups and local churches accepted shared responsibility for maintenance and the general upkeep of the parks (mowing, trash removal, graffiti reporting, etc.). As partners, they received a stipend of either cash, special services, or availability of department resources to the church or neighborhood association. The work has been done at a lower cost than union maintenance crews could do it for, and local involvement has resulted in a higher level of maintenance and lower levels of vandalism. In Naperville, Illinois, the city and park district (the park district is a separate taxing district) have partnered with the Riverwalk Foundation to develop and maintain a downtown riverwalk. In celebration of the city's 1981 sesquicentennial anniversary, volunteers developed the riverwalk and, since then, it has become a focal point of the community. Its covered bridges, fountains, landscaping, and distinctive shepherd's-crook light poles have become symbolic of Naperville's ties to its historic past as the oldest settlement in DuPage County. The city, the park district, and a community foundation have all worked together to ensure the continued success of this area. Fittingly, City Hall and the park district headquarters are adjacent to the riverwalk, and the high school is within walking distance. Numerous major park and recreation facilities are linked to the riverwalk, and it continues to figure prominently in community festivals and special events.

Revenue Structure Plan

How much revenue an organization needs, and from where that revenue should come, is detailed in the *revenue structure plan.* The purpose of the revenue structure plan is to help the financial manager to understand the organization's expenditure needs and its potential sources of revenue. A revenue structure plan is typically prepared on an annual basis and conforms to a fiscal year. All sport and leisure service organizations should develop a revenue structure plan. Commercial and nonprofit leisure service organizations might identify a small number of income sources, but the expenditures may be distributed across multiple divisions or profit centers. Conversely, public agencies might identify many different sources of income to cover expenses in a single leisure service enterprise. Figure 4.1 illustrates an example of the different types of revenue sources reported by state park agencies in 1997.

The revenue structure plan focuses attention on the need to strive for an acceptable balance in income sources. Table 4.3 depicts how one municipality's income is derived. As might be expected, property taxes constitute the largest source of income for the municipality, and sales tax is the second largest source of revenue. In today's changing fiscal environment, some public leisure service organizations are generating more than 50 percent of their income from non-tax sources. In this example, there are 11 sources of income for the municipality. A private nonprofit or commercial leisure service organization's revenue structure would be different and would likely show a higher percentage that is derived from charges for services or other types of earned income.

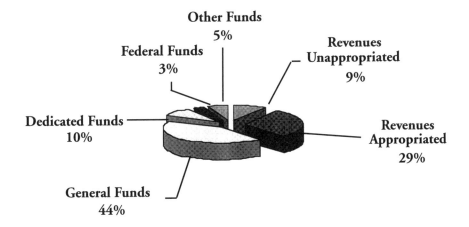

Figure 4.2. Example revenue structure for state parks

Property Tax	Utility Tax	Sales Tax	Shared State Tax	Other Taxes	Licenses & Permits
32.3%	14.3%	29.5%	11.6%	9.6%	2.6%
$17,854,577	$7,906,750	$16,317,115	$6,420,521	$5,316,027	$1,448,228

Fines & Forfeitures	Income on Investments	Inter-governmental Services	Charges for Services	Other	Total
2.8%	5.8%	7.2%	6.5%	17.4%	100%
$1,551,597	$3,221,994	$3,976,524	$3,574,485	$9,606,298	$77,194,116

Table 4.3. Example of a revenue structure for a municipality.

It is important that any revenue structure plan be based on an established fiscal policy. That policy should articulate the revenue goals and describe, in general terms, how revenue should or may be generated. For example, Indy Parks developed its revenue structure model and identified two major funding categories: enterprise funds and underwriting (see Table 4.4). The establishment of these two categories helped to further identify and classify revenue sources and place them on a service continuum with fair market pricing (where user fees cover full costs) at one extreme and city budgeting (where all costs are covered by tax revenues) at the other. Each program or service can be matched to a point on the continuum, depending on a variety of factors such as need, ability to pay, community willingness to support, consistency with the mission of the city and the department, vision of the city and the department, and consistency with the core principles of the organization. Appropriate revenue sources for those programs and services could then be emphasized.

Enterprise Funding	Fair Market Price *(fee covers total cost)*
	Fee Schedule *(fee covers partial costs)*
	Sponsorships *(sponsor gets exposures as benefit)*
Underwriting	Self-funding *(funds shift from another department budget)*
	Donor Base *(corporate, individual giving, and grants)*
	City Budget *(tax revenues)*

Table 4.4. Revenue structure for enterprise funding for Indy Parks.

Developing the revenue structure plan as guided by fiscal policy maintains consistency and promotes efficient exploitation of revenue sources. Furthermore, following the fiscal policy ensures that revenue generation activities will be supported by policy makers.

Summary

Income generation is an important aspect of financial management in sport and leisure service organizations. The various revenue sources discussed in this chapter provide the funds necessary to conduct programs, offer services, and maintain equipment and facilities. There are five types of income: compulsory income, gratuitous income, earned income, investment income, and contractual receipts. All of them provide different levels and types of funding for sport and leisure service organizations. Not all sport and leisure service organizations will secure income from the same sources. Understanding and awareness of income sources, along with the relating of that knowledge to policy directions, allow sport and leisure service managers to more effectively meet the revenue demands of their organization.

References

Crompton, J. L. 1987. *Doing more with less in parks and recreation services.* State College, PA: Venture Publishing, Inc.

McLean, D. D. (Ed.). 1993. *Models of change in parks and recreation: Proceedings of a national conference.* Bloomington, IN: Department of Recreation and Park Administration, Indiana University.

McLean, D. D. (Ed.). 1993. *Models of change in parks and recreation: A 2-part training video.* Bloomington, IN: Department of Recreation and Park Administration, Indiana University.

Chapter 5

Pricing

Introduction

One of the most challenging tasks associated with financial management in sport and leisure service organizations is that of setting prices. In setting prices, the financial manager must be able to collect and appropriately analyze relevant data, make reasoned predictions about consumer behavior, and be creative in developing pricing strategies to help achieve the financial objectives of the organization. This chapter discusses the purposes of pricing in sport and leisure service enterprises and explores the ways in which prices are established and adjusted. In addition, this chapter examines the effects of pricing on consumer behavior.

Price quantifies the financial and other resources that a consumer of sport and leisure services exchanges with the provider of those services. The nature, amount, and source of the resource that is exchanged vary tremendously, but there will always be an exchange in the consumption process. Every service has a price, and every pricing strategy is designed to achieve particular purposes.

Purposes of Pricing

In most situations, pricing is used to recover the costs of production, but it can also be used to create new resources, establish value, influence behavior, and promote efficiency and equity.

Pricing to Recover Costs

Cost-recovery pricing is best illustrated by its application in public, private not-for-profit, and commercial organizations. Though not exclusively, commercial organizations produce and deliver services on a *for-profit* basis, which means that the agency uses pricing to recover more resources from the consumer than were used in production and delivery. Organizations in the public and private not-for-profit sectors typically price their services on a *break-even* basis (i.e., approximately the same amount of resources are recovered through pricing as are expended in production and delivery), and public sport and leisure organizations frequently offer *subsidized* services which are priced in order to recover only a certain portion of their production and delivery costs.

Cost-recovery pricing assumes that the production costs are known and can be apportioned and assessed to a known number of consumers who are to pay the price. Production and delivery costs include fixed and variable costs, and the consumers (i.e., those who pay the price) may include nonusers as well as direct users of the service. The method for calculating prices based on cost recovery will be described in detail later in this chapter.

Pricing to Create New Resources (Added Value Pricing)

Where pricing is used to recover more resources than constitute the cost of production and delivery, value is thereby added to the service, and new resources (profits) for the organization are created. The sport and leisure service organization can retain those new resources to develop additional services, support other existing services, or maintain the support of investors by paying dividends or increasing the value of stock.

Pricing to Establish Value

While most people like to believe that "the best things in life are free," they also accept that, usually, "you get what you pay for." The latter assertion reinforces the suggestion that price is used as an indicator of the relative quality or value of a product. For example, a sporting event for which the admission price is $40 is expected to be much better than one that charges $2 at the gate; a $19 resort room is not likely to be as nice as a $200 room; a golf putter that sells for $15 is inferior to one that sells for $150; and so on. When the price for a particular sport or leisure service is determined, the value of that service is established in the minds of the consumer. It is not unusual, therefore, to find sport and leisure services which are priced well above the full cost-recovery level simply to establish and maintain a perceived level of value or quality.

Public and private golf operations provide a challenge for appropriate pricing.

Pricing to Influence Behavior

When consumers pay a price for a sport and leisure service, they recognize that the service has value to them. The price is considered fair; otherwise, they would not have paid it. If, however, that fair price is increased because of failed performance or irresponsible behavior on the part of the consumer, the price may no longer be consistent with the value of the service. For example, $50 for 10 canoeing lessons may sound like a good price, but only if the student attends all 10 lessons. If he attends only one lesson, it is a very expensive lesson. In this case, the student is encouraged to attend all 10 lessons because of the price. He would not likely be so motivated if the price of all 10 lessons were only 49 cents.

Similarly, the price of admission to a session of roller skating may seem reasonable, unless the skater violates safety or other rules of conduct and is ejected from the facility without a refund of the admission price. The fear of having the experience reduced, but not the price, or having to pay the full admission price for re-admission to the same session, strongly influences the value-conscious skater to conduct himself according to the established standards.

Many sport and leisure service organizations use pricing to promote desired behaviors. Consider the following examples:

- Lower early-registration fees are charged as an incentive to participants to sign up for programs early enough to give the agency adequate preparation time.

- Late fines or replacement fees are charged by libraries or movie rental stores to encourage users to return books and videos promptly and in good condition.

- Performance bonds are required of teams to make it seem too costly to withdraw from a tournament at the last moment.

- Care of facilities and equipment is promoted through the assessment of damage/ cleaning deposits from groups renting recreational facilities and areas.

Pricing to Promote Efficiency

The sport and leisure service industry is subject to seasonal and other fluctuations in demand. There are times when the demand for certain services or products exceeds the supply, and there are times when the supply far exceeds the demand. Pricing is often used to shift the demand from peak periods to low periods and, thereby, promote efficiency. For example, the summertime demand for a commercial campground with 100 sites will normally exceed its capacity, but many sites will be empty during the spring and fall (especially on weekdays). If the campground operator added 50 new sites to accommodate the summer campers, he would be offering an inefficient solution, because the off-season surplus would then be even greater. A more efficient response might be to raise prices during the summer and lower them during other times. Some campers have flexibility in their vacation and travel plans and can be enticed, by the price differential, to camp during the off-season rather than during the busy summer months.

Bulk pricing, in the form of season passes or ticket blocks, can also promote efficiency by reducing the cost of selling individual tickets and reducing the uncertainty in estimating demand. Many amusement theme parks, for example, have abandoned the inefficient practice of selling individual tickets or coupons for attractions in favor of the all-inclusive admission price.

Pricing to Promote Equity

Equity refers to fairness in the allocation of resources. Equity decisions are based on response to need and merit and, therefore, may result in unequal allocation of services. Pricing can be used to promote equity by redistributing the wealth of those who pay a higher price for a service to more needy or deserving people who would pay a lower price for the same service. For example, an adult may pay $5 to use a public swimming pool, while a child may pay only $2 for the same opportunity. This price structure is considered fair because children have fewer financial resources than adults, and because they need to develop aquatic safety skills and have available healthy recreation activities in their growing years. Pricing promotes equity by making the swimming pool more accessible to a needy or deserving market (the children) through fees that are made more affordable by the higher financial contribution of a more resourceful and less needy market (the adults).

The Appropriateness and Feasibility of Pricing

As stated earlier, every sport or leisure service has a price. That price, however, may be or may include a non-monetary resource that the consumer is required to give up in exchange for the service. Only certain types of services can appropriately or feasibly be priced in direct monetary terms. In other words, charging a fee for a service is not always desirable or practical.

An example of a type of service for which it may not be desirable or practical to charge a user fee is a *public service.* Public services, such as neighborhood parks and playgrounds, trails, parades, and ecological reserves, are of value and benefit to a broadly defined community and, for that reason, have traditionally been supported by public funds (i.e., taxes) rather than user fees. The customary practice of having no direct user charges, coupled with the difficulty or inefficiency of limiting access for the purpose of charging admission, makes public services unlikely candidates for pricing.

A type of service for which pricing may be more appropriate and feasible is a *merit service.* Merit services are those which indirectly benefit the community, but are most beneficial to those who receive the service. Many of the facilities and programs provided by public recreation agencies qualify as merit services. For example, a minor soccer league is good for the community because it provides positive, wholesome outlets for the energy of young girls and boys. It also promotes many of the qualities of leadership and responsible citizenship. Aside from benefiting the community indirectly, participation in the soccer league promotes the physical health of those who participate and also provides a great deal of personal enjoyment. Because of the benefit received by the community, it is appropriate for some community resources (e.g., playing fields built and maintained with tax dollars) to be used in support of the league. On the other hand, the individual participant benefits the most, so it is also considered appropriate and desirable for each boy or girl to pay a fee in order to play on a league team. Because player registration and game scheduling are required for the successful operation of the soccer league, it is feasible to charge a fee for individual participation.

Public, private not-for-profit, and commercial sport and leisure service organizations might also provide what are classified as *private services.* Though more common in commercial agencies, private services are those that are exclusive and that benefit only the individuals who use the service. It is, therefore, considered to be both desirable and feasible for the agency to charge a fee. Tennis lessons, dog grooming classes, weight training, movies, amusement parks, lake or ocean cruises, sky diving, river rafting, and professional sporting events are just a few of the thousands of private sport and leisure services available to consumers. Participation in them is at the discretion of the consumer and, while they may be highly enjoyable and beneficial to the participant, their value to the general community is not readily apparent, and there is little reason for financial support of the services by anyone but the direct consumers.

It is important to recognize that a service is not inherently public, merit, or private. A weight-training facility at a particular university, for example, may be open to all students by virtue of the mandatory activity fee. Viewed as a benefit to all, it would be considered a public service in that campus community. Another university may provide access to its weight-training facilities only to those who pay the voluntary student activity fee. In recognition of the extended value of personal physical health to the university community, the university may subsidize the activity fee. In this case, the weight-training facility is a merit service. A third university, meanwhile, may determine that weight training benefits only the user of the facilities and that all costs of maintaining and operating a weight-training center need to be recovered from single usage or semester pass fees charged to individual users. The sometimes challenging task of classifying sport and leisure facilities, programs, and activities as either public, merit, or private services is central to the debate about whether user fees should be charged.

The Nature of Price

Price, as a quantification of the resources exchanged by a consumer for a desired service, is usually expressed in monetary terms. The price of a hot summer afternoon at the swimming pool, for example, is said to be $3—the amount charged by the pool owner for admission to the facility. There are, however, other non-monetary elements of price that may play an equal or more important role in the decision about whether or not to purchase the service than the dollar amount displayed on the price tag. In addition to the monetary cost, the consumer of a sport and leisure service will incur opportunity costs, psychological costs, and effort costs.

Monetary Price

The monetary price of a sport or leisure program or event includes direct and indirect expenditures attributable to participation in that activity. Obviously, the registration or admission fee will be one part of the monetary price. Another part will be money that had to be paid for services that facilitate the individual's participation in the program. These facilitation costs include the following:

- Transportation: all the costs of getting to and from the activity, including fares, gasoline, maintenance, depreciation, insurance

- Clothing and Equipment: the costs of specialized clothing and/or equipment required for participation in the activity

- Proxy: the costs of someone else fulfilling other obligations of the participant while he or she is engaged in the activity (e.g., expenses for child care, pet boarding, house sitting, employment substitution)

- Refreshment/Sustenance: the additional cost of purchasing meals or refreshments during the time of the activity

- Qualification: the costs directly associated with making the individual eligible to participate in the activity (includes preparatory training and/or certification, medical clearance, membership fees, etc.)

- Reference: the costs of acquiring artifacts, such as souvenirs and photographs, that help the participant to later recall and describe the experience

Opportunity Price

By participating in a sport or leisure activity, an individual dedicates to that activity time and other resources that could have been utilized in alternate ways. The participant always pays the price for lost opportunity. Fathers who go out in the evening to play basketball with their co-workers give up the opportunity to spend that time with their families. College students who spend the weekend skiing lose the opportunity that those two days presented for rest, study, and preparation for an upcoming exam. Children who take piano lessons forfeit the opportunity to watch after-school cartoons on television. A recreational seamstress may spend carefully saved money to take a quilting class but, in so doing, lose the opportunity to buy a new sewing machine. The opportunity cost of time can be measured in hours and minutes; the opportunity cost of lost wages or spent savings can be measured in dollars and cents; and the opportunity cost of not studying can be measured in grade points. There are, however, opportunity costs that defy quantification, such as family cohesiveness, spiritual health, a clear conscience, a sense of accomplishment, and so on. Though not always measurable, the opportunity price is perceivable by the consumer and is considered in the purchase/participation decision.

Psychological Price

Participants in sport and leisure activities experience a certain amount of psychological stress. The stress may result from the uncertainty of a contest's outcome or the anxiety associated with performing at a level near the limits of the participant's capabilities. Other forms of stress manifest themselves as boredom, fear, or even embarrassment. All these conditions are a part of the psychological price of the activity. Participation may require the individual to step out of his or her personal comfort zone and place his or her self-esteem or social position at risk. By participating, the individual exchanges the psychological position of comfort for the expected stresses and anticipated outcomes and, thereby, pays the psychological price.

Effort Price

Sport and leisure activities usually require substantial physical or mental exercise and, by so doing, exact a price of personal energy. Some programs may be too expensive for certain individuals—not because the monetary, opportunity, or psychological price is excessive, but because the prospective participant is "just not up to it."

Figure 5.1 presents a summary of the many costs that constitute the price for a man to spend his hot summer afternoon at the community swimming pool. It provides examples of the monetary, opportunity, psychological, and effort prices that the man must be willing to pay in order to go swimming.

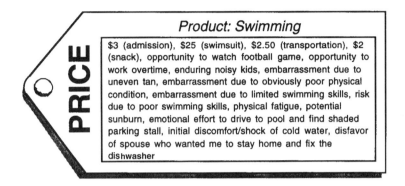

Product: Swimming

$3 (admission), $25 (swimsuit), $2.50 (transportation), $2 (snack), opportunity to watch football game, opportunity to work overtime, enduring noisy kids, embarrassment due to uneven tan, embarrassment due to obviously poor physical condition, embarrassment due to limited swimming skills, risk due to poor swimming skills, physical fatigue, potential sunburn, emotional effort to drive to pool and find shaded parking stall, initial discomfort/shock of cold water, disfavor of spouse who wanted me to stay home and fix the dishwasher

Figure 5.1. The varied elements of the price tag for going swimming.

Approaches to Establishing Price

One of the easiest ways to establish a price is to just pick a number and decide that it will be the dollar price for the service. This *arbitrary* approach ignores market conditions and requirements for cost recovery, and settles on a price with which the financial decision-maker is most comfortable. For example, the director of a summer sport camp may decide to charge $20 just because $20 is a nice round number. Unfortunately, the positive simplicity of this approach is usually overshadowed by the negative ineffectiveness of such a strategy in meeting the financial goals of the organization.

Another relatively simple approach is to establish a price that is consistent with the price charged for the same or a similar service by a competing service provider. *Competitive pricing* can be an efficient and effective strategy if the competing provider has similar goals, production resources, costs, and market conditions. For example, the price for a recreational swimming session at a new YMCA Family Fitness Center may reasonably be set at the same amount as is charged for admission to the local public swimming pool because the costs of operation are comparable, the range of aquatic services is similar, the market is identical, and both agencies are pricing their services at the break-even level. If, however, the YMCA has a wave machine in the new pool and requires more lifeguards than the public recreation agency, then charging the same as the public agency would likely result in reduced profits or increased operating deficits.

A third approach to pricing sport and leisure services is to charge whatever the market is willing to pay. This *market pricing* strategy assumes that consumers are willing to pay at least the amount required by the organization for cost recovery and then seeks a higher amount that will optimize financial returns. Using the market pricing approach, a college athletic department with a nationally ranked basketball team may decide to charge non-student spectators $20 per game because that is the amount that these basketball fans have demonstrated a willingness to pay. These same fans, however, may only be willing to pay $5 per game if the basketball team goes for three seasons losing every game by as many as 50 points.

Finally, a *cost-recovery pricing* strategy is based on the principle of seeking a return from the consumers that represents a predetermined portion of the resources that are required to provide the sport or leisure service to them. That portion may be less than, equal to, or greater than 100%, depending on the organization's financial objectives and how the service being priced is supposed to help achieve those objectives. Clearly, two pieces of information are essential before determining price based on cost recovery. The first is accurate information about the costs of providing the service, and the second is information about the extent to which the pricing strategy is expected to generate revenues equal to those costs. The latter item of information is referred to as either the *subsidization rate* or the *markup*.

Calculating Costs for Unit Pricing

In order to calculate the costs incurred in the provision of service to each consumer, the financial manager needs to know what the fixed and variable costs are, how much contingency is required, and how many consumers are likely to participate in the program or purchase the service at a given price. Estimating *demand* (i.e., the quantity desired at a given price) requires an understanding of the needs, interests, capabilities, constraints, and opportunities of the target market. Although demand has been discussed in detail in Chapter 1, it is appropriate here to emphasize that estimation of demand is an art founded in science and measurement. In other words, "knowing" how many people will participate in a sport or leisure program requires an educated guess.

Contingency refers to being prepared for the unexpected. There is obvious wisdom in adding to the itemized costs of a product an amount that can be used if additional costs arise. How many contingencies should be built into the costs? Some managers are comfortable with only 5 percent of the costs being contingent, while other, more cautious financial managers may want to have an amount as much as 15 percent of the itemized costs be available to deal with contingencies. For longstanding, established programs, or for programs requiring limited financial investment, the reduced risk would justify a relatively small contingency, but new, untried, or short-term programs, as well as those for which the consequences of financial failure are severe, should have a relatively high contingency built into their cost estimates.

Fixed and variable costs are the financial resources that are used in production and delivery of the sport or leisure service. They can be itemized and are the basis of cost-recovery pricing. *Fixed costs* are those financial costs that the sport or leisure service organization incurs, regardless of the status of the program. They are unavoidable, even if nobody registers for the program or attends the event. Figure 5.2 identifies the fixed costs associated with the maintenance of a skating rink. If the facility is maintained as a rink, but nobody comes to skate, there will still be mortgage installments due and bills to be paid. There will still be a portion of the agency administrators' salaries that are actually rink-related costs, because maintaining the rink partly justifies the administrator's position. There will be the direct costs of installing and removing the ice surface at either end of the skating season. And even this unused and empty facility would require repairs and upkeep, as well as basic utility services.

Variable costs are those costs that result from the actual operation of the sport or leisure service. The more the service operates, the greater the variable costs will be. Operating at full capacity, the skating rink lights would be on, the dressing rooms and spectator areas would be heated, showers would deliver thousands of gallons of hot water, floors would need cleaning, supervisory staff would be retained, and so on. The cost of operating the rink will vary depending on its use; hence, the term *variable costs*. Figure 5.2 identifies sample variable costs for the rink to operate for a seven-month skating season.

COST SUMMARY

Kotkawagan Ice Rink

(October - April)

Fixed Costs

Capital costs	$4,300/month x 7 months	$30,100
Administration (overhead)	$375/month x 7 months	$2,625
Ice installation/removal		$2,000
Basic maintenance	$2,000/month x 7 months	$14,000
Basic utilities and service	$1,100/month x 7 months	$7,700

TOTAL FIXED COSTS	$56,425
HOURLY FIXED COSTS (FOR 2250 HOURS)	*$25.08

Variable Costs

Utilities and maintenance	$11/hour x 2250 hours	$24,750
Staff	$9/hr x 2250 hours	$20,250

TOTAL VARIABLE COSTS	$45,000
HOURLY VARIABLE COST	$20
TOTAL COSTS	**$101,450**
HOURLY COST	*$45.09

*Recoverable hourly costs based on expected 2,250 hours of ice-time sold.

Figure 5.2. Sample cost summary for ice rink.

The actual cost of one unit of a product is calculated by applying the formula:

$P=(F+V)/N$ where P=the cost of a unit, F=the total fixed costs, V=the total variable costs, and N=the number of units expected to be sold.

Using the data from Figure 5.2, the recoverable hourly cost of operating the ice rink is calculated by applying the formula:

P=(F+V)/N

P=($56,425 + $45,000)/2,250 hours

P= $45.09/hour

To calculate the price that should be charged in order to recover all costs, a revised formula that considers contingency may be used.

P=C(F+V)/N   where P=the average price per unit, and C=the contingency rate.

If the operator of the ice rink chooses to build in a 5% contingency into the pricing model, then the average price for one hour of ice time will be:

P=((F+V)+C(F+V))/N

P=(($56,425 + $45,000)+ .05($56,425 + $45,000))/2,250 hours

P=($101,425 + $5,071.25)/2,250 hours

P= $47.33/hour

Note that the $47.33 per hour cost calculated in the preceding example includes *all* of the costs associated with providing the specific activity. This approach to cost quantification is referred to as *activity-based costing* (ABC) and is different from traditional approaches to accounting which often ignore major fixed costs (e.g., capital, administrative overhead) and often do not relate costs to specific activities or program components.

The advantages of ABC over traditional cost measurement strategies include the following:

- ABC helps to identify manageable contributing factors to cost (thereby facilitating improvements to operational efficiency).

- ABC allows cost comparisons for the same activity provided by different units within the organization or for different market segments.

- ABC generates data for benchmarking and comparing the cost of an activity provided in-house or by contracting out.

- ABC tells the true story of cost and facilitates appropriate pricing based on cost-recovery objectives.

Subsidization and Unit Pricing

Once the cost-based price has been determined, the next step in establishing the unit price for a particular consumer or target market is the application of a rate of subsidization. The *rate of subsidization* refers to how much of the unit cost is going to be recovered from sources other than the consumer. In the public sport and leisure service organization, subsidization means using tax revenues to reduce or eliminate user fees for services. Private not-for-profit and commercial sport and leisure service organizations may subsidize some programs or services by using the profits generated by another of their enterprises to reduce or eliminate the consumer's contribution to meeting the costs of the programs or services. Using the profits of one program to reduce the price of another is often called *cross-subsidization.*

A common pricing strategy involves subsidizing different market segments at different levels. For example, the pricing strategy for the public skating rink could reflect a political decision to keep skating activities very affordable for special populations in the community while, at the same time, expecting commercial ventures to pay the full share (or more) of the costs of any public facilities or services that they use. The sample subsidization rates displayed in Table 5.1 demonstrate a commitment to youth recreation.

Subsidization rates are used to convert the average per unit cost of a sport or leisure service to the final consumer price(s) for the product. The appropriate formula for calculating price is:

$$Pm=(1-Sm)(((F+V)+C(F+V))/N)$$ where P=the price to be charged to a specific market (m) for one unit, and Sm=the subsidization rate applied to market m.

Note that the subsidization rate can be as high as 100% (a free service) or as low as a minus percentage (a profit-generating service). A service that is "marked up" 30% is subsidized at -30%, and priced at 130% of its cost.

The prices charged to various skating groups for one hour of ice time are shown in Table 5.1. The price for youth programs such as minor hockey, figure skating, and ringette are subsidized 35% and calculated as follows:

$$Pm=(1-Sm)(((F+V)+C(F+V))/N)$$

$$Pm=(1-.35)(\$47.33/hour)$$

$$Pm = \$30.77/hour$$

User Group	Subsidy Rate	Price
Minor Hockey	35%	$30.77/hour
Figure Skating	35%	$30.77/hour
Ringette	35%	$30.77/hour
Public Skating	0%	$47.33/hour
Open Skate	100%	Free
Gentlemen's Hockey	10%	$42.60/hour
Junior A Hockey (practice)	-25%	$59.16/hour

Table 5.1. Sample subsidy rates and hourly prices for ice rink rental.

The subsidization rate for the Junior A hockey club (a commercial enterprise) is minus 25%, which means that the hourly cost will be marked up to establish a price for this user group. The formula given above can be used to calculate the price to be charged ($59.16/hour, which is 25% greater than the cost to be recovered).

Pm=(1-Sm)(((F+V)+C(F+V))/N)

Pm=(1-.(-25))($47.33/hour)

Pm = $59.16/hour

Other Considerations in Establishing Price

While cost recovery is usually the most important consideration in establishing prices, there are other factors to keep in mind when determining how much to charge for a sport or leisure service. The potential customers' willingness to pay the established price is certainly an important consideration, as is their sensitivity to price changes.

Willingness to Pay/The Going Rate

When cost-recovery goals are easily met because the calculated unit price is below an amount that all or most consumers are accustomed to paying or willing to pay, it may be appropriate (and, perhaps, necessary) to price the sport or leisure service at a higher "going rate." Conversely, a service that costs more to produce than the consumers are willing to pay may also need to be priced at a going rate that results in a financial loss. In either case, the reasons for pricing at the going rate may be varied and may also include protection of perceived value, protection of consumer self-esteem, and promotion of competition.

A sport or leisure service that is highly valued by consumers may not necessarily be costly to produce. However, if that low-cost service is priced too low, the potential appeal of and commitment to it may actually be diminished because of the commonly held belief that "you get what you pay for, and if it doesn't cost much, then it's probably not very good." Even if a private not-for-profit organization's excellent fitness program incurs a cost of $10 per participant, it might be wise to charge around $30 per participant if that is what he or she is used to paying for services of similar value (i.e., perceived personal benefit) or for similar services offered by another provider. In this example, the consumers have indicated a willingness to pay $30 and thereby have implicitly suggested that a significantly lower price would probably generate doubts about the quality of the product. The $30 price tag helps to protect the perceived value of the service. The "problem" of what to do with the $20 profit that would be realized by this not-for-profit organization may be quickly resolved if the organization also has a worthwhile program for which the production costs exceed the price that consumers are willing to pay. All the organization needs to do is to shift the profits of the former program to cover the losses of the latter. Clearly, consideration of the willingness of patrons to pay the going rate is important in pricing decisions, especially when the sport or leisure service organization uses cross-subsidization to achieve its financial objectives.

Consideration of the going rate in pricing decisions is also important for protecting the self-esteem of consumers. Generally, people like to feel that they have earned what they receive. When they receive benefits from a sport or leisure service, they feel better about themselves if they worked, sacrificed, or somehow paid a fair price for those benefits. Pricing decisions should allow for consumers to maintain or enhance their self-esteem in the knowledge that they will have "paid their dues." At the same time, pricing decisions should protect consumers' self-esteem by demonstrating sensitivity to the desire to believe that all basic needs and, perhaps, a few leisure wants are available and affordable to everyone. In other words, prices should not make a consumer feel that it is impossible to satisfy perceived needs, but instead should make him or her feel that paying the price is an appropriate way to demonstrate deservedness of the benefits derived from consuming the sport or leisure product.

Sometimes the going rate is used as a means to promote competition. For example, a state park agency may be able to provide serviced campsites at an average cost of $8 per night, but will choose to charge the going rate of $15 per night in order to help the neighboring commercial campground stay in business. The commercial campground also charges $15 per night, but its average campsite costs are $12. The state park is able to produce campsites at a lower cost because it does not pay off a mortgage on the land, does not pay local property taxes or sales and income taxes, and does not pay directly for marketing. In some respects, the state park has an unfair advantage and could exploit that through its pricing. The state park, however, cannot always satisfy the demand for camping, but is required to facilitate extensive use of the park. It needs the commercial campground to stay in business in order for the state park to continue to attract visitors and to avoid expanding the public campground to the detriment of protected natural areas. By establishing prices that are consistent with the going rate, regardless of production costs, the state park promotes competition and ensures adequate camping opportunities for overnight visitors.

It should be noted that the going rate for a particular service might vary according to product and market conditions. Products that are seasonal in their appeal will have a lower going rate in the off-season than during periods of high demand. Products oriented towards children or economically disadvantaged population segments also tend to have a lower going rate than those offered to adults and wealthier persons. There are several appropriate justifications for differential pricing that are based on willingness to pay and the going rate:

- *Customer Characteristics.* Both the willingness to pay and the going rate may vary because of age limitations/opportunities, income, ability, intensity of consumption, etc.

- *Product Levels.* Consumers are willing to pay more for advanced levels or elitist leisure and sport opportunities and less for basic services.

- *Distribution.* Differential pricing may reflect the advantages of one service location or time over another. For example, concert tickets are priced according to the location of reserved seats, and rental fees for sports facilities are higher during prime-time hours.

- *Merit.* Prices and expectations of price differentials may reflect the historical contribution of the consumer to the product. For example, lower program registration fees for club or association members serve as recognition and expectation resulting from the earlier payment of membership. Bulk pricing (such as season passes and ticket packs) is also a practice based on recognition of the contribution and merit of the high-quantity/frequency customer.

Sensitivity to Changes in Price

Consumers of sport and leisure services respond to changes in prices in several different ways. In some cases, an increase in price will result in an increase in consumption because the price increase is thought to be an indication of improved service quality. Most often, however, increases in price have the opposite effect on consumption. When the price goes up, the attendance goes down.

The degree to which consumption decreases with a given increase in price will differ between consumer markets. Some groups of consumers are more sensitive to price changes than others, and it is important for the financial manager in sport and leisure service organizations to understand and be able to make sound decisions based on an understanding of price-induced fluctuations in demand.

The measure of demand fluctuations is referred to as *elasticity of demand*. The measure of price-induced demand fluctuations is called *price elasticity of demand*. More specifically, price elasticity of demand is defined as the percentage change in a quantity consumed that is caused by a percentage change in price. For example, suppose that a 1.0 percent increase in the admission price results in an 0.5 percent decrease in sales to a particular market segment. The price elasticity of demand for this market segment and this product would be –0.5.

Allowing that an increase in price practically always results in a decrease in demand, the calculated value of price demand elasticity would always be negative. An important academic/practical contradiction deserves attention at this point. Because elasticities are always negative values—and to avoid confusion when comparing those values—economists usually ignore the negative sign. Thus, an elasticity of –2.5 would be considered greater than –2.4 (in spite of what is learned in elementary school mathematics).

Consider the following illustration, which uses admission price and attendance data from A.J.'s Aussieland Theme Park:

To calculate the price elasticity of demand for any of the four market segments, use the appropriate data from Table 5.2 and apply the following formula:

Price Elasticity = Change in attendance/(Sum of attendance/2)

Change price/(Sum of prices/2)

Example: For the child market segment in 2001-2003, the price elasticity of demand would be:

Price Elasticity = (120,000 ñ 150,000) / ((120,000 + 150,000)/2)

(3.50 ñ 3.00) / ((3.00 + 3.50)/2)

= -1.44

Market Segment	Season	Price	Attendance
Child	2001	$3.00	150,000
Child	2003	$3.50	120,000
Child	2005	$4.00	100,000
Youth	2001	$4.00	105,000
Youth	2003	$5.00	99,500
Youth	2005	$6.00	92,000
Adult	2001	$7.00	60,000
Adult	2003	$8.00	52,500
Adult	2005	$10	42,000
Senior	2001	$6.00	35,00
Senior	2003	$6.50	28,000
Senior	2005	$7.00	23,000

Table 5.2. Sample price and attendance data for four market segments.

Other elasticities were calculated in an identical manner and are presented in the following table:

Market Segment	Season	Price	Attendance	Elasticity
Child	2001	$3.00	150,000	
Child	2003	$3.50	120,000	-1.44
Child	2005	$4.00	100,000	-1.36
Youth	2001	$4.00	105,000	
Youth	2003	$5.00	99,500	- 0.24
Youth	2005	$6.00	92,000	- 0.43
Adult	2001	$7.00	60,000	
Adult	2003	$8.00	52,500	-1.00
Adult	2005	$10	42,000	-1.00
Senior	2001	$6.00	35,00	
Senior	2003	$6.50	28,000	- 2.78
Senior	2005	$7.00	23,000	- 2.78

Table 5.3. Sample data and computed elasticities for four market segments.

Note that the calculated elasticities for the child and senior markets are both "greater" than 1.0 (remember to ignore the minus sign). This means that a greater percentage of change was observed in attendance than was affected by price. As demonstrated by their change in demand, the children and the seniors appear to be relatively sensitive to price changes. In fact, they are so sensitive that the additional revenue received from increased admission fees paid by the 120,000 remaining customers in 2003 was $30,000 less than the amount received in 2001 from the 150,000 customers who paid the lower fee. Market segments with an elasticity of greater than 1.0 are said to be *relatively elastic*. They are markets for which a change in price results in an opposite change in revenue (i.e., increasing prices produce decreasing revenue; decreasing prices produce increasing revenue).

The calculated elasticities for the youth market segment are "less" than 1.0, which indicates that the youth market is relatively insensitive to price changes at A.J.'s Aussieland. Market segments with an elasticity of less than 1.0 are said to be *relatively inelastic.* They are markets for which a change in price results in a parallel change in revenue (i.e., increasing prices produce increasing revenue; decreasing prices produce decreasing revenue).

The adult market is called a *unitary elastic* market segment because price changes, although they cause a decrease in attendance, do not result in either an increase or a decrease in revenues. Unitary elastic markets have a price demand elasticity of approximately 1.0.

For the purpose of comparison, the linear demand curves for three markets that share a common point on their demand curves are presented in Figure 5.3.

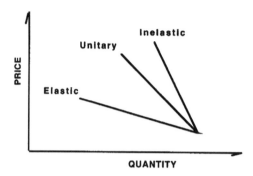

Figure 5.3. Comparison of demand curves for elastic, inelastic, and unitary elastic markets.

From Figure 5.3, it is evident that markets that are less sensitive to price changes (inelastic) are represented by steep demand curves. Conversely, the demand curves for more price-sensitive (elastic) markets will be less sloped.

Adjusting Prices

It is natural to expect that a drop in sales or attendance will result from an increase in price. When a price increases, there will inevitably be a portion of the market that feels that the new price is too high and, therefore, cannot or will not pay the higher amount. Some of those customers will need time to adjust to the new price and may eventually find the resources or the will to return and continue participating. Others will not be able to convince themselves that the higher price is worth paying, but could be convinced by the service provider. In doing so, the sport and leisure service provider is challenged with finding a way to adjust or redefine the consumer's reference price. *Reference price* is the amount that the consumer feels that the service might or should cost and is derived from the consumer's experience with similar services and/or from introductory information provided by the sport and leisure service organization. The reference price for a youth soccer camp, for example, might be $40. Last year the consumer paid $45 for a basketball camp with a similar format, and her neighbor reported paying $38 to register his daughter in the children's soccer camp offered by the YMCA. Hence, $40 seems to be a reasonable expectation (reference price).

The sport and leisure service organization only needs to adjust the soccer moms' reference price if it is significantly different from the *objective price.* The objective price is defined as the actual price charged for the service. For example, the registration fee for youth soccer may be $55.

Expecting to pay $40 and then being presented with a bill for $55, the consumer would be inclined to consider the program to be a bit expensive. She may even consider it to be much too expensive. The words or expressions that a consumer uses to describe the difference between the reference price and the objective price are referred to as the *subjective price.* Essentially, the subjective price is how the consumer feels about the objective price, based on his or her reference price. The subjective price is a word or expression, not a number. Examples include the following: "expensive," "reasonable," "cheap," "bargain," "rip-off," "prohibitive," "a good deal."

There are several effective approaches to adjusting the consumer's reference price. One approach is to inform the consumer of the actual costs that the price is supposed to recover. For example, the soccer camp may cost the agency $65 per participant. Knowing this, the consumer would be inclined to adjust her reference price upward and recognize that the objective price ($55) is really a pretty good deal. A second approach to changing the consumer's reference price is to emphasize the value or the benefits of the product to the consumer. In the youth soccer camp example, the sponsoring agency could point out that participation in the program provides the boy or girl with a wholesome, health-promoting way to spend time, a positive social environment, opportunities to experience success and failure (and help in learning how to deal with them), skill development, leadership experience, etc. Surely these benefits are worth at least $55! The third approach involves comparing the cost of the service with a similar service or activity offered elsewhere. The consumer could be informed that the price for the local soccer camp is $55, but that a similar program in a nearby community would cost $80. Furthermore, the soccer camp is $15 cheaper than both the basketball and volleyball camps offered by the same agency. The fourth approach to adjusting the reference price is to enhance the image of the product in the eyes of the consumer. In order to raise the reference price for the youth soccer camp, promotional emphasis could be placed on the success achieved by camp alumni or on the international reputation of the camp director.

Figure 5.4 shows the relationship of past experience and direct communications to the establishment of reference prices. It also identifies four approaches to adjusting reference

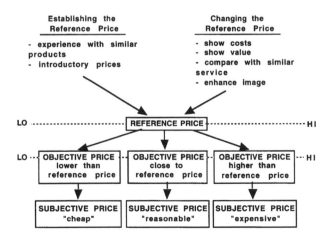

Figure 5.4. Relationship of reference price to subjective price.

price. The opportunity to influence the reference price is important to the sport and leisure service manager, because the reference price is the price with which the objective price is compared in order to establish a subjective price. Purchase decisions are based on subjective price.

Summary

The price of a sport or leisure service is the quantification of the level of exchange between the service provider and the customer. It is what the customer gives up in order to receive the service. In addition to financial resources, the price includes opportunity, effort, and psychological stress. Monetary pricing helps the leisure service organization to recover costs of production, manage consumer behavior, and establish value for the service. Pricing of certain services is desirable and necessary, but others may not be suitable for direct pricing. There are several ways to establish a price, but the most common approach is to determine production costs and then price according to particular cost-recovery objectives. It is important for financial managers to understand and consider the sensitivity of sport and leisure service consumers to price changes. Price changes will affect demand and consumption, which ultimately will affect revenue and profits.

Chapter 6

Grantseeking

Introduction

Grantseeking is an art at which a few people have been highly successful, while many more have been moderately successful. Yet, for most, it remains somewhat of a mystery. Grantseeking does not need to be approached as a mystery. It is a systematic, logical process for articulating needs and matching those needs with the goals and qualifications of a granting agency. Unfortunately, many sports and leisure service managers are deterred from grantseeking by a process that they believe will require them to write a complicated proposal. While some organizations do require proposals that are detailed and strongly supported with additional sources of information or money, there are many one-page grant proposals that have been quite successful. Although there is no guaranteed formula for success, there are procedures that, when followed, increase an applicant's potential for success. In today's competitive budget environment, it has become more common to use grantseeking as part of the sports and leisure service organization's revenue plan. Successful grantseeking provides opportunities to extend programs and services in ways that might not otherwise be possible. This chapter describes the grantseeking process and suggests approaches that have proven to be successful in a variety of situations.

Why Pursue Grants?

Indiana University's Bradford Woods Outdoor Center is a 2,600-acre outdoor campus located about 20 minutes south of Indianapolis. During its 55-year history, it has evolved from a youth camp facility to a multifaceted outdoor education resource and demonstration center that includes camping, professional development, environmental education, a retreat center, and a training center. For its first 35 years, Bradford Woods operated with little change. Its primary function was to provide summer camping opportunities and dedicated areas for outdoor youth-serving agencies. By 1978, Bradford Woods was operating with a significant financial deficit. The university determined that changes needed to be made in order for Bradford Woods to become more financially self-sufficient. Divestiture of the property, which had been bequeathed to the university in 1941, was not an available option, so a new director was brought in and given a charge to diversify operations and create new opportunities. One of the early strategies for increasing its financial strength was to focus more intently on the use of grants to support operations, programs, and capital improvements. This approach has made Bradford Woods increasingly more effective in securing short-term and multi-year grants. For example, the 1998–99 revenue budget for Bradford Woods was more than $2.25 million, of which about 20 percent came from the parent institution. Another 15 percent came as gratuitous income through an ongoing aggressive program of grantseeking. The 1998–99 capital improvement budget for this outdoor education center was $150,000, of which 80 percent came from grants.

Park-like settings provide users with leisure experiences that encourage them to return.

Sometimes Bradford Woods is more successful than at other times—it varies from year to year—but the management team's approach to grantseeking has yielded very positive results. In many ways, Bradford Woods' need for and approach to grantseeking is typical of that experienced by many public and nonprofit organizations.

The Grantmaking Environment

According to the Foundation Center's 1998 edition of *Foundation Giving,* the United States had nearly 42,000 grantmaking foundations in 1996. That year, grantmaking organizations awarded $13.8 billion in grants. Of that amount, the largest share (18 percent of the grants and 16 percent of the money) was given to children and youth service organizations. Recreation organizations, on the other hand, received almost 2 percent of the grants and 4 percent of the dollars. This small share still amounted to $552 million, excluding the significant state or federal grant dollars that were also awarded (*Foundation Giving,* 1998). Thus, grantmaking organizations can be viewed as a potentially important source of income for sport and leisure service organizations.

Foundation granting organizations are divided into three categories: independent foundations, corporate foundations, and community foundations. Independent or private foundations are what they appear. They are not specifically connected with an organization, corporation, or community. Private foundations have most frequently been created by a single individual or family through a bequest of funds. These bequests often have some restrictions placed on the grantmaking. These independent foundations make grants to other tax-exempt organizations to accomplish their charitable purposes. They do not program directly, but provide money to organizations that do program.

A foundation typically has assets it has invested. The investments generate revenue that is usually used to provide money for grants. Independent foundations must make charitable expenditures of approximately 5 percent of the market value of their assets each year. If an independent foundation has assets totaling $100 million, it will need to award at least $5 million in grants. Of course, it may award even more than that.

A foundation is generally organized as a nonprofit organization under appropriate state codes and registered as a (501 (c) (3)) charitable organization with the Internal Revenue Service. They typically have a board of directors and frequently, but not always, hire an executive director. The board of directors makes decisions for grant awards. Independent foundations are the largest single source of grants. In 1996, independent foundations accounted for 88.7 percent of all granting organizations and awarded 77.3 percent of all grant dollars (see Table 6.1).

Type	Number	Grants*	Assets*
Independent	36,885	$10.7	$226.5
Corporate	1,946	$1.8	$9.5
Community	411	$0.9	$15.9

*Dollar figures are in billions

Table 6.1. Foundation statistics for 1996 (Foundation Center, 1998 giving).

A corporate foundation, as the name suggests, is linked to a corporation and frequently focuses its giving in those communities where the corporation has operations such as offices, factories, or other interests. Funds for these foundations come primarily from the corporation, but granting decisions are, in most cases, separate from corporate decision-making processes and officers.

Community foundations represent a relatively new phenomenon. The focus of these locally instituted foundations is on their communities and on investing into the community. Some large corporate foundations, such as the Lilly Foundation, have made major commitments to community foundations as a way of enhancing their efforts to achieve their noble purposes. The purposes of community foundations vary somewhat, but tend to be much like those articulated in the following mission statement:

"The _____ Community Foundation is committed to improving and strengthening the community of the metropolitan region. Our mission is to:

- Develop the widest range of endowed funds and services to donors on behalf of the region and its counties and communities;

- Administer a growing grantmaking program focused on helping where the needs are greatest and the benefits to the region are most extensive;

- Support the development of the services and institutions of the charitable sector of the region; and,

- Serve as a catalyst for community-based convening consensus building and problem solving in the region."

In today's rapidly changing and competitive society, securing grants is essential to fulfilling the missions of public and nonprofit sports or leisure service organizations. The availability of traditional funding sources has forced organizations such as Bradford Woods to seek alternative funding opportunities. At the same time, the diminishing role played by government in social service areas has increased the demand upon grantmaking organizations. It is, therefore, essential that grantseekers learn the art of matching their seemingly infinite needs with the finite offerings of grantmakers. The following step-by-step discussion of the grantseeking process is designed to help sport and leisure service managers to learn the art.

The Grantseeking Process

Successful grant preparation involves far more than just writing and asking. A well-planned grantseeking process involves six steps (Figure 6.1) that take the applicant from idea generation to grant administration. Each step requires the development and assessment of time-tested approaches to grantseeking. Grantseeking should be viewed as an opportunity to increase resources and thereby allow the organization to accomplish its mission in ways that would not normally be possible.

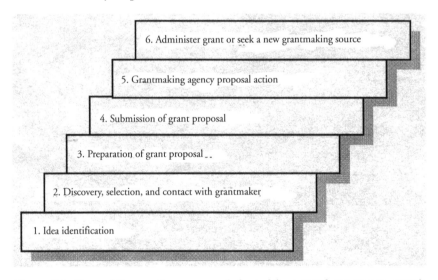

Figure 6.1. Steps of the granting process (adapted from Smith & McLean, 1988).

Step 1: Identifying a Potential Idea

Beginning with the end in mind is a key element of grantseeking. Step 1 involves *identifying a potential* idea that lends itself to the grantseeking process. The identification of a potential idea is not as difficult as it may at first appear. There are many good ideas that are worthy of a grantseeking, but the key is to mature the idea into a problem statement and then match it to a willing grantmaker.

The development of a good idea is a problem-solving process. It does not initially seek to match ideas with potential grantmakers, but instead seeks to identify ideas that cannot be met with existing resources. The following criteria can assist an organization in determining whether the idea has potential merit with a grantmaking organization:

- Is the idea new or innovative, and does it meet an identified need among potential or existing constituents? Can it solve an existing problem or enhance the potential for the solution of a problem?

- Is there a general recognition of the need among community or organizational members?

- Is funding available within the organization to support the idea? If no, then what external sources and amounts can be considered?

- Are local or organizational funds available as a matching support for a potential grant (e.g., other government or nonprofit organizations, individuals, in-kind contributions, etc.)?

- Are the community and the organizational members willing to support a grantseeking process?

- Does the idea support the organization's mission and strategic plan?

Once an idea is generated, it needs to be refined. The most important part of this phase of the process is to clearly identify and describe the problem. This phase will require sound research to show that a problem exists. Just because someone may "think this is a problem" does not make it a problem in the eyes of the granting organization. It is becoming more common for grantmakers to require documentation of the needs and to justify the problem. If other, similar types of projects already exist in other organizations, the grantseeker may be asked to show how his proposal is different. At this stage of the process, the development of the idea should be the primary focus. Collection of data to justify the need should be started, but only sufficient to begin phase 2 of the process.

Step 2: Discovery, Selection, and Contact with a Granting Agency

Of the thousands of grantmakers serving U.S. communities, grantseekers must identify those that are most closely linked in their purposes for applying for the grant. Grantmakers can be divided into (1) government organizations, (2) corporations, (3) national or international philanthropic organizations, (4) regional or local or community philanthropic organizations, and (5) individual foundations. Identification of the philanthropic organization that best fits your problem can be daunting; fortunately, assistantship is available.

Several organizations exist that assist grantseekers in their search for the perfect match. For example, the Foundation Center has branch libraries with staff in Atlanta, Cleveland, New York, San Francisco, and Washington, D.C. In addition, there are cooperating collections in over 200 public and university libraries, where support materials and publications are available. The Foundation Center publishes several directories, including the two-volume *The Foundation Directory* and the single-volume *National Guide to Funding in Arts and Culture,* and *The Foundation Grants Index.* The Foundation Center suggests that, through its resources, searches can be accomplished by using one of three approaches: geographical, subject, or type of support.

The *Chronicle of Philanthropy* is another way to secure information about grants. *The Chronicle* is especially useful if the intent is to make grantseeking a part of the organization's funding and growth strategy. *The Chronicle* is a bi-weekly newspaper that tracks what is going on in the philanthropy arena and provides detailed information about grantmakers, types of grants that are being awarded, trends in grants, and so forth.

The Grantsmanship Center is another frequently used source of information about grantmaking organizations. Its primary focus is on fundraising training and provision of publications to support those efforts. One of its key publications is *Program Planning and Proposal Writing*. It also publishes *The Grantsmanship Center* magazine.

Many foundations provide information to grantseekers that can be informative. Examples of different types of information provided include annual reports, grant guidelines, web sites, newsletters, press releases, and grants lists. The Foundation Center directories and *The Chronicle of Philanthropy* can help to secure this information.

Searching for Grantmakers

There is no single best way to search for a foundation that will support the identified problem. It is a time-consuming and sometimes frustrating process. This discovery phase, however, is a necessary second step towards successful grantseeking. The search can be conducted by looking through the various resources available from one of the three previously mentioned sources, by making direct contact with foundations, by securing support and ideas from other individuals, or through electronic information searching. No single source will be sufficient. It requires a combination of sources to identify and select the one or more grantmakers that may match a particular problem statement.

The search will likely turn up several potential grantmakers, from whom some basic information should be secured. First, the name, contact person, and address of the foundation should be noted. Second, financial information related to the organization should be collected. This information should include the total assets of the grantmaker, the total grants paid in the most recent reporting year (many foundations issue annual reports), the dollar value range of grants awarded (high to low), and the average period of time for which the grantmaker is willing to fund a project. Total assets consist of the economic resources available to the grantmaker. They make up the principle which the grantmaker has available for investment purposes and from which it draws the interest income that allows it make grants. Third, the grantmaker's areas of focus (in order of importance) should be noted. Fourth, the grantseeker needs to know if there are any funding restrictions on the geographic locations of the grantmaker. Many grantmakers place geographical restrictions upon where the grants are awarded. Private grants are frequently restricted to the area where the benefactor either lived or had some special ties. Fifth, there may be restrictions or specific types of support that are identified by the grantmaker. The population that is served, such as children, the disabled, or the elderly, is another important piece of information for the grantseeker. Finally, the grantseeker should identify the types of recipients that the grantmaker has made awards to in recent years. Figure 6.2 depicts the results of this information search as applied to the Lila Wallace-Reader's Digest Fund.

1. Name of the Foundation: Lila Wallace-Reader's Digest Fund

2. Assets: $633,212,206 (December 1997)

   Grants: 1997 Grants Paid $27,208,364;

   1997 Grants Approved: $26,884,913

   Grant Ranges: $400,000 to $1.5 million

   Funding Periods: up to 5 years

3. Focus:

   1. efforts to build audiences for the performing, visual, literary and folk arts

   2. invest in programs that enhance the cultural life of communities and encourage people to make the arts and culture an active part of their everyday lives

   3. funds and supports programs to improve literacy instruction for adult and

   4. to create and improve urban parks.

4. Geographic limits: none

5. Types of support: Resources are allocated to organizations invited to apply for grants, generally as part of larger initiatives or programs that have far-reaching national, regional or multi-state impact.

6. Populations served: not identified

7. Examples of recipients: Urban Parks Improving the Quality and Increasing the Quantity of Parks in Mid-Sized Cities. The Fund is supporting local organizations in seven mid-sized cities and the Trust for Public Land (TPL), a national nonprofit land conservation organization, to create new parks in undeserved neighborhoods and enhance existing park space. TPL is helping to acquire and develop the space. Local organizations are developing collaborations among community groups and residents for the design and programming of the parks. The Fund has invested $6.5 million in this effort since 1994. Grants in this category were made in 1994. Some examples include:

   - Austin Parks Foundation, Austin, Texas Trust for Public Land/Austin - $800,000

   - Baltimore, Md. - $420,428 Trust for Public Land/Washington, D.C. - $463,300

   - Boston Natural Areas Fund, Boston, Mass. - $432,823 Trust for Public Land/Boston - $400,300

   - Clean-Land Ohio, Cleveland, Ohio - $423,700 Trust for Public Land/ Cleveland - $460,300

   - Urban League of Portland, Portland, Ore. - $420,730 Trust for Public Land/Portland - $450,100

   - The Providence Plan, Providence, R.I. - $419,432 Trust for Public Land/ Boston - $440,200

   - San Francisco Foundation, San Francisco, Calif. - $520,500 Trust for Public Land/San Francisco - $440,000

Figure 6.2. Example of a search result.

Selecting a Grantmaker

Selection of the appropriate grantmaker from which to secure potential funding is based on the research completed in the early part of this step. If the research has been thorough, then the grantseeker will know the grantmaking landscape and be able to make an informed judgment. It is hoped that several grantmakers will emerge as potential sources of funding. If this occurs, the grantseeker must make decisions about how to select the grantmakers with the highest potential to fund the project. Using the collected information, the grantseeker compares the various grantmakers with the specific criteria for the grant. Table 6.2 provides an example of how to evaluate the information gathered from the various grantmakers. The decision to select a single grantmaker is based on finding the one that most closely matches the funding problem. If there are no foundations that seem to match the funding problem, then maybe it is appropriate to rethink the problem or to rethink the type of grantmaker being sought.

Grantseeker	Grantmaker	Criteria
Problem Statement	Focus	These two should closely match so that the problem statement is similar to the focus of the grantmaker.
Appropriateness	Examples of Recipients	Examples provide additional information depicting how previous resources have been expended. This is a guide and should not be considered an absolute.
Location of needed funding	Geographic limits	Many grantmakers are restricted in where they will provide funding. This provides a quick eliminator of some foundations.
Required support	Types of support	Provides detailed discussion of the types of support that a grantmaker will provide. Grantseekers must make sure they match in this area.
Population	Population served	Another quick eliminator, but should be used with caution. It may require looking at examples of recipients or calling the grantmaker for more information.

Table 6.2. Grantseeking selection criteria.

While some grantmakers may seem better suited to a particular problem or idea, there may be other grantmakers who have not been considered. Figure 6.3 depicts a prospect worksheet that a grantseeker can use to assist in the decision-making process. Being too limiting in the selection of a potential granting source can lead to a frustrating and defeatist process. Keeping options open and being creative in the approach to seeking a grantmaker will allow an organization to have a higher degree of success. Most grantseekers are not successful in their first try. An attitude of perseverance is an essential quality for all grantseekers.

Contacting the Grantmaker

Depending on the type of grantmaker that is contacted, the nature of the relationship between the would-be grantseeker and the potential grantmaker will vary. Large grantmakers may simply send a packet with a form letter telling about themselves and their expectations. Smaller, specialized, and regional grantmakers may take a more personal interest. In one community, the grantseeker made personal contacts with the grantmaker over a period of several years and had established a credible relationship. Many have done the same thing with local foundations in their areas.

Date:	Funder:	Your Organization
1. Name, Address, Contact Person		N/A

2. Financial Data:
    Total Assets
    Total Grants Paid
    Grant Ranges/Amount Needed
    Period of Funding Project		

3. Subject Focus		
4. Geographic Limits		
5. Type(s) of Support		
6. Population(s) served		
7. Type(s) of Recipients		
8. People (Officers, Trustees, Staff, Donors)		

Application Information:
    Does the funder have printed guidelines/Application forms?
    What type of initial approach is required?
    What are the deadlines?
    Board meeting date(s)?		

What are the sources of information?		
Notes:		
Follow-up:		

Figure 6.3. Funding prospect worksheet (after Foundation Center worksheet).

If personal contact is made, some questions need to be addressed by the grantseeker. The questions can include the following: (1) How do they want the proposal written? (2) Do they provide technical assistance, including a review of proposal drafts? (3) How are proposals reviewed, and how are decisions made? and (4) Are there budgetary requirements and preferences (examples include matching funds, in-kind services, payment preferences, and so forth). The contact is an important source of information and future reference for the grantseeker. The contact could prove invaluable in the future.

Securing Grant Guidelines

It is important to secure a copy of published grant guidelines from the potential grantmakers. Many grantmakers have their guidelines printed and available for distribution. Figure 6.4 provides an example of the grant guidelines from a philanthropic organization that supports nonprofit agencies.

We strongly recommend that prospective applicants submit the following in the form of a letter of inquiry before a full proposal is sent:

- Information about the organization's purposes and specific activities.

- A brief description of the program for which funds are being sought, including the time period to be covered.

- The principal outcome(s) expected.

- Budgets for the program for which funds are sought, as well as for the organization.

- The amount being requested of the Foundation.

- Funding received to date for the program, as well as sources from which funding is being sought.

- The names and qualifications of the key personnel who will be responsible for the program.

- The most recent audited financial statements of the organization and its operating subsidiaries, if any.

- IRS certification of 501(c)(3) status of the organization.

- E-mail address for contact person at the organization.

Figure 6.4. Grant guidelines from the Surdna Foundation.

Step 3: Preparation of the Grant Proposal

A grant proposal has several elements. Each element either builds on or supports the other parts of the proposal. Collectively, they provide a comprehensive and detailed justification and plan for what the grantseeker sees as a problem and for which they hope to secure funding. Unfortunately, there is no standardized format for preparing grant proposals. One grantmaker may require a full funding proposal of 10 or more pages, while another may require a single-page summary of the proposal. Paying careful attention to the grantmaker's guidelines increases the chances that the proposal will be looked at. Figure 6.5 illustrates elements of a grant proposal as suggested by four different grantmakers and grantwriting support organizations.

The elements of a grant proposal, as depicted in Figure 6.4, will vary according to the grantmaker's requirements, but there appear to be some commonly agreed upon elements of a proposal. The six common elements are a cover letter; an executive summary; a statement of need; a project description; organizational information, including key personnel and/or credentials, a budget, and an evaluation process; and the grantseeker's commitment and ability to complete the project.

The Foundation Center	Corporation for Public Broadcasting	LRR.Net	The Grantsmanship Center
		Cover Letter	Cover Letter
Executive Summary		Summary or Cover Sheet	Abstract / Summary
			Introduction
Statement of Need	Statement of Need	Problem Statement or Needs Assessment	Need
Project Description	Approach	Methodology	Plan of Operations
	Methods of Evaluation	Evaluation	Evaluation
	Project Timelines	Program Goals and Objectives	Budget and Cost Effectiveness
Budget	Budget	Budget	
Organization Information	Credentials	Qualifications	Key Personnel
Conclusion			Commitment and Capability
	Supporting Materials	Appendices	

Figure 6.5. Comparative analysis of elements of a grant proposal.

Cover Letter

The cover letter is the first formal introduction of the grantseeker to the grantmaker. It should be a clear and concise statement about the organization's purpose and why a grant is being sought. A linkage needs to be made between the grantseeker's needs and desires and the grantmaker's purposes. This match clarifies the grantseeker's intentions and provides a gateway to the grantmaker's goals and objectives. The cover letter should be addressed to a specific person, rather than to the grantmaking organization, and it should include a brief description of the content of the proposal. The letter should not be overly long. One page should suffice in most cases. It is important to use the cover letter to commit to a follow-up visit or telephone call.

Executive Summary

The executive summary is a one- to two-page short description of the project. It contains all of the information, in summary form, that is in the full proposal. This snapshot of the proposal allows the grantseeker to set the stage for the proposal, and in a clear and concise way. It provides a narrative that explains the problem and its importance, the proposed solution (the projects and anticipated results), budget needs (including what has already been committed), and information about the organization and its competence. The executive summary should be written last and needs the considerable attention that a short summary requires. It is often much easier to write a 10–15-page proposal than a one- or two-page summary. It takes practice and several rounds of editing to write a good executive summary. The first draft should not be the final version.

Statement of Need

The statement of need is the most critical part of the grant proposal. It provides a statement and justification of the need or the problem to be resolved by the proposed project. This statement should facilitate the reader's understanding of the issues. It presents facts that support the project's need and validates the grantseeker as the best organization to meet the need. It provides information about five areas: (1) involvement of beneficiaries of the grant; (2) statement of need in terms of the participants or beneficiaries; (3) explanation of how needs were identified; (4) supporting statements and statistical data and authoritative documentation or statements; and (5) linking the needs and proposed solutions to the goals and strategic plan of the organization. The Foundation Center's *Proposal Writing Short Course* suggests six points to follow in preparing the arguments:

1. Determine which facts or statistics are going to best support the project. Emphasis in this section is on accuracy and detail to ensure that a valid case is built for the issue or problem. Eliminate information that is not germane to the proposal.

2. Determine whether it is reasonable to portray the problem as acute. If this is an acute problem, then explain why the organization should receive the grant.

3. If the problem is an issue that may seem unsolvable, then give the reader hope about the organization's involvement and potential to solve the problem.

4. Could the project be presented as a model solution? Determine if that is the best approach for this grant. If the grantseeker has a model solution and it fits the grant proposal, then include it. If not, then don't make it part of the proposal. Using a model solution can increase the base of potential grantmakers.

5. Demonstrate that the project addresses the need differently or better than other projects that may have preceded it. Be sure not to be critical of other projects that are competitive or have preceded this proposal. Show collaboration where possible. This characteristic is frequently viewed as a strength by grantmakers.

6. Avoid circular reasoning, where the absence of a problem is presented as a problem. For example, "The problem is we have no community center in our community. Building a community center will resolve that problem." It is better to focus on what a community center would mean to the community. "The problem is the lack of available facilities for community members to use, and especially youth-at-risk and gang-related issues."

Project Description

The project description should contain four subsections: goals and objectives, methodology, staffing and administration, and evaluation. The proposal has already dealt with the issue of need. This section describes how the proposal, when funded, will operate and solve that need. It should provide sufficient detail so the grantmaker will clearly understand the process and be able to see how it can meet the described need. *Goals and objectives* establish a foundation for measuring outcomes of the project. Each provides a clear level of distinction. Goals separate the problem or need into achievable work units. For example, a problem statement that reads, "How can we reduce the rise in juvenile crime and its impact upon at-risk youth in our neighborhood?" might have several goals that could read:

1. Determine who the at-risk youth are and who has the greatest potential to engage in criminal behavior.

2. Establish an outreach program to reach these youth.

3. Establish a collaborative program of after-school activities and neighborhood resources that meet the needs of youth.

Goals provide a general direction. They take the broader problem or need statement and divide it into workable units so it can be addressed. For the grantmaker, it shows that the organization has established a clear direction and has a plan that will lead to a solution.

Objectives are a natural subdivision of goals and more clearly delineate how the goal will be established. Objectives are more specific, are based on a goal, and are measurable. There are four different types of objectives that are commonly written. The *behavioral objectives* suggest some type of human behavioral impact. An example would be, "Over a period of nine months, targeted youth will have a more positive feeling about themselves." Objectives should not try to address more than a single outcome. An objective that states, "Over a period of nine months, targeted youth will have a more positive feeling about themselves and about their families" should be written as two separate objectives. One would deal with self and the second with families.

Performance objectives deal with proficiency and skill development. For example, take the statement "At-risk youth participating in the program over a six-month period will develop and exhibit study skills that allow them to improve their school performance." This objective may appear to have two outcomes, but the actual outcome is improved school performance. This is a measurable outcome. The development and exhibiting of study skills are processes that facilitate the measurable outcome.

Product objectives suggest a deliverable item or hands-on product that other people can use or that is used by the grantseeker. An example is the statement "To develop a manual for outreach workers that provides them with proven approaches to reaching at-risk youth." Here, both the product and the users of the product are clearly defined. A *process objective* looks at how a methodology was implemented and modified. It suggests, in many cases, an assessment process (e.g., "Methods used in the outreach program will be documented and assessed to determine which are most effective").

Methodology describes how the problem will be solved once the grant is awarded. This detailed section will lead the grantmaker to a clear understanding of how the grant will be administered. Smith and McLean (1988) suggest that several items should be considered, including the following:

1. The overall designs of the project, which should include an overview of how the project will be administered from start to finish. This is a narrative that begins by restating the problem or need statement and then summarizing the entire design process. The emphasis is upon providing a concise statement of process and then expanding upon it in detail.

2. Specific activities that are planned, and the sequencing of these activities within the project.

3. The relationship between planned activities and the stated goals and objectives. Tying together the activities with the goals and objectives is essential to the grantmaker's understanding of how outcomes will be achieved. Goals and objectives do not stand alone, but they must always be tied to process.

4. Identifying the specific procedures used to implement the program. A discussion of *how* the procedures will operate, as well as *when* they will be implemented. This may include a discussion of the sequencing of actions that must occur before planned activities are implemented.

5. Explaining how program participants will be selected.

6. Identifying project completion timelines for each phase of the proposal.

7. Discussing plans for collaborations with other organizations.

8. Describing the project "deliverables," such as newsletters, process manuals, training materials, publications, seminars, and workshops. (p. 38)

Staffing and administration are important parts of any grant proposal. This section explains the competence of the organization's members who will be administering the grant. One of its purposes is to convince the grantmaker that the organization has the ability to successfully carry the project to completion. Included are the key people to be involved in the project, along with their experience, education, and training, as they will relate to the proposed project. Résumés for existing staff should be included in the appendix with a narrative summary in the text.

When new staff are proposed as part of the grant project, it is necessary to justify these positions and demonstrate how the staff will have adequate responsibilities related to the project. Projects that propose new positions but fail to provide for continuation of the positions after the conclusion of the grant may find it a detriment to successful grantseeking. Finally, a project that appears to be relying only on new staff will be less attractive than one that has a mix of permanent and new staff.

Organizational Information

The introduction to this section is a description of the grantseeker's qualifications or credibility for the proposed project. A detailed discussion is not essential in this section. This introduction tells the grantmaker about the organization, its mission, its purpose, a brief history, and its goals and objectives. There is a discussion about the organization's current programs, activities, service statistics, strengths, and accomplishments and a discussion of its strategic plan and its progress towards achieving it. Also included is a discussion about the function and size of the board, as well as its involvement in the organization. The grantmaker should be able to get a feel for the composition, commitment, and involvement of the board. Any special constituent groups that serve as volunteers should be identified and described with respect to how they support the organization's mission. The staff will be involved in a variety of activities focusing on the organization's mission. Finally, a description of what these organizational activities are—as well as the identification of the services provided to the various constituencies—should help in emphasizing the appropriateness of the expertise of the organization, especially as it fits with the proposal.

Budget

The budget can be a key factor in successful grantseeking. Convincing the grantmaker that the budget reflects the needs of the grant is important. A well-constructed budget with a supporting narrative, when appropriate, is a positive reinforcement to the grant proposal. Budgets normally contain two primary sources of funds: those requested from the grantmaker, and those provided by the grantseeker. The grantmaker normally provides money, but may also provide other types of resources. The grantseeker can provide a variety of different types of resources. These include money from the operating budget, in-kind services (such as staff or secretarial assistance), or external resources (such as sponsors or volunteers). *In-kind donations* are services rendered by individuals who are already part of the organization, and the cost of their services is figured and added to the budget. For example, a secretary who makes $30,000 a year and has 10 percent of her time assigned to the project would represent $3,000 in in-kind services. In-kind services could include office space, utilities, and other services. A budget should clearly reflect the types of in-kind services provided. The budget process follows the budget procedures explained in Chapter 9. As a guide, the budget should

- Include exactly what the narrative of the grant has proposed;

- Provide complete information about each staff position, including rate of pay, percent of time allocated to the project, fringe benefits, mileage rate, per diem rates, honorariums, and so forth;

- Include actual costs for supplies and services related to the project; and

- Include items paid for by other sources.

Figure 6.6 depicts how a sample budget for a project might be formatted. A supporting budget narrative would only be necessary to explain unusual or unclear costs. A budget narrative could be framed in one of two ways: A footnote style provides a descriptor for different budget items and is linked to the budget. If this is insufficient, a budget narrative could be written as part of the document. In some cases, grantmakers provide a budget form that grantseekers must complete.

Item	Number	Cost	Total Cost
Printing of Envelopes & Stationery	300	$80.00	$80.00
Questionnaire Printing	150	$1.50	$225.00
Questionnaire Mailings	150	$1.75	$262.50
Data Input (student hours)	40 hrs	$12.00	$480.00
Data Analysis (student hours)	40 hrs	$12.00	$480.00
Telephone Interviews (student hours)	60 hrs	$12.00	$720.00
Qualitative Data Analysis (student hours)	60 hrs	$12.00	$720.00
Travel			
Dissemination of Data - Conference	partial	$1500.00	$1250.00
Dissemination of Data - Workshop	partial	$1500.00	$1250.00
Sub-Total			**$5,467.50**
Overhead		$532.50	$532.50
TOTAL			**$6,000.00**
In-kind Contributions	**% or time**		
Co-Primary research time	5%	$2,993.05	$2,993.05
Co-Primary research time	5%	$2,675.80	$2,675.80
faculty benefits	38.73%	$2195.55	$2195.55
Clerical staff	50 hrs	$9.15	$457.50
clerical benefits	25.01%	$114.42	$114.42
TOTAL			**$8,436.32**

Figure 6.6. Sample grant budget.

Evaluation Process

The purpose of the evaluation section of the proposal is to explain how the project outcomes will be assessed. It provides the grantmaker with a measure of effectiveness of the grant dollars awarded. More and more grantmakers are requiring some type of evaluation process. Evaluation should not be considered to be a post-project process, but should be integrated throughout the project. The evaluation process should include an assessment of the process, as well as an assessment of the progress towards outcomes throughout the process and of the final outcomes of the project. Grantmakers see a well-prepared evaluation process as an important criterion in their decision making. Many grantmakers require major written components explaining how success would be measured, who would conduct the evaluations, and how the results will be disseminated. A checklist for the evaluation narrative would include the following:

- Explain how the evaluator and the process will be selected.

- Include an evaluation procedure for each goal and objective.

- Identify interim outcomes and match them to timelines for the project, as well as to reporting periods.

- Describe data-gathering methodology and line it to goals, objectives, and timelines.

- Describe any instruments or tools to be used and how they support the project.

- Explain how evaluation data will be used and disseminated to other publics.

- Describe the evaluation reports.

- Explain the process evaluation and how it will be used to enhance the project's progress and outcomes.

Commitment and Capability

What is the potential for success of the project if a grant is awarded to the grantseeker? This is a question that every grantmaking organization asks itself and must attempt to answer through a careful review of the grant proposal. A section that discusses the commitment and capability of the organization helps the grantmaker to answer this question. The grantseeker can explain how similarly funded projects have been successful, how the presence of staff, facilities, and other resources all contribute to the potential success of the proposed project. A concise discussion of strengths, resources, and successes allows the grantmaker to gain a clearer picture of the grantseeker's capability. The section does not need to be long, but should provide support to the other sections of the proposal.

Step 4: Submitting the Grant Proposal

The culmination of the grantwriting process is the submission of the grant proposal to the selected granting organization. All of the components described in step 4 are included in the proposal submission. It is essential that the submitted grant proposal have a professional look. The proposal should be bound if it is large, should conform to good writing style, and should be easy to read. Before sealing the package for delivery to the grantmaker, the grantseeker should be sure to complete one final review to ensure that all materials are included and in the intended order.

Step 5: Grantmaker's Decision

The grantmaker can make one of several decisions regarding a grant proposal. It can be to (1) award the grant in full, (2) make a partial grant award, (3) defer consideration of the proposal to a later date, or (4) deny the grant request. If the final option is taken, the grantmaker is under no obligation to the grantseeker to explain why the proposal was rejected. In the same regard, the grantseeker should not read a worthiness or value issue into a grant rejection. A grant rejection may be due to a lack of available funds or an overabundance of similar proposals, or it may have fallen outside the guidelines of the grantmaker. In some cases, the grantmaker will ask for changes to be made and then to have it resubmitted. Whether the grant proposal is rejected, funded in part, or needs modification, the grantseeker should call the grantmaker and ask how the proposal might be strengthened. This feedback may be important in strengthening the grant proposal for future submissions.

In cases where only portions of the grant were funded or where there was a decision to defer to a later time, the grantseeker must decide whether to accept the decision of the grantmaker or to withdraw the proposal and seek another grantmaker. This can be a difficult decision, as the grantseeker has invested considerable energy in the process. If the grantseeker determines that it may have a better opportunity elsewhere, then it may be appropriate to seek another grantmaker. Regardless of the decision, the grantmaker should be contacted and information should be gathered regarding the decision-making process and how the proposal might be strengthened or reconsidered for full funding.

Even when full funding is awarded, the grantseeker still must choose to accept the grant. A grantmaker may attach conditions to the funds, and the grantseeker will have to determine if they are appropriate. An important deciding factor in the acceptance of a grant is whether the project can be accomplished and whether it remains consistent with the values and mission of the organization.

Step 6: Grant Administration

Grant administration involves managing the project for which the grant was awarded, along with maintaining appropriate communications with the grantmaker. Some grantmakers choose to have little contact with the organization after an award is made, but most require some type of ongoing contact. The grant administration should consider the following:

- Where feasible, have a single point of contact from the grantseeking organization to the grantmaking organization. This simplification enhances communication and reduces the potential for confusion.

- Don't leave questions about the grant unanswered. Make contact with the grantmaker to resolve issues before they become problems.

- Always make contact with an individual, and not with an organization.

- Include the project name and grant identification number on all correspondence.

- All correspondence should be clear and specific. Do not assume people know the issue being discussed.

- Always seek permission before making changes in the budget.

- Make regular progress reports to the grantmaker. Any deliverables such as news letters, reports, brochures, and annual reports should be provided.

- Stick to the timeline. If changes are required, seek approval from the grantmaker.

- At the conclusion of the report, submit all required information in a timely and complete manner. (Smith and McLean, 1988, pp. 60–61)

Knowledge of all the requirements of the grantmaking organization, as well as the criteria of the grant, will ensure a more effective administration process.

Summary

Grantseeking is neither a complicated nor a mystic process. It can be a time-consuming process, and those organizations that are successful have taken the time to implement the six steps of grantseeking. Careful attention to detail, the time taken to learn the grantseeking process and potential grantmakers will often pay off with successful grants. There is no substitute for good ideas that can be matched to willing grantmakers. The decision to award a grant is based on the sustained efforts of the grantseeker to find a grantmaker that is a good match for a proposed project.

References

Smith, S. H., & McLean, D. D. (1988). *ABC's of grantsmanship.* Reston, VA: American Alliance for Health, Physical Education, Recreation and Dance.

Chapter 7

Philanthropy and Fundraising

Introduction

In contemporary government enterprises and among nonprofit organizations, the traditional reliance upon support from the general fund and from fees and charges is waning. The productivity expectations placed on leisure service organizations are increasing, while budgetary resources are holding steady in many organizations and declining in others. Partnering with philanthropic and nonprofit organizations and individuals is increasingly becoming an attractive and necessary approach to securing additional resources. It is not unusual for a forum conducted by the National Association of State Park Directors, for example, to have as much as 60 percent of all presentations focused on partnering, friends' groups, and philanthropy. One state reported the simultaneous creation of almost 200 friends' groups with nonprofit fundraising status. Furthermore, many and varied training programs on fundraising that are designed for leisure service professionals are offered by major fundraising organizations and universities.

This chapter looks at the process of philanthropy and fundraising as it applies to leisure service organizations. It provides a background discussion on philanthropy and fundraising and describes several approaches to philanthropic fundraising.

Philanthropy

A charitable act is a social exchange that occurs each time a gift is made. The decision to make a gift comes after being asked by someone else, someone who is trusted by the donor. A gift implies a considerable level of confidence and trust in both the asker and the charitable organization's ability (and faithfulness) to do what is "right" with the donation.

Philanthropy is synonymous with charitable giving. While charitable giving has been perceived as giving for the social good, the social good is increasingly being interpreted in a broader context of issues. In the narrowest sense, charitable giving is giving resources to the poor and needy or to organizations that assist them. This perspective of giving has been broadened to include all types of philanthropy, which can be defined as an act of trust on the part of a donor towards the organization that will receive and use the donation.

The philanthropic process is uniquely American. No other region in the world has the same level of giving, nor the social and governmental structure to allow such massive levels of giving. In 1997, over $143 billion was donated to charitable causes. Of that amount, $110 billion was donated by individuals, and the balance was donated by foundations from investment income.

Philanthropy is an activity of and resource to individuals and nonprofit organizations. It is nonprofit organizations working in conjunction with individuals and public and private organizations that secure different types of donations from individuals and other nonprofit organizations and foundations. Sometimes referred to as the *third sector,* philanthropic organizations focus on meeting social needs that are neglected by other sectors. In public park and recreation organizations, for example, there has been a steady decline in financial resources made available from the public purse to fulfill the public recreation mission. To counteract this, public agencies have turned to the philanthropic sector. The National Park Service is probably the leader in this movement, although other federal land-managing agencies, state park agencies, civic recreation departments, and many nonprofit sports organizations are close behind. The Florida Park Service produces a *Citizen Support Organization Handbook* for the express purpose of extending the resources of the Florida Park Service. Hundreds of American cities have developed foundations to support their social service programs. Many state sports corporations are highly dependent on charitable giving for their support. Philanthropy has become intertwined with daily services and programs provided by sports and leisure service organizations.

Both independence and volunteerism characterize philanthropy. Independence is a characteristic in the sense that individuals and organizations making donations give independently of conditions that could have been associated with the gift. In philanthropy, the gift is given voluntarily; that is, the donor does so of his or her free will with the intent of promoting a particular purpose or meeting a particular need.

Why Fundraising is Important

Many public and private sector leaders have been reluctant to embrace fundraising as a tool for expanding their organization's abilities to provide services. There are many good reasons to use fundraising to develop and sustain public and nonprofit sport and leisure service organizations. The *Philanthropy and American Outdoors Workshop* suggests 10 reasons why organizations should include fundraising in their revenue structure plan:

1. There is growing evidence that public agencies at all levels of government are becoming increasingly dependent upon external philanthropic support. Traditional services offered by public agencies are either dwindling or being replaced by for-profit enterprises.

2. Philanthropy is one of America's most distinctive virtues. Giving to *public/society benefit purposes* and giving to *leisure, sports, and environment and wildlife* experienced significant increases in recent years.

3. The "Greening of America"—Contributions to environmental causes including our parks, forests, open spaces, and wildlife is big business— almost $4 billion annually. The numerous nonprofit environmental

and park support organizations hope to benefit as current generations pass unprecedented wealth to the baby boomer generation—an estimated $8 trillion by 2010.

4. Tax-law changes are having an impact on the amounts and kinds of gifts Americans make today. Capital gains, appreciated property, estate planning, charitable trusts, endowments, gift annuities, bequests, etc., are becoming part of our everyday language in the public and private nonprofit community.

5. Leisure service organizations are well positioned to make the case for philanthropic support. They are in the quality-of-life and resources business.

6. Socially and environmentally oriented public service professionals have those desired qualities to make fundraising a success: a dedication to fulfilling a public trust, a desire to work with both the general public and those with affluence or influence (hopefully, both), a willingness to ask the hard questions, and an ability to communicate a sense of urgency.

7. Partnership building is here to stay and is critical in obtaining the diverse philanthropic support available.

8. Individual citizen donors and volunteers are marching to a different drummer today, demanding accountability, ownership in what they give to, and a direct voice in how the philanthropic dollars are spent.

9. We are faced with what Andrew Carnegie called "the proper administration of wealth." He formulated three alternative ways of disposing of wealth: bequest it to one's relatives, endow it to the public good, and administer it during one's lifetime for public benefits. Carnegie preferred and practiced the third alternative.

10. From fundraising to the stewardship of gifts received, leisure service organization professionals demonstrate their public trust. (p. 6)

The Role of Fund Development

The roles of fund development can be many. Regardless of how the organization is structured, it is how the philanthropy dollar is used and how effectively the donor or potential donor perceives that use that is of most importance. Some of the roles that have been identified include the following:

- Building community: Leisure service organizations have long been involved in building communities. They are seen as contributing to the quality of life of communities. The Riverwalk Foundation in Naperville, Illinois, focuses on securing funding that will build the quality of life along the community's river that runs through the downtown. Other community foundations have focused on improving the community.

- Funding opportunities to invest in human capital: This is a frequent source of giving. Leisure service organizations have their foundations in human capital and continue to strengthen their involvement in this area.

- Seeking a design to allow the accomplishment of objectives: The City of Baltimore, Maryland, when faced with a $500,000 annual deficit in its golf course operations, reorganized them as a nonprofit corporation. The nonprofit corporation was able to receive gifts, but more important, it reorganized golf operations in such a way as to relieve the public from a significant tax burden.

- Offering a means for donors to fulfill their aspirations: Friends of Zoos, Friends of Parks, Friends of Wildlife, Sports Corporations, and similar types of friends groups provide donors with the opportunity to give of both their time and money. There are among the most popular approaches to giving in the United States.

Why People Give

Understanding why people give is as important as asking for money. Not all people are motivated to give for the same reasons. Several reasons have been suggested for giving. For some, it fulfills social, religious, or philosophical convictions. Religious organizations receive the largest amounts of charitable contributions. Social and philosophical reasons are inherent in society as motivations for giving. When Ted Turner, founder of the Cable News Network and other major cable television channels, pledged $1 billion to the United Nations' efforts, it was for philosophical and social reasons.

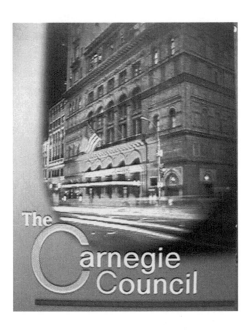

The use of brochures and reports aid organizations in securing external funding and grants.

The government has made charitable giving an obvious tax advantage, both at the federal and state levels. Every philanthropic organization makes sure that its potential and actual donors understand the tax advantages of giving. Another reason for giving is for gratitude or for a commitment to public service that will lead to a better society. Some individuals hope to gain appreciation and public recognition for their efforts. In some cases, givers may hope for redemption. Some give out influence in the form of guilt or competitiveness by challenging others to give at the same level or by offering a matching grant as an incentive. Other philanthropists want to create a memorial to themselves or others who are dear to them. Many structures and funds in the United States have been created as a memorial to an individual or a family (e.g., the Rockefeller Fund). An observant walker on any college campus will note the names on benches, fountains, and buildings which were made possible by the conspicuous generosity of a successful alumnus or friend. Finally, some donors want to keep their life's work in the family and make sure that it is perpetuated for future generations.

Charitable Organizations

Most charitable organizations are organized under the Internal Revenue Service (IRS) tax code as 501(c)(3) classification. In order to qualify for 501(c)(3) status, an organization must meet certain requirements. Included for foundations (which are the most common in support of leisure service organizations) are articles of incorporation that have been filed with the appropriate state authorities. Requirements for incorporation vary in each state. The IRS also requires that the organization provide a detailed narrative of all of the activities of the organization—past, present, and future. The Florida Park Service has provided the following narrative as an example to consider:

Activities of Charitable Organization Established to Support the Park System

- *Development of Educational Media:* The development of at least five educational videos relating to the resources, management practices, and recreational opportunities in Florida state parks.

- *Promotion of Florida State Parks:* Undertake a program to promote Florida state parks through the production of three driving tours of three representative Florida ecosystems. Also, help sponsor traveling exhibits on Florida state parks.

- *Development of Endowment Fund:* Commence the establishment of a dedicated endowment fund for the support of major needs in Florida state parks. The fund will be established and administered by a committee of the board of directors.

The charitable organization also needs to identify its sources of income, describe its actual and planned fundraising program in detail, and provide the names, addresses, and titles of the officers of the board of directors. If public officials are involved in the organization, they must be mentioned by title. Many of these organizations receive administrative support from the organizations they are serving. If so, this must be noted in the IRS submission. Additional information requested by the IRS includes activities and operational functions focusing on the assets of the organization, as well as financial data for the current year and the three previous years.

Fund Development

Fund development is a planned process that involves promotion of understanding, participation, and support. It is a process of involving the public to give of its time, talent, and resources to play an active part in achieving the organization's goals. Figure 7.1 illustrates a perspective of the development of donors. The development process involves the three stages shown to the left in Figure 7.1. They are the contact phase, the growth phase, and the commitment phase. Fund development is a process of finding and nurturing potential contacts until they become committed to the cause of the organization. Such a process can take years to accomplish.

Fund development is a strategic marketing process designed to bring together potential donors with the nonprofit organization in such a way that both benefit from an exchange. The donor may be giving for altruistic reasons or for financial benefit. The marketing process is different from the type of marketing that a commercial organization practices. While there are some similarities, there are also some significant differences. The product that a commercial organization sells is a tangible benefit or commodity to the customer. In some sense, charitable organizations provide the same advantages, in terms of tax benefits, but as previously discussed, they also provide some philosophical, social, and cultural benefits that commercial organizations are not well suited to provide. The marketing campaign of the charitable organization focuses on securing committed donors.

The three phases depicted in Figure 7.1 are further divided into eight levels within the pyramid. The *initial contact phase* is important for maintaining a base of new and committed donors. The *universe of suspects, or consumer base,* is seen as all individuals who might be contacted. This is a global population of potential donors from which the organization could potentially draw. In reality, only a small part of the population is going to become actual donors. With limited funds available for the search for new donors, the charitable organization must begin to narrow its list of potential donors. Some organizations maintain profiles of donors to assist in efforts to target the most responsive prospects. Table 7.1 illustrates three characteristics by which a population was segmented by a cultural organization. The elitist group was seen as its primary long-term benefactors, while the other two groups were seen as less promising sources of donors.

Socio-Demographic Title	Population Characteristic	Targeted Nonprofits
Elitist	Top tier individuals socio-economically; cutting edge foundation and corporate support; planned gifts	Arts & Culture International Affairs
Elite and Democratic Access	All of the above, plus mass appeal, mass 'events'	Higher Education Environment
Mass Appeal	Some of the above Direct mail; advertising campaigns	Health Care Education Social Services

Table 7.1. Population titles and characteristics as donors (Golan, 1998).

The narrowing of the population of donors to those who *might give* is critical to the charitable organization. Whether the winnowing is done through a mass mailing, telephone calls, or individual contact, the charitable organization needs to maximize the efficiency and effectiveness of the contact. Researching and knowing of potential donor sources is critical and is discussed in more detail in the section on annual campaigns. First-time contributors are the lifeblood of an expanding donor pool. Not only does this group represent a new source of money, but also a new contact. The charitable organization immediately moves the new donor to the *growth phase.*

In the growth phase, the donor begins to receive more frequent or sustained contact from the charitable organization. The intent is to encourage the donor to change from a once-a-year minimal contributor to one who makes multiple annual donations. The goal is to create a commitment to the charitable organization's goals and mission that will continue to grow, along with donations. As depicted in Figure 7.1, there are three levels of contact and giving used in this phase, each one requiring a higher level of involvement on the part of the charitable organization and resulting in a higher level of giving by the donor.

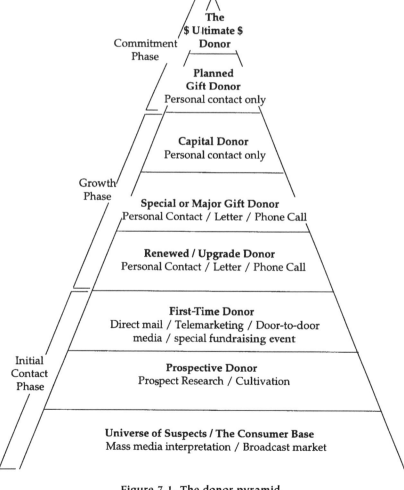

Figure 7.1. The donor pyramid.

The growth phase typically occurs over several years. Of greatest importance in the growth phase is the matching of donors' desires with organizational needs. Growth in this phase comes when the donors see their gift as something that meets their desires. They have become committed to the charitable organization or some aspect of its operations and are willing to commit some of their financial resources to it. At this level, personal contact becomes more and more important to the success of the effort.

A few donors will move from the growth phase to the *commitment phase,* and, as might be expected, the level of their gifts will increase. The frequency of gifts may decrease, although this is not always the case, but the size of their gift and its impact on the charitable organization will be significant. These are the donors who will give $1 million or more to endow a chair, or $500,000 to build a community structure, or $200,000 to endow a scholarship fund.

Finally, as illustrated in Figure 7.1, the once-large pool of donors continues to get smaller as the charitable organization moves towards securing the *ultimate donor.* The willingness of the donor to give is a function of both economics and commitment to the charitable cause. An individual with a desire to give much, but whose economic resources are limited, may always be a special or major gift donor. The ultimate donor has the economic resources to make a gift that has a major impact on the charitable organization's ability to achieve its mission. As each organization strives to develop the ultimate donor, it would be unwise for it to focus all of its energies on this limited field of donors. It must rely on diverse, multi-tiered fundraising and donor development efforts.

Fundraising Sources

A successful fundraising program draws upon at least seven different sources of potential funds. These include individuals and/or memberships, boards and board relations, corporations and industry councils, foundations, special events, government, and planned giving.

Individuals constitute the most significant source of all philanthropic dollars available to charitable organizations. Major donors are cultivated over a period of time and provide the core of success to many charitable organizations. These individuals are important because they generate an enduring personal loyalty to the charitable organization. Typically, these individuals have the interest and wealth necessary to act on their enthusiasm for the benefit of the charitable organization. Major donors have become benefactors for risky projects, providing necessary capital to successfully undertake a project that the charitable organization might not otherwise fund. Finally, these individuals have extensive contacts and can bring others (and their money) to the charitable organization. Although they will be few, the major individual donors should be recruited and nurtured with great care. Individuals are drawn to charitable organizations because they believe that they have the ability to make a difference. For example, the Riley Foundation has supported Bradford Woods summer camp programs for individuals with disabilities for over 50 years, during which time it has funded many major capital improvements. The Riley family established and made the initial investment in a foundation that supports the Bradford Woods summer camp program, along with many other programs for children with disabilities. Cultivating major donors requires a long-term commitment on the part of the board and the chief executive officer (CEO) of the charitable organization. It requires personal communication from peers, prompt acknowledgment of communication and gifts, and the dissemination of advanced news of the charitable organization's activities.

Corporate and industry councils have been consistent givers to philanthropic causes. Since 1950, they have given about five percent of total contributions (about $8 billion annually). Many corporations restrict their giving to local communities where they have operations. They do so for many reasons, including strengthening the community, enhancing board connections, stimulating economic development, and providing educational outreach. Most corporations have a separate corporate foundation into which they make donations and from which they award grants. Gaining access to corporate foundation grants is facilitated by continuous nurturing of a relationship between the foundation and the sport and leisure service organization. The Battle Creek, Michigan, Parks and Recreation Department, for example, has consistently worked with the Kellogg Foundation to insure a steady source of capital income for park and recreation facilities.

Boards and board relations are an important source of income and prospective donors. Board members of charitable organizations have usually made large donations or are expected to contribute during their tenure on the board. In addition, board members identify and work with potential major gift givers.

Charitable organizations and support foundations occasionally reach out to other *foundations* for sources of funds. Many foundations only give to intermediary foundations or charitable organizations. The search for and use of foundations as a major income source requires considerable effort, but can result in sizable contributions.

Special events can be a major source of income for some charitable organizations. The extent to which special-event fundraising is used depends upon the purpose and focus of the charitable organization. Sports organizations, cultural groups, and symphonies are a few examples of groups that use special events extensively. Whether it is a "run for youth" or a "jazz festival in the park" or a "riverwalk festival," the purpose is the same: to raise community awareness about the charitable organization and its function and purpose, and to raise money. Special events bring in diverse donor groups that might not otherwise be interested in the charitable organization. A positive spin-off of special events is the publicity it generates and the potential it offers for board development. On the negative side, the cost-benefit ratio of a special event can sometimes be quite low. Special-event fundraising is not always an effective long-term single-focus strategy, but it does serve as an important ingredient in the mix of effective fundraising.

Government at all levels can be perceived as a potential supporter for charitable causes. Such support frequently comes in the form of grants to leisure service organizations, but may also include special supportive legislation. The value of the latter is well understood by the Miami–Dade County Parks and Recreation Department, which maintains a full-time liaison with the state legislature. This person's assignment is to lobby for the department's interests. Government is an especially important source of funds for capital projects. However, capital development funds from the government are not usually forthcoming without an intense amount of lobbying and preliminary work. The cost and uncertainty associated with seeking government funding may sometimes be too great. Many small communities have learned not to hold out too much hope for the government to provide them with money that may not be forthcoming, or have found that when government funding does come, it is too little to support what was planned.

Planned giving is discussed later in this chapter. It is a core process that helps to make a charitable organization self-sustaining and also allows it to grow.

Goal Setting, Relationships, and the Gift Pyramid

Any successful fundraising effort is grounded in goal setting. Figure 7.2 illustrates the relationship of organization goals to gift-giving potential, as well as to the organization's statement of mission, to the board, and to the staff. A sport and leisure service organization's mission statement answers the following: (1) who is served, (2) what services are provided, and (3) how the services are delivered. The mission statement is a starting point for the charitable organization's fundraising efforts. Some charitable organizations call their mission statement a "statement of purpose." The Parks and Wildlife Foundation of Texas, Inc., identifies its purpose as being "to provide private support for the efforts of Texas Parks and Wildlife Department." It further states that, together, the department and the foundation play a leading role in ensuring both the protection of Texas' unique heritage and the provision of full outdoor opportunities for future generations.

Figure 7.2. Goal relationships in fundraising.

The *staff* play an important and ongoing support role in fundraising. The annual giving program is a major focus of the charitable organization's employees and volunteers. They are the behind-the-scenes workforce that ensures the success of the campaign without becoming directly involved in the publicly visible parts of the process. Public appeals are reserved for the CEO, members of the Board of Directors, or honorary spokespersons. The activities of the staff will vary according to the size and nature of the organization, their level of expertise in fundraising, and the expectations of the board when it comes to staff involvement.

Opportunities for gifts represents the range of potential program areas and services to which donors might give. They are defined by the charitable organization and represent the development and accomplishment of their mission. The leaders of the organization develop and implement strategies that build on their individual and collective strengths. Such strategies might include signing letters, attending top-level meetings with potential donors, making strategic calls, attending media opportunities with donors, attending receptions, and generally creating a high level of public visibility. The board defines the opportunities for gifts with the help of significant input from the chief executive officer and the support staff. The strategy to actually receive the proposed gifts is part of organizational goal development.

Each charitable organization has a unique perspective on its expectations of the *board's role* in fundraising. All boards of directors have multiple responsibilities. They have a general responsibility to govern the organization in such a way as to ensure the success of its mission—which also assumes a fiduciary, programmatic, and capital responsibility. Secondly, the board should be responsible for the recruitment and selection of board members who agree with the mission of the organization and can potentially give to the organization. Most boards have some type of annual retreat, where they discuss the charitable organization's mission and functions, build board relationships, and strengthen staff and board relationships. Board members are expected to make major efforts in securing funds for the charitable organization. These efforts may include an expectation for them to personally make donations. One major symphony, for example, expects each board member to make a minimum annual contribution of $650,000. Failure to do so means removal from the board. While not all boards have this same type of requirement, almost all expect contributions and fundraising efforts from their members.

Goal Setting

The annual campaign involves the establishment of fundraising goals. The goals should be realistic and designed to meet the charitable organization's identified needs. Goal setting begins by examining the charitable organization's financial needs for the coming year. This examination involves constructing an operating budget which shows all committed and desired services and programs. If the charitable organization is committed to providing funds to another organization, this is taken into account as part of the committed monies. Another goal-setting activity is the identification of which programs and functions will require external funding and which can be supported either by internal funding sources or through direct cost recovery from sales, fees, etc.

The act of setting an achievable goal for contributed income is based on several factors, such as the history of giving to the charitable organization, the level of current giving, current economic conditions, the frequency of past appeals and their effectiveness, and the attractiveness of the programs. Table 7.2 illustrates a budget that defines a gift goal. In general, projected contributed income should be set at 90 percent of the previous year's donation level. This practice allows for the incidence of donors who may not continue contributing to this charitable organization. The remaining 10 percent of the gift goal must be met through the contributions of new donors, or else the need projection should be reduced.

Budget	Amount	Totals	Goal
Expenditure			
Committed Funding	$750,000		
Desired Funding	$450,000	$1,200,000	
Income			
Earned Income	$350,000		
Deferred Income/Investment Income	$600,000		
Special Events	$50,000	$1,000,000	
Desired Contributed Income (Goal)			$200,000

Table 7.2. Example goal setting using a budget.

The Gift Pyramid

The rule of thirds (see Table 7.3) represents a commonly accepted standard for planning levels of giving. It is a useful tool in goal setting. The rule of thirds suggests that a third of your funding goal will come from 10 to 15 gifts; the next third will come from the next 25 donors; and the final third will come from all other gifts. The rule of thirds reminds fundraisers not only where their potential donors are coming from, but also where these fundraisers should concentrate their energies. Obviously, the rule of thirds is to be used as a guide and not as a formal expectation.

	Gift Level	Gifts Needed	Prospects Needed	Total Dollars
TOP THIRD	$250,000	1	1	$250,000
	$150,000	1	2	$150,000
	$100,000	3	6	$300,000
	$75,000	4	8	$300,000
				$1,000,000
MIDDLE THIRD	$50,000	10	16	$500,000
	$25,000	15	45	$375,000
				$875,000
BOTTOM THIRD	$10,000	20	75	$200,000
	$5,000	40	100	$200,000
	$2,500	50	125	$125,000
	Under $1,000	Many	Many	$100,000
				$625,000
			GRAND TOTAL	$2,500,000

Table 7.3. Rule of thirds—gifts/prospects needed for a $2,500,000 capital or endowment campaign.

Fundraising Strategies

A successful fundraising process requires a variety of strategies designed to take advantage of different donor levels. A fundraising campaign recognizes different types and levels of donors and makes appropriate overtures to them. While direct mail or telephone solicitation will secure a first-time donor and may retain a donor in the early stages of commitment, it will not likely entice the individuals at the top of the gift pyramid. Hence, diversifying strategies for fundraising is essential. This section looks at annual campaigns, planned giving, special events, and support organizations as differing strategies. These strategies do not represent all those that are available, but they do constitute a major portion of the types of strategies that effective leisure service organizations utilize.

There are four types of fundraising campaigns. The annual campaign focuses on raising funds for annual operating expenses. Programs of planned giving take a longer-term perspective and focus on different types of gifts that may be available for years. Special events are a less effective way of securing income, but they do raise the level of awareness of the charitable organization in the community. Capital campaigns (which are described elsewhere in this book) reflect the need for nonprofits to invest in construction, land acquisition, or other major purchases.

Annual Campaigns

Annual campaigns are the primary source of income for annual operating funds for many organizations. An annual campaign is an organized process that raises a specific amount of money over a specified period of time. Examples include the United Way, public radio and television stations, the Boy Scouts, and the Girl Scouts. The development of a well-planned annual campaign requires a considerable amount of effort on the part of the nonprofit staff, its board, and its volunteers. The annual giving campaign has two primary functions: (1) to acquire new donors and (2) to retain donors and upgrade their level of giving.

The annual giving campaign generally results in low levels of donations ($1 to $50), but this is more than offset by the number of donations that are typically made at that time. Annual giving campaigns are seen as a predictable source of income because they tend not to fluctuate significantly from year to year. The donations received are intended to provide a short-term benefit to the organization by allowing for the operating functions to continue. These donations are typically unrestricted, allowing the organization's managers to determine how best to use the money.

The two most common methods of conducting an annual campaign are mail and telephone solicitations. Direct mail is the least expensive way to conduct an annual campaign. Most nonprofits dependent upon annual campaigns use some type of direct mail strategy. The development of a successful mailing list requires considerable effort. Returns from cold, or untested, lists can be as low as 1 percent, while on a more predictable, or tested, list, as high as 66 percent. The more refined the list, the higher the expected return. Greater accuracy and currency in the mailing leads to a higher rate of return. Another factor affecting the rate of return is how well those who receive the mailing know the charitable organization. This factor is termed "name recognition." Organizations with greater name recognition can expect a higher rate of return from direct mailings.

When retention is the goal of the mailed message, additional strategies are developed. The strategies should include multiple (two or more) mailings (or contacts requesting donations) per year, thank-you notes, newsletters, and other methods of communication. Effective direct mail campaigns should accomplish the following:

- Raise funds cost-effectively

- Dramatically increase the number of donors to an organization

- Increase the visibility of the organization among the general public

- Help identify better prospects for other giving strategies

- Identify potential volunteers and new workers for the organization

- Reach a greater number of those you want to reach in the way you want to reach them

- Give more control to the development aspect

- Provide instant gratification

- Give the nonprofit organization the opportunity to tell the full story

- Be individualized/personalized and segmented to a specific audience

Telephone solicitations have a higher rate of return. They are usually reserved for those individuals from whom a donation is realistically anticipated. Often a letter to the potential donor precedes the telephone campaign. Telephone campaigns are more costly and time-consuming than direct mail campaigns and are therefore expected to result in larger donations and provide a greater percentage of revenue. Staff, volunteers, and board members should all be involved in telephone campaigns.

Planned Giving

Planned giving is an inclusive term that addresses the scope of philanthropic giving. Although it may involve the annual campaign, more frequently, planned giving is associated with major fund drives. Planned giving is an effort by the organization to ensure its future through a program where donors are identified, contacted, nurtured, and made part of a giving program that benefits the organization and the individual. In many instances, the results of the planned giving are deferred, with the actual donation occurring years in the future.

Table 7.4 identifies six different types of planned giving approaches. *Outright gifts* are gifts of money or other tangible property given with an immediate benefit to the nonprofit. Such gifts may be given without regard to how they will be used, or the donor may choose to put specific conditions on the gift. The larger the gift, the more likely some parameters will be established. *Bequests,* by contrast, are made available to the charitable organization only after the donor dies and the will has gone through probate. Bequests are the single most important source of income for charitable organizations. Bequests allow the donor to retain control of the donation throughout his lifetime while simultaneously reducing the estate tax for the donor's heirs. Bequests can come in many forms. They can be for a fixed amount of money, a percentage of the total estate or a part thereof, or a specific item in estate (e.g., land, stock).

Type of Gift	Form of Gift	Benefit to Donor	Benefit to Nonprofit
1. Outright Gift	• Cash • Securities • Real Estate • Insurance • Personal Property	• deductible for income-tax purposes	• funds available for immediate use by the organization • frequently without restriction or terms of trust
2. Bequests: Anything one owns at the time of death may be passed on to an organization or person through one's last will and testament. Moreover, all forms of life income gifts may be in testamentary form to benefit family or friends and will then become available for use by named organizations.			
3. Life Income Gifts A. Pooled income funds	• appreciated securities • cash	• variable income that may provide hedge against inflation • no capital gains tax on appreciated gift	• ensures future funding
B. Charitable remainder unitrusts	• real estate • securities • cash	• same as pooled income funds plus • can be tailored to donor's situation • permits deferred income • includes real estate	• ensures substantial future funding
C. Charitable remainder annuity trusts	• cash • securities	• fixed income • tax deduction in year that gift is made • no capital gains tax on appreciated gift: alternative minimum tax may apply	• ensures substantial future funding
D. Charitable gift annuity	• cash • securities	• fixed income for lifetime • tax deduction in early years of gift	• portion of funds can be available to organization • ensures future funding • upon death of insured, remaining payable to organization
4. Charitable Lead Trust	• real estate • securities • cash	• allows property to be passed to others with little or no shrinkage due to taxes	• provides organization with current income for the length of the trust for a period of 10 years
5. Revocable Charitable Trust	• real estate • securities • cash	• all or part of amount placed in trust is available if needed by donor • removes burden of managing assets	• very high percentage of revocable trusts are not revoked and thus provide future funding
6. Insurance Policies A. Organization is made owner and beneficiary of policy currently in force	• life insurance	• donor gets income tax deduction for value of policy when transferred • future premium payments may be deducted as gift • donor can make large future gift at small present cost	• organization may borrow on policy • organization may cash in policy • organization may receive face value of policy at insured's death
B. Paid-up policy is given to organization	• life insurance	• tax deduction based on current value of policy	• organization may keep policy and receive face value upon death of insured
C. Organization is named beneficiary of policy, but not owner	• life insurance	• enables donor to make large future gift at small present cost • donor may change beneficiary later • donor may borrow on policy	• upon death of insured, organization will receive face value of policy

Source: KPMG Peat Marwick, *Management Issues*
Note: This table was revised by the AAFRC Trust for Philanthropy. The trust gratefully acknowledges the advice of the National Committee on Planned Giving. The contents of the table are the responsibility of that trust. This table is for information purposes only and is not a substitute for legal or other professional advice.

Table 7.4. Overview of some planned giving instruments.

A *life income gift* is given to the charitable organization as an irrevocable gift. The asset is invested by the organization, with all or part of the income earnings paid either to a single beneficiary or to multiple beneficiaries for a specified period of time. The charitable organization can use that part of the investment income from the gift that is not given to the beneficiary. Once the beneficiary dies or the predetermined period of income to the beneficiary expires, then the full benefit of the gift is made available to the nonprofit organization.

A *pooled income fund* can be compared to a mutual fund in the sense that the contributions of multiple donors are pooled together and managed as a single investment. The obvious advantage is the size of the fund, which allows for a greater return and broader investment opportunities. The investment generated from the principal provides support to the charitable organization after the donor's death.

The *charitable remainder annuity trust* provides income to both the charitable organization and the donor. The donor makes a fixed contribution to the nonprofit that can be added to at any time. The charitable organization manages the contribution, and the donor receives a guaranteed return on the contribution annually. The donor can determine when the return begins (e.g., after retirement) or can set it for a fixed length of time (e.g., 20 years). This is known as deferring income. If the return on the investment is greater than the amount promised the donor, then the charitable organization retains it as earnings. The charitable organization eventually receives the returns. The *charitable remainder unitrusts* are very similar to a charitable remainder annuity trust, except that instead of a fixed amount, the return to the donor will vary, depending on the market.

The final type of life income gift is a *charitable gift annuity*. This is a combination gift and investment, and it is among the oldest and most popular of the methods of making a life income gift. While similar to the others previously presented, the charitable gift annuity immediately becomes the property of the charitable organization, which then guarantees the donor a lifetime income.

A *charitable lead trust* provides assets to the charitable organization for a specified period of time, but not indefinitely. It allows the donor to preserve assets for himself while providing income for a charitable organization. The income received by the charitable organization is either a percentage of the trust assets as annually revalued or a fixed dollar amount. A charitable lead trust can be in the form of property, securities, or cash.

A *revocable charitable trust* puts the resources (real estate, cash, or securities) in control of the charitable organization, but allows the donor to access the trust, if desired. The donation is placed in a trust so that it might be available to the donor, if desired. Not only does this type of trust remove the burden of managing the assets, but in many cases, the trust ultimately is given to the charitable organization.

When *insurance policies* are given, they are placed wholly or partially in the control of the charitable organization. There are three methods of providing life insurance proceeds to such an organization. The first is to make the charitable organization the owner and beneficiary of a policy currently in force. The donor secures an income tax deduction for the value of the policy when transferred, and all future insurance premiums are treated as charitable donations by the IRS. The charitable organization has the option of cashing in the policy for its current value, borrowing on the policy, or waiting until the death of the benefactor to receive its value. The second method is for a benefactor to give a paid-up policy to a charitable organization. To the donor, the advantage is a tax deduction based on the market value of the policy. The charitable organization benefits immediately by knowing that, upon the death of the donor, it has a certain amount of income. The third method is for the charitable organization to be the owner and the beneficiary of the policy. In this instance, the benefactor can make a large future gift at a small present cost. The charitable organization receives the face value of the policy upon the death of the benefactor. One problem with this, however, is the fear that the donor may borrow against the policy or change the beneficiary at any time.

Special Events

Special events provide a unique opportunity for the charitable organization to put its mission forward to the public, to secure new potential donors, and to generate a profit. Special events come in many forms and might include runs, festivals, dinners, social outings, dances, and other types of creative approaches to raising money. Special events are seen as an attractive and relatively easy method of raising money, but they are very time-consuming, require considerable effort to be successful, can be financially risky, and may not generate a profit. The easiest way to ensure the financial success of a special event is to have someone underwrite it in advance. When this occurs, all the proceeds become profit. An underwritten special event can also put a higher level of pressure on the organization to be successful. Both the frequency and the number of special events by different organizations make it increasingly difficult to conduct a special event that successfully raises money.

Support Organizations

Support organizations are increasingly popular among leisure service organizations. At the federal, state, and local levels, "Friends of the Park" or "Friends of the Zoo" or "Friends of the Botanical Garden" or "Friends of the Sports Club" have grown dramatically in the past decade. The National Park Service has 64 cooperating associations. In 1997, these cooperating associations earned $90 million and contributed $19 million to various sites in the National Park system. In Ohio, the state park system has over 4,000 volunteers who annually contribute over two million hours of service. In Oregon, a state parks trust program has been established and has grown from four to 12 organizations since the mid-1970s. In 1997, the combined trusts raised $1.2 million. The trusts also receive land and gifts for the state park system. In Maryland, friends groups actually run two smaller parks and have purchased cabins that are then rented by the state park as revenue sources. In Indiana, the state park division of government is cooperating with a private foundation in the development of a new state park. The state is purchasing the land, and the foundation is undertaking the major development.

The Florida Park Service views support groups, or citizen support organizations, as valuable sources of volunteers to support ongoing operations. These support organizations may provide guides, as well as documents, in exhibit or interpretive areas, and they may also conduct tours or special programs. All support groups are member based and may or may not have a membership fee. Members of the support groups can provide special educational needs, serve as a communication liaison to the community, develop special exhibits, and help in other ways. In addition, most support groups are organized in such a way that they are able to receive funds, seek grants, and accept gifts and bequests of money or tangible property.

Support groups are usually organized as tax-exempt organizations under the umbrella of the parent public or private nonprofit organization. Each support group must operate according to rules and procedures that have been approved by the parent organization. Funds, volunteers, members, and potential partners are directed to the parent organization in order for it to fulfill its mission. Generally, the parent organization has developed a set of priorities and has identified needs to be met (such as volunteers for special events, funding for capital and interpretive projects, operation of concessions area, etc.). The priorities are generally agreed upon in advance by the support group and the parent organization.

A well-organized support group has a board of directors and a variety of committees who focus on meeting the needs of the parent organization. The committees work interdependently and independently on different projects. The committees become highly engaged in the process and meet the needs of individual members, as well those of the support group and the parent organization.

Support groups require the same care and nurturing that annual campaigns and planned giving programs require. Members of support groups are donors and often give considerably more than just their time. The parent organization should find effective ways of nurturing support group members. These can include member-only lectures, special recognition, newsletters, group travel tours, estate planning seminars, and others—all designed to keep members active.

Although support groups are formed to support the parent organization, they do require a certain level of independence and autonomy. The delicate balance between independence and interdependence is an ideal that parent and support organizations need to achieve. Some parent organizations have complained that they have lost control of their support groups, and some support groups protest that they are just "rubber stamp" organizations. Not only should there be sufficient independence to allow the support group to make decisions and be flexible enough to respond to changing demands and economic conditions, but there should also be accountability and shared vision.

Summary

Philanthropy and fundraising are an increasing part of the budget and fiscal operations of sport and leisure service organizations. Managers of these organizations must be well versed in the different strategies and methodologies of fundraising and know how philanthropy can assist their organizations. Leisure service organizations have been among the recent beneficiaries of support groups and philanthropic efforts. Sport and leisure service organization managers who ignore the impact of philanthropy will find their organizations left out of a key source of income.

References

Barrett, R. D., & Ware, M. E. 1997. *Planned giving essentials.* Gaithersburg, MD: Aspen Publishers, Inc.

Edwards, R. L., & Benefield, E. A. S. 1997. *Building a strong foundation: Fundraising for nonprofits.* Washington, DC: National Association of Social Workers.

Golan, J. 1998. *Comments on fundraising: Winning strategies and practices with a special eye to Carnegie Hall.* From lecture notes of November 10, 1998, from a lecture given to a graduate philanthropy course at Indiana University.

Greenfield, J. M. 1994. *Fundraising fundamentals.* New York: John Wiley & Sons.

Hopkins, K. B., & Friedman, C. S. 1997. *Successful fundraising for arts and cultural organizations.* Phoenix, AZ: Oryx Press.

Ross, J. R. (Ed.). 1997. *Philanthropy and Americans outdoors: Fundraising and partnering workshop.* Bloomington, IN: Indiana University.

Section C

Expenditure Management

Management of revenue includes accounting for all income received by the sport and leisure service organization. In addition to personal integrity, the financial manager needs skills in bookkeeping, accounting, and financial reporting in order to deal with another very important management concern—that of managing expenditures. Chapter 8 is not intended to serve as an all-encompassing treatment of the very complex world of business accounting, but it does provide an introduction to and overview of the most commonly used accounting and reporting tools, along with a discussion of the basic principles and generally accepted accounting practices. Chapters 9 and 10 explain why budgets are such important tools and describe how budgets are prepared and managed. A description of the budget styles or formats that are most frequently used by sport and leisure service organizations emphasizes the need for detailed attention to all aspects of planning to receive and spend financial resources.

Chapter 8

Accounting/Reporting

Introduction

One of the most important factors that, from a financial management perspective, separates successful sport and leisure service enterprises from those that fail is the system of keeping records and reporting financial activity. The system of keeping financial records is called *accounting*, and its purpose is to allow the sport and leisure service manager to find and easily understand information about the history of transactions and about the current financial condition of the organization. This chapter presents the basic principles of accounting and explores its use in reporting important findings to the financial manager.

There could be as many ways in which financial information is recorded and organized, records are managed, and reports are summarized and interpreted as there are people who need the information. Highly customized accounting systems might meet the very specific needs of financial managers and decision makers, as well as help to keep confidential information as cryptic as possible, but therein lies their weakness. If a highly customized accounting system is so unique that it is understood only by the user, others who may need specific financial information in order to regulate or cooperate with the organization may find it difficult or impossible to do so. This may result in penalties and/or loss of opportunity. For example, imagine a taxpayer tossing out the tax department's forms and submitting her annual tax return using a different method of reporting that she developed to match her shoebox filing system. Not a good idea! Imagine asking the bank for a business loan and providing a financial report that uses budget classifications, record systems, and report formats that are completely incompatible with those of the potential lending institution. Also not a good idea!

There is a need for order in business, and that need is probably nowhere greater than in the area of financial management. The established order for recording and reporting financial information in sport and leisure service organizations is referred to as Generally Accepted Accounting Principles (GAAP). These principles are described in publications by such recognized organizations as the Financial Accounting Standards Board or are derived from familiarity with the professional body of knowledge and prevalent practices. It is important to note that the principles and practices discussed in this chapter are "generally accepted," not "universally applied."

Stock and Flow

In developing an understanding of and appreciation for accounting, it is important to differentiate between the concepts of *stock* and *flow*. Stock refers to the financial resources available to the sport and leisure service organization at a given point in time. It is a measure of what the organization owns and what it owes. Stock information is used by financial managers to report on and make decisions on the basis of the current financial condition of the organization. To use a sports analogy, stock information is the score at a particular point in an athletic contest. At the beginning of the game, both teams have 0 points of stock. At the end of the game, the home team may have 45 points and the triumphant visiting team may have 52 points. Obviously, coaches' decisions made when the stock (score) is 0-0 at the start of the contest will be very different from those made when the clock is about to run out and the stock (score) is 50-43.

Flow refers to the movement (increase or decrease) of financial resources during a certain period of time. Reports of flow focus on the net change (loss or gain) in resources, but also provide information about the nature and extent of financial activity that brought about the eventual loss or gain. In the sports analogy, flow is the activity between the start of the game and the final buzzer. The official score sheet, coaches' comments, and newspaper articles describing the game are forms of flow reports. They describe how the game moved from a score of 0-0 to a score of 45-52. Measuring and reporting flow helps managers to know how the organization moved from one stock position to another.

Financial managers use *balance sheets* to report point-in-time (stock) conditions, while the *income statement* (also called a *profit and loss statement* or an *operating statement)* is used to report on financial activity (flow) between two points in time.

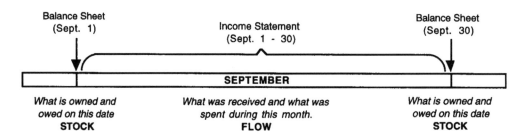

Figure 8.1. The relationship of balance sheets and the income statement in detailing stock and flow.

The Balance Sheet

What the organization owns and what it owes at a given point in time are recorded on the balance sheet (see Figure 8.2). Things that are owned are referred to as *assets* and are detailed on the left side of the balance sheet. Assets may be tangible items or properties such as cash, equipment, inventories, buildings, land, etc., or they may be valuable intangible items such as trademarks, names, or patents. Furthermore, assets may be classified as "current" (i.e., something that is or can be converted into cash within one year) or "fixed" (i.e., something that cannot readily be converted into cash). Assets are economic resources that are owned or controlled by the organization and which may benefit future operations.

What the organization owes are called *liabilities* and are recorded on the right side of the balance sheet. Liabilities include short-term (current) and long-term financial obligations or commitments to staff, contractors, lenders, suppliers, etc. The current value of investment made by the owner(s) is also a liability in the sense that it is a financial resource that is owed to the owner(s). The value of the owners' investment in the organization is more commonly termed *equity*. Both liabilities and equity appear on the right side of the balance sheet and are equal in combined value to that of the assets. Remember, the left side of the balance sheet is equal to (i.e., balances) the right side.

Figure 8.2. Placement of information on the balance sheet.

The simple equation which describes the balance sheet is:

$$Assets = Liabilities + Equity$$

Figures 8.3 and 8.5 are sample balance sheets for the Ruth Norton Quilting Center. One describes the financial condition of the quilting center on February 1, and the other describes the conditions on February 29. Figure 8.4 is a sample income statement covering operation of the quilting center between February 1 and February 29.

Notice in Figure 8.3 the current asset item called "accounts receivable." This item includes all amounts that the organization expects to receive in the near future due to services actually rendered or goods actually sold to customers. For example, the quilting center may have issued an invoice to a customer and is waiting for a $250 check as compensation for tutoring services recently provided. The accounts receivable category differs from cash in that the former represents money due but not yet received; and it differs from inventory in that the latter is the value of goods or service-related goods that the organization holds but has not yet exchanged for currency.

Ruth Norton Quilting Center
Balance Sheet
As of February 1, 2002

Assets		Liabilities	
Current Assets		**Current Liabilities**	
Cash	$4,000	Accounts payable	$8,550
Accounts receivable	250		
Inventory/Supplies	7,000	**Long-term Debt**	
Fixed Assets		Mortgage	48,000
Building	90,000		
		Equity	44,700
Total Assets	$101,250	**Total liability and equity**	$101,250

Figure 8.3. Sample balance sheet (February 1, 2002).

On the right side of the balance sheet shown in Figure 8.3 there is a liability category identified as "accounts payable." This short-term liability item presents the value of all goods or services received by the organization and for which payment is imminently due. For example, the pile of utility bills on the director's desk represents some of the ongoing or regular payable accounts.

The Income Statement

Financial transactions that occur during a specified period of time (a fiscal period) are summarized in a document called the income statement. A typical income statement (illustrated in Figure 8.4) reports all expenditures and all income during the business period and identifies the difference between the two totals as either a profit or a loss. Revenue and expenditure categories used in the income statement mirror the income and expenditure categories used in the organization's formal budget document.

Ruth Norton Quilting Center
Income Statement
February 1–29, 2002

Revenue		Expenditures	
Tuition	5,378	Wages	6,500
Consulting	3,075	Fabric supplies	1,200
Sale of Materials	1,450	Utilities	375
Royalties	1,367	Advertising	125
		Mortgage	1,400
		Auto Lease	350
Total Revenue	$11,270	Total Expenditures	$9,950
Net Revenue / (Loss)	$1,320		

Figure 8.4. Sample income statement (February 1–29, 2002).

It is natural to expect that the net revenue or net loss shown on the income statement would be evident in the difference between the balance statements prepared for the first and last days of the period of financial activity. That is, it seems that the $44,700 equity shown on February 1 (Figure 8.3) should increase by the $1,320 profit realized in the following 29 days (Figure 8.4). While it may occasionally be so, such a clear relationship is rarely this discernable. The reason it is not is that the balance sheet contains some information that reflects future financial activity. Note that the balance sheet in Figure 8.3 lists accounts receivable and accounts payable. Each of these items, respectively, indicates expected in-flows and out-flows of cash during the period covered by the next income statement (Figure 8.4). The balance sheet for the end of the reporting period, however, may have different asset, liability, and equity amounts, simply because those amounts will include expected receivables and payables for the period immediately after (see Figure 8.5).

The February 29 balance sheet is based on the stock described on the February 1 balance sheet, the flow described in the February 1–29 income statement, and additional economic activity for which there are new accounts receivable and payable.

Internal Control

Most large sport or leisure service organizations employ trained accountants and book-keepers to control financial operations, accounting, and reporting. These people will record transactions, pay bills, deposit funds, and maintain accounts. They will also help the sport or leisure service administrator to establish a petty cash fund and thereby reduce some potential organizational barriers to efficient program management.

Computers have become an integral part of fiscal management processes.

Ruth Norton Quilting Center
Balance Sheet
As of February 29, 2002

Assets		*Liabilities*	
Current Assets		**Current Liabilities**	
Cash	4,220	Accounts payable	89,000
Accounts receivable	100		
Inventory/Supplies	6,900	**Long-term Debt**	
Fixed Assets		Mortgage	47,200
Building	90,000		
		Equity	46,020
Total Assets	$101,220	**Total liability and equity**	$101,220

Figure 8.5. Sample balance sheet (February 29, 2002).

Petty Cash

Most expenses of the sport and leisure service organization are paid by check, but sometimes it is impossible or inefficient to draw a check to make a payment. For example, on-street parking or postage stamps may cost so little that the expense of writing the check would exceed the cost of the item. Furthermore, it would be very difficult to find a parking meter that accepts checks! To help the organization deal with small expenses, a *petty cash fund* may be established.

In establishing the petty cash fund, clear guidelines or rules regarding its use must be articulated. One guideline might be a limit on the amount of expenses to be paid from this fund. Expenses in excess of $20 are usually paid by check. Another guideline might describe the types of expenses that may be paid with petty cash funds. Petty cash funds are not typically used to pay recurring expenses such as utilities or subscriptions, regardless of the size of the expense. Yet another guideline or rule concerning the petty cash fund might concern management of the fund: Somebody should be appointed as custodian of the fund and held responsible for its proper management.

The petty cash fund is created by the treasurer upon writing a check to the custodian or manager of the fund for a fairly small amount of money, usually $50–$100. The check is recorded. The fund manager cashes the check and places the cash in a petty cash secured envelope or cash box. Authorized persons within the organization may then claim funds in advance or as reimbursement for minor (petty) expenditures. Petty cash funds are issued after the claimant submits a petty cash voucher (with attached receipts where possible). Pads of blank petty cash vouchers like the one shown in Figure 8.6 can be purchased at most stationery or office supply stores.

PETTY CASH VOUCHER

Date: _____
Amount: $ _____
For: _____
_____
_____
_____
Account: _____
Received by: _____

Figure 8.6. Example of a petty cash voucher.

After the claimant has been paid, the petty cash voucher is kept in the petty cash box. The money in the box and the face value of all the vouchers in the box should always add up to the original amount of cash issued to establish the fund. When the money in the petty cash box is almost spent, the vouchers and receipts are submitted like any other invoice, and a check for the total value of the vouchers is issued to the fund manager. The check is cashed and the money returned to the petty cash box in order to bring its total back to the level of funds originally established.

It is important to note that petty cash is not a budget line. It is a means of payment only. Any expense which is paid using petty cash is charged to the appropriate budget account.

Periodically, the fund manager should prepare a petty cash reconciliation statement. This simple form (shown in Figure 8.7) helps the manager to monitor the fund and anticipate cash replenishment needs.

The petty cash fund offers convenience, but, because of that convenience, it also has the potential to be abused. Great care should be taken to manage the petty cash fund according to established principles and practices of accounting.

Petty Cash Reconciliation Statement

Date: _____

Opening cash on hand	$ _____
ADD	
Payments to petty cash fund	$ _____
SUBTRACT	
Total amount of vouchers paid	$ _____
Cash on hand (this should be the same as the amount of cash in the cash box)	$ _____

Figure 8.7. Sample petty cash reconciliation statement.

Reporting

There are many kinds of reports that can be generated by accountants and bookkeepers. Two of the most useful for financial managers in sport and leisure service organizations are described below. They are *budget statements* and the *project report*.

The Budget Statement

The sport or leisure service organization budget is a revenue and spending plan for a period of time, usually a year. The goal of the financial manager is to ensure that revenues reach the expected level and that expenses do not exceed the projected amounts. This two-pronged goal is referred to as "staying within the budget," and the realization of this goal must be a priority for the financial manager. The budget statement is a useful tool that allows the manager to review the financial activity of the organization with respect to the budget.

The sample budget statement shown in Figure 8.8 lists key budget classes and the amount of money projected as revenue or expenditure for that class. As of the date listed at the top of the budget statement, the actual receipts and expenditures are reported, along with any commitments for revenue or expenditure that have been made. The budget statement also shows the portion (percentage) of each budget item that has been received or spent and reports the balance remaining.

In the preceding example, 50 percent of the budget period has elapsed, but less than 50 percent of the revenues have been received and less than 50 percent of the expenditures have been made. Noticeably, several expenditure items are at or near 75 percent, and a major revenue category is at 33 percent. Is this disparity an early warning of budget problems? Not necessarily.

The budget statement only tells the manager how much of the budget has been received or spent at a particular point in the fiscal period. It does not indicate how much of the revenue *should* be received or how much of the expenses *should* have been paid at that time. The manager must use his or her knowledge of seasonal and other fluctuations in demand and cost in interpeting the budget statement and making judgments about how well the organization's finances are being managed.

Pine Creek Resort
Recreation Services Department
Budget Statement
June 30, 2002 (50% of Budget Period)

	Budget	Actual	Committed	%	Balance
REVENUE					
Guest Service Assessment	120,000	60,000	0	50.0	60,000
Bike Rentals	18,000	5,920	0	32.9	12,080
Supply Fees	2,000	831	0	41.6	1,169
Total Revenue	140,000	66,751	0	47.7	73,249
EXPENSES					
Personnel	108,000	42,000	2,000	40.7	64,000
Equipment Maintenance	9,000	6,850	0	76,.1	2,150
Program Supplies	1,500	988	0	65.9	512
Transportation	4,500	2,123	1,200	73.8	1,177
Promotion	2,000	1,112	400	75.6	488
Administration	12,000	5,857	0	48.8	6,143
Contingency/Enterprise	3,000	800	500	43.3	1,700
Total Expenses	140,000	59,730	4,100	45.6	76,170

Figure 8.8. Sample budget statement.

Project/Event Report

In addition to the budget statement, many sport and leisure service managers find the project report to be particularly useful. This report compares projected and actual revenues and expenditures for specfic programs or events and includes commentary that helps future organizers of the program/event to understand what contributed to the financial success or failure of the project. A sample project report is shown in Figure 8.9.

The project report is a document that helps organizers of future events. It is rarely used in financial audit situations or for legal or highly technical documentation. For these reasons, the project report should be accurate and, more important, easily read and understood.

Frosty Frolic Festival Association
Project Report

Project/Event: Snow-Pitch Softball Tournament

Date: Feb 11–13, 2001

	Project Budget	Actual
REVENUE		
Community grant	1,000	1,000
Corporate sponsorships	500	600
Registration fees	800	800
Concession sales	1,100	1,400
Total Revenue	3,400	3,800
EXPENSES		
Publicity/Administration	400	380
Referee honoraria	900	900
Equipment purchase/rental	400	450
Awards	150	150
Facility fees	50	60
Kick-off reception	850	980
Insurance	610	670
Total Expenses	3,360	3,590
Net Income (Loss)	40	210

Signed by: Hugo ZoBell
Comments:

Kick-off reception exceeded budget estimate due to requirement to use the catering service under contract to the facility. Original estimate was based on service club catering. Colder than anticipated weather necessitated change in menu (more hot drinks).

Figure 8.9. Sample project report.

Summary

In order to effectively and efficiently manage the financial resources of a sport or leisure service organization, the manager must have a basic understanding of accounting principles and practices. By following generally accepted accounting principles, reports that are meaningful, timely, and accurate can be prepared for use in executive decision making. The report or financial statement that indicates the single-point-in-time condition of the organization is the balance sheet. The income statement (also called the profit and loss statement, statement of receipts and disbursement, or operating statement) details financial activity between two dates for which balance sheets are prepared. Where available, trained accountants and bookkeepers help to prepare financial reports. Sport and leisure service administrators may, however, be responsible for maintaining and being accountable for a petty cash fund. Rules governing the use of the petty cash fund should be understood and followed by all users. A particularly useful report that helps the sport or leisure service manager to be aware of the state of the budget is the budget statement. This report shows how much of each budget category has been received or spent at a particular point in the fiscal period. For specific programs, projects, or events, the project report is a common form of reporting on the financial outcomes of the project.

Chapter 9

Budget Preparation

Introduction

Budgeting is a process that focuses on providing managers with information and tools to manage fiscal resources and operations. Well-constructed and well-understood budgets ultimately allow managers to make more informed decisions. In that context, budgeting is linked to organizational goals and objectives and is a tool to help achieve them. Further, budgeting allows sports and leisure service organizations to translate their organizational visions into realities. Budgeting, then, is an essential component of the larger management process of any organization. In today's competitive and changing society, sport and leisure service organizations cannot function effectively without a clear understanding of how good fiscal management contributes to their day-to-day success.

Few decisions facing sport and leisure service organization managers are more daunting than those made concerning how to allocate limited fiscal resources. It is the decision making in sport and leisure service organizations involving the allocation of human and fiscal resources that affects the organization's ability to achieve its vision. This chapter discusses the process of budgeting for sport and leisure service organizations and should provide the manager with tools to measure and monitor the impact of budgeting on the organization.

Budget Processes

What is a Budget?

Budgeting is one of the most important tasks that a sport and leisure service manager can be engaged in. The budget is a financial plan and frequently translates the operational and strategic plans of the organization into achievable activities over a specified period of time. This period of time is typically one year. A budget is a document depicting the anticipated revenues and expenditures of an organization over a specified period of time. Budgets anticipate expenditures and revenue and are linked to organizational and individual work plans. Edginton and Williams (1978) originally described 10 advantages of budgeting. Modified for today's fiscal environment, nine are presented here:

1. Budgeting is a systematic process that brings structure to the organization.

2. Budgeting requires the manager to do advance planning for the organization, which reinforces strategic and long-range planning.

3. Budgeting provides a starting point for building organizational and individual work plans.

4. Budgeting moves the organization towards measurable and quantifiable outcomes in both human and material terms.

5. Budgeting encourages standardization in fiscal operations, encouraging an efficiency that unifies approaches to spending and revenue accounting. It allows an organization to be more efficient.

6. Budgeting, in the absence of other measures, allows managers and subordinates to communicate on a common level. It reinforces other measures of effectiveness in the organization.

7. The budget is an essential part of a complex decision-making process in most organizations.

8. The budget provides policy-setting bodies with a measurement tool used in formal evaluation.

9. The budget serves as a policy body's mechanism for control.

Budgets are classified as two types: *operating* budgets and *capital* budgets. Operating budgets deal with current expenditures for a specified period of time, while capital budgets cover longer periods of time in attempting to address major projects requiring significant investments of dollars. Capital budgets are funded for more than one year at a time and are adjusted on an annual basis. Capital budgeting is discussed in detail in Chapter 12. Almost all managers work with operating budgets. Fewer work with capital budgets, yet they contribute to the construction of capital budgets in important ways.

The Budget Cycle

Budgets usually span a one-year period, called a fiscal year. A fiscal year is not always the same as the calendar year. The most common fiscal year period is from July 1 through June 30 of the ensuing year. The U.S. Government's fiscal year is October 1 through September 30. Many private nonprofit and commercial sport and leisure service organizations use January 1 through December 31 as their fiscal year. It is acceptable and common to refer to a fiscal year by the year in which it ends. If a fiscal year begins July 1, 2001, and ends June 30, 2002, the fiscal year is referred to as FY2002 (fiscal year 2002).

The importance of a fiscal year lies in the spending and accounting process. Money can be *allocated, encumbered,* and *expended* within a given fiscal year. *Allocated monies* are those dollars that the legislative/policy body has approved for use by the sport and leisure service organization. *Encumbered monies* are those dollars that have been committed, but have yet to be paid out. As an example, a municipal parks and recreation department, which purchased new playground equipment for $34,000 in March, issued a purchase order for the purchase. The department recorded the money as being committed or encumbered, but not spent. After an invoice was received, the department issued a check, and the money was no longer encumbered, but expended. *Expended funds,* then, are those funds paid out for services and items purchased, leased, and rented and for which invoices have been received and checks issued.

A fiscal year provides a fixed starting and stopping point for budget administration. Policy-setting or legislative bodies and managers need to be able to establish budgetary guidelines for their organizations. The fiscal year is recognized as an accounting standard. It allows organizations to accomplish fiscal planning for a fixed period of time. It allows government organizations to match anticipated tax revenues against projected expenditures. It allows commercial and nonprofit enterprises to plan for revenues and expenditures.

Budget cycles can take up to 24 months, and some organizations may have longer planning cycles. Figure 9.1 illustrates three fiscal years and includes the budget preparation time and the budget closeout period. The length of time required to construct a budget will vary from organization to organization. It is mandated by the organization's governing body. Accounting bodies prefer to finalize or close out an organization's end-of-the-year budget within 30 to 90 days. Even when some funds remain encumbered, budgets can be closed out with the knowledge that encumbered funds remain to be expended.

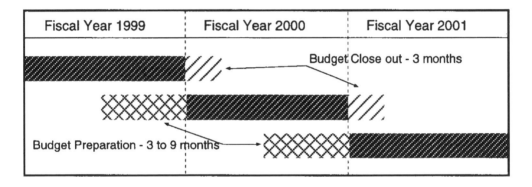

Figure 9.1. Three-year budget calendar.

Budget Preparation Cycle

A typical budget preparation cycle includes four tasks, as depicted in Figure 9.2. In a government agency, the budget cycle is usually prescribed by the legislative authority, such as a city council, a park board, a county council, or a state or provincial government. For nonprofit organizations, a board of directors defines the budget process. Nonprofit organizations which depend on the United Way for part of their operating budget may be required to follow a United Way budget presentation process in full or in part. Commercial enterprises may have a specified set of instructions and procedures to follow, or they may be flexible in their approach to budget development. Regardless of the type of sport and leisure service organization, there are some commonalities that each type of organization can follow in the development of a budget.

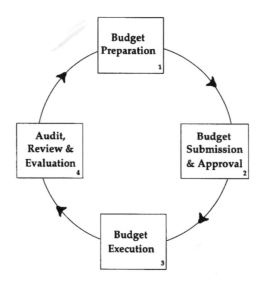

Figure 9.2. Budget preparation cycle.

An example of a municipal budget cycle (Figure 9.2) includes activities and deadlines. A budget preparation document includes such items as specific directives from the legislative body, any restrictions on budget growth, identification of budget deadlines, budget formats, budget decision guidelines, and specific instructions that either may be applicable only to this budget period or may be new to the organization. The guidelines are typically transmitted in a letter, along with support documentation from the head of the legislative body or her designated administrative officer. The organization is expected to comply with all of the guidelines prescribed by the legislative authority.

The budget guidelines include a budget calendar, which is an orderly chronological timetable showing the dates when necessary action must be taken in preparing the budget. A budget calendar may initiate the process as much as 12 months in advance of the start of the budget. (The example in Table 9.1 begins six months in advance.) The budget guidelines and calendar are provided so the legislative, executive, and departmental entities will avoid encroachment on one another, and so that orderly performance in the budget preparation can be achieved. The development phase is the most critical phase of the budget process and the only phase for which completion dates are established. Dates should be established for the following:

- Distribution of instructions and forms

- Preparation of revenue estimates

- Return of the completed budget request forms

- Completion of review and preliminary preparation of work assigned to the central budget agency

- Completion of executive review and executive determination of final budget content

Date	Action to be completed
2 January (-180)	Mayor's budget policy letter requesting department heads to submit proposed work program and budget estimates for ensuing fiscal year. Necessary forms and revisions to budget manual are transmitted with the letter.
1 February (-150)	City administrative officer (CAO) approves staff budget assignments, which are thereafter distributed to the staff.
1 March (-120)	Service betterment budget estimates, if any, received from department heads.
10 April (-80)	CAO reviews tentative Capital Improvement Expenditure Program (CIP) and, upon approval, transmits it to the Public Works Priority Committee.
10 April (-80)	CAO submits annual salary recommendations to City Council.
10–30 April (-80 to -60)	Hearings conducted by the Public Works Priority Committee to determine final priority of capital projects to be included in CIP for ensuing year.
10–17 April (-80 to -73)	Preliminary budget hearing held by CAO and Budget Coordinator with the Assistant Budget Coordinator and staff analyst for each department.
18–28 April (-74 to -92)	CAO, assisted by Budget Coordinator, conducts departmental budget hearing with each department head, at which time the staff analysts' recommendations for that departmental budget are presented and the department head is given an opportunity to express his or her viewpoint.
1 May (-60)	Final date for submission by City Controller of the official estimates of revenue from all sources (other than general property taxes).
1 May (-60)	CAO submits official estimate of revenue from general property taxes.
1–5 May (-60 to -55)	Mayor, assisted by CAO, conducts budget conferences with each department head. Attended by council members, press, and taxpayer groups.
5–12 May (-55 to -48)	Final budget decisions made by Mayor, who is assisted by CAO.
12–31 May (-48 to -30)	Budget printed under supervision of CAO.
1 June (-29)	Mayor submits budget to City Council.
1–20 June (-29 to -10)	Council considers Mayor's budget and makes modifications as it deems necessary.
20–25 June (-10 to -5)	Mayor considers any modifications made by City Council and may veto such changes.
25–28 June (-5 to -2)	Council considers Mayor's veto of any items and may vote to override Mayor's veto by a two-thirds' majority.
1 July (0)	Beginning of fiscal year—budget takes effect.

Table 9.1. A public budget preparation cycle.

- Submission of the budget to the legislative body

- Completion of public hearings

- Preliminary legislative determination of the content of the appropriation ordinance or budget to be approved

- Final action by the legislative body

- Executive approval or veto of the adopted budget and legislative action thereon

- Completion of administrative action, if any, needed to actuate budget appropriations

- Beginning of the fiscal year

The calendar should also include the following:

- Schedule showing responsibilities of the various officials and departments to specific items

- Excerpts of legal and administrative rules that govern budget formulation and execution

It is recommended that each sport and leisure service organization develop its own budget calendar using the legislative and administrative body's calendar as a guide. The calendar should provide information similar to that found in the legislative body's calendar, although it should be specific to the organization. Commercial or nonprofit organizations which may not have as formal a legislative process would be wise to develop a budget calendar along the same guidelines.

Funds

Budgets are constructed around accounting funds. Funds can come from either an independent fiscal source, property taxes, or other income sources. They are segregated from the regular operating budget for the purpose of carrying on specific activities. Funds are unique to government and nonprofit organizations. Funds are a separate group of accounts that are managed independent of each other. Funds have come about because government organizations have legal restrictions placed on them regarding how specific revenue may be expended. A local option hotel/motel tax may be restricted by state or city code for use to support greenways, greenbelts, or convention and meeting facilities. These funds can be divided into three categories: governmental funds, proprietary funds, and fiduciary funds. Each is described below and depicted in Table 9.2.

Governmental Funds	Proprietary Funds	Fiduciary Funds
General Fund Special Revenue Fund Capital Projects Fund Debt Service Funds Special Assessment Funds	Enterprise Funds Internal Service Funds	Expendable Trust Funds Nonexpendable Trust Funds Agency Funds

Table 9.2. Types of government-based funds
(Aronson & Schwartz, 1996; Reed & Swain, 1998).

Included within the three types of funds are sub-funds that are common to most public sport and leisure service organizations. Most governmental fiscal operations are conducted through four types of funds: (1) general fund, (2) special revenue fund, (3) capital projects fund, and (4) debt service fund. Proprietary and fiduciary funds are also present in public agencies. The general fund is the fund most common to all public organizations. It supports all operations not assigned to other funds. In public park and recreation agencies, this fund will vary from less than 30 percent to more than 90 percent of the operating budget. Included in it might be personnel services, maintenance operations, supplies, contractual services, and the like. Sources of revenue at the governmental level are most frequently property taxes, but they also may include sales taxes, special taxes, intergovernmental grants, and licenses and permits.

Public parks and open spaces provide important opportunities for recreation activities.

The *special revenue fund* is made up of services provided from revenues that have been specifically designated for that purpose. User fees and charges are the primary source of revenue for special revenue funds. Fees collected from recreation programs and services are a common source of revenue. These fees are deposited in the special revenue fund and used to pay for recreation programs and services. The fund can also be used to partially defray or wholly pay for operating expenses, personnel services, supplies and material, etc. Use of these funds may be restricted by law.

A *capital projects fund* focuses on the acquisition, design, and construction of capital or major projects that have an economic life of greater than one year. These projects include aquatic complexes; recreation centers; sports complexes; ice arenas; city, county, and state parks; and other buildings and structures. It also includes the purchase of major pieces of equipment. Funding for a capital projects fund can come from a variety of sources, including special taxes, intergovernmental grants, and proceeds from the sale of revenue or general obligation bonds.

A *debt service fund* is used to pay the organization's long-term debt and, in the case of government, the general obligation debt from the sale of bonds. Any organization involved in capital projects of significant size has probably engaged in long-term debt. Revenue for the debt service fund primarily comes from taxes, grants, special assessments, and intergovernmental grants.

A *special assessment fund* consists of money targeted for a specific project or task. Assessments are made to specific individuals or organizations for an identified service or benefit to be received.

A *proprietary fund* is designed to provide for ongoing activities as a self-sustaining operation. An enterprise fund receives the bulk of its revenue from user charges, but typically supports a major operation or enterprise and, by definition, only needs to generate 50 percent of its operating budget. Examples of enterprise fund operations include civic centers, aquatic complexes, and major parks, zoos, and sports complexes. The distinction between a special revenue fund and an enterprise fund may be clouded by various state codes.

Internal service funds transfer money between different departments within the same organization for services rendered. For example, if the program division at the YMCA needed 8,500 brochures, and its printing services department provided the brochures, the program division would be billed internally for the cost. This fund allows organizations to track the cost of services provided internally.

Fiduciary funds are used to account for assets received and held in trust by either a government or an organization. The organization can be perceived as a trustee, custodian, or agent for the funds. Three types of funds are common to fiduciary funds: The *nonexpendable trust fund* requires that the principal remain unspent, but allows the expenditure of income generated from an investment of the principal. The income may be spent in the general fund or assigned to specific programs or other funds. A nonexpendable trust fund may accrue income to the principal from a variety of sources, such as donations, grants, and bequests. An *expendable trust,* by contrast, allows spending from the principal. Art endowment and zoo endowment programs are common examples of expendable trusts. Individuals are encouraged to contribute to a specific endowment, and the agency uses the money contributed for day-to-day operations or for special projects. An *agency fund* allows an agency to have specific control over a set of designated monies. Examples might include lottery funds used to finance parks and recreation or a boat tax for fish and wildlife.

Less common funds include annuity funds, endowment funds, loan funds, and operating funds. An *annuity fund* holds funds that remain after an annuity contract has expired. These funds can be used in any manner so deemed by the organization unless specific restrictions are placed upon them. An *endowment fund* is most frequently used by nonprofits, but has the same characteristics as a nonexpendable trust. A *loan fund* is a separate fund set aside with the monies available for loan for specific functions or services. One example of a loan fund is the provision of loans to faculty, students, and staff at a university. An *operating fund* is made up of all those monies that are available to a nonprofit board for use. The operating fund fulfills the same role as the general fund in a government.

Budget Presentation Format

There are many different ways to format and present a budget. Table 9.3 provides information for 20 different budget formats. Each budget format provides decision makers with different kinds of information. Depending on the goals of the sport and leisure service organization, one or more appropriate budget formats are selected. The *object classification budget* is the most common format for public, nonprofit, and commercial organizations. It is a budget format that allows managers to use the budget as a tool to accomplish goals and objectives. Expenditures are classified into a specific category (called a code). However, as government and nonprofits become more entrepreneurial and develop revenue-generating operations, the object classification budget cannot meet all of the requirements and is frequently paired with another budget type, such as the program budget. (Chapter 10 discusses selected budget formats in detail.)

Budget Preparation Activities

Budget preparation is the responsibility of the chief executive officer (CEO) of the sport and leisure service organization. This person may be the director, the executive director, the superintendent, the manager, or the owner. The CEO sets the agenda and the tone for budget preparation for all members of the organization. Budget preparation should be a cooperative endeavor among the organization's members and the external budget agency, if one is present. Cooperation among participants in the budget process is a key element in the success of the organization. It should be viewed as a shared process rather than a competitive process.

Effective budget preparation engages all members of the organization. Budget preparation should be taken to the lowest levels of the organization, thus fostering understanding, input, and commitment from organization members. This process may necessitate training for members of the organization, as well as an enhanced level of trust. Decentralizing budget decision making to the lowest possible levels results in an increased commitment to the budget and to the organization's purpose and direction. Ultimately, the CEO defines each member's role in the budget's preparation and sets the tone for budget operations.

A single individual should be tasked as the budget preparation officer (BPO). The budget preparation officer ensures conformity in the budget preparation, collects and collates all of the data submitted by different budget managers, identifies discrepancies, and resolves disputes. The officer also ensures that the budget conforms to the guidelines proposed by both the CEO and the legislative body and is linked to the department's strategic or long-

Type of Budget	Description	Purpose / When Used	Advantages	Disadvantages
Object Classification Budget	Looks at operations as categories (objects) and classifies expenditures into those categories	Most common of budget types in use by government and non-profit corporations and provides ease of budget classification and management	• Relatively easy to establish • Process is uniform and follows standardized procedure • Category development is pre-determined	• Does not provide for flexibility to meet needs • Requires detailed cost elements at the program level • Categories too generalized to provide budget detail
Line Item Budget	Similar to object classification, the item represents a specific object and it is placed in a line for classification purposes	As common as object classification and provides similar ease of budget classification and management	• Allows some flexibility in budget preparation • Allows for multiple system utilization • Allows for budget adjustment with minimal difficulty	• Requires detailed planning and preparation • Some loss of reporting accuracy because expenditures collapsed into lines
Activity Budget	Budget areas are divided into "activity areas" and focus on cost to perform a specific function	Allows agencies to have a clearer delineation of the costs associated with different functional activities of the organization	• Clearly defines services as activities • Allows comparison of costs between activities • Provides clear picture of where budget funds are allocated	• Can be difficult to set up and requires detailed accounting system • Some budget activities don't comfortably fit • Reduces some levels of flexibility
Function Budget	Similar to the Activity budget, this allows the agencies to group activities under major functions	Grouped activity budgets are tracked and administrators are able to view their change in costs across time	• Comparison of functional costs available • Helps budget agency understand where money allocated • Provides for comparison of costs across functions	• Budgets may not lend themselves to easy comparison • Uses Object Classification concept and suffers from same disadvantages
Performance Budget	Used to measure end results of activities based on performance outcome measures	Similar to the program budget most frequently used with operations that can have repetitive measures, such as maintenance operations and other reoccurring operations	• Highly standardized units of measurement and cost • Provides for high control and detailed accuracy • Effectively integrated with computer based management of operations	• Requires high level of sophistication in organization reporting procedures • Not particularly useful in non-repetitive situations • Fixed approach to budget management and decisions

Table 9.3. Types of budget formats and their uses (adapted from Kelsey, Gray, & McLean, 1993).

Type of Budget	Description	Purpose / When Used	Advantages	Disadvantages
Planning, Programming Budgeting System	Implemented by the Kennedy administration and identifies the relationship between costs and end results of programs	Used to measure the outcome of budget operations. Focus is on the end result rather than the cost of the program	• Focuses on service goals • Focuses on end results rather than just costs • Provides for a comparative analysis of programs and services	• Requires an equitable measurement system to be established • Difficulty determining importance of need and value • Not always able to make comparisons across the entire organization
Zero Based Budget	Focuses on actual cost of programs, assuming that all programs must be regularly justify all operations	When the agency needs to assess operations and to justify those operations retained to decision makers	• Encourages regular review of value / importance of programs • Provides for increased flexibility and creativity • Enhances difficult decision making about service elimination • Facilitates orderly review of operations and services	• Increased justification and reporting required • May increase competition within the organization • Tends to increase tension within the organization at expense of morale
Program Budget	Focuses on explaining why expenditures are required and tied to agency goals and objectives	Used when there needs to be a fuller explanation of the programs and when costs can be clearly identified along with identification of outcomes	• Provides narrative justification • Focuses on values of programs / services rather than just costs • Creativity and flexibility are enhanced	• Requires a level of sophistication in the delivery of services and accounting • Limited budget-cost detail provided • May sell program beyond its ability to deliver
Fee Budget	Determines actual cost of providing services or operations and allocates to specific categories	When the budget operation requires a detailed accounting of costs and allocation to specific expenditure areas	• Provides a more detailed accounting of actual costs • Provides significant detailed information • Breaks down into per-participant costs	• Use may be restricted to specific program types • Requires detailed knowledge of needs before initiating the budget • May not include all costs because of accounting system used

Table 9.3. Types of budget formats and their uses (adapted from Kelsey, Gray, & McLean, 1993).

Type of Budget	Description	Purpose / When Used	Advantages	Disadvantages
Unit Budget	Used frequently in large organizations, it groups costs by different organizational units. It may employ a different budget process within the unit.	Useful for looking at operational costs across the whole organization. It does not suggest all units are similar, rather shows where funds are being expended.	• Provides a clear description of costs • Relatively simple to present and comprehend • Opens the budget process to multiple constituencies	• Is not a stand alone budget system • Does not show budget detail or division operating costs • Requires top down policy and procedures setting
Fund Budget	Used to identify multiple sources of income for an organization	Allows tracking of multiple sources of funds to different budget areas. More frequently used as an income rather than an expense budget	• Shows sources of funds • Provides some limited projection data on fund sources	• Not really an operating budget • Requires another budgeting system to be developed to support
Character Budget	Organizes expenditures according to the past, present and future directions of the organization	It takes into account long and short term debt and obligations and develops a budget picture over time.	• Provides a picture of budget operations over multiple years • Isolates major expenditure commitments • Enhances future budget planning	• While a good planning budget, it does not facilitate day to day operations • May be confusing to those not familiar with it • Detailed long term budget planning required
Increment / Decrement Budget	A traditional approach of adding a percentage to the existing budget without regard for need or importance.	Makes the budget process relatively simple, addressing issues of increase with a static figure	• Provides for hassle-free and predictable growth • Simplifies the budget process - requires minimal decision making	• Provides no flexibility based on need or demand • Encourages status quo • Discourages creativity and flexibility
Running Budget	Budget that is developed and modified based on income sources and expenditure needs. Driven by income and expenses are expected to conform.	Allows organizations who don't have a stable source of income to modify their budget based on income sources. Provides flexibility to the budgeting process.	• Provides day to day accounting system • Functions on a time-line fiscal chart • Tied to revenues and income	• Supplemental budget process required for budget administration • Requires constant attention to budget process • Time consuming to establish

Table 9.3. Types of budget formats and their uses (adapted from Kelsey, Gray, & McLean, 1993).

Type of Budget	Description	Purpose / When Used	Advantages	Disadvantages
Enterprise Budget	Developed to manage enterprises that are self-sustaining or can generate more that 50% of their operating budget.	For those operations where it is intended, the operation will pay for itself or most of its operation through revenue generation.	• Allows organizations to create flexibility in the budgeting process • Typically allows the organization to carry revenues over from one year to the next • Allows maximum flexibility to the organization's budget	• May have specific restrictions within a given state • Frequently cannot spend funds outside of the enterprise area • Dependent upon revenues and marketing of programs and services
Benefit Cost Budget	More common in private enterprise and is used to compare costs with measured benefits.	Allows organizations to develop levels of services based on a predetermined cost / benefit ratio.	• Allows for program comparisons • Encourages evaluating needs and satisfaction • Encourages sound decision making on program retention and/or expansion	• Measurement of benefit still difficult to determine • May be viewed as a superficial budget process • In simplest form does not take into account complexity of need
Enterprise Fund Budget	A budget type focusing on a service or facility that generates revenue that is applied back to the service or facility. Other budget processes can be used in conjunction with this.	Used when 50% or more of the operating revenue is generated by the program or facility and when state code allows for the implementation of enterprise budgets.	• Based on revenues or income generated • Provides service to those using it • Revenues and surplus funds (profit) returned to budget for future use	• "Parks for Profit" image may hurt agency • Detailed accounting and budget adjustments required • State Code may restrict level of utilization
Capital Budget	Separate budget for major expenditures such as equipment and facilities.	Typically used as a separate budget within the organization's budget process and identified specifically for this purpose.	• Focuses on major expenditures • Provides operating budget with clear picture of operations	• Is a separate budget process, frequently mandated • Generally viewed over a 5 year or longer period and no guarantee of funding

Table 9.3. Types of budget formats and their uses (adapted from Kelsey, Gray, & McLean, 1993).

Type of Budget	Description	Purpose / When Used	Advantages	Disadvantages
Mission Driven Budget	Focuses on organization's mission (external) rather than costs (internal) and most often used with total quality management budget	This budget increases flexibility to budget managers, allows for greater flexibility and responsiveness in meeting demands and encourages entrepreneurship among staff.	• Increases autonomy in budget administration • Simplifies the budget process and creates a predictable environment • Pushes budget planning and administration to lowest levels of organization	• Requires a level of sophistication among those who budget • Total Quality Management training required for all employees • Appropriate measurement and control processes must be established
Results Oriented Budget	Also called outcome budgeting, ties the budget to customer expectations.	Tied to measures of customer expectations and allows for flexibility in administration of the budget, but requires long term planning and measures of effectiveness.	• Budget managers focus on long term issues based on known acceptable levels of service • Focus on outcomes • Enhances accountability among staff	• Requires detailed measurement processes • Requires community input in measurement levels • High level of budget sophistication desirable
Activity Based Costing	A budget strategy that measures actual costs of all program efforts.	Used when costs of delivery of services are essential to know and incorporate into the budget process.	• Provides detailed knowledge of costs. • Allows the organization to build fees and charges based on realistic knowledge of costs • Increases effectiveness of decision making.	• Very costly to initiate the process. Typically can't be done by organizational staff. • Requires detailed reporting and allocation of expenditures by all staff. • Time consuming

Table 9.3. Types of budget formats and their uses (adapted from Kelsey, Gray, & McLean, 1993).

range plans. The department budget preparation officer briefs each member of the organization who has contributed to the budget, coordinates closely with the department executive officer, and prepares the final budget document for submission to the legislative or policy body.

The Relationship of Strategic Planning to Budget Preparation

The budgeting process is intricately linked to strategic planning. An organization, during the process of development of the strategic plan, should engage in aligning the budget with the strategic plan. Budget preparation decisions should be based upon achieving the strategic plan. Strategic planning is about achieving organizational futures. Linking the budget to strategic planning becomes a visible method of moving from planning to action. All budget decisions should focus on the organization's values, vision, mission, and action plan. A strategic plan is not intended to address all operations of the organization. Rather, the emphasis is upon those action items necessary to achieving the organization's vision. Strategic planning complements and enhances, but does not replace effective evaluation of day-to-day operations, special initiatives, capital projects, etc. Strategic planning is another budget preparation component that the budget preparation officer and budget manager must consider. (For more information on strategic planning, see McLean, Bannon, and Gray, 1998.)

Budget Preparation Philosophies

How budget needs are estimated depends upon the type of preparation philosophy adopted by the organization. An *open-ended budget* allows an organization to submit a budget that provides an optimum program for the organization. The budget is not hindered by restrictions on spending, but it does require decision makers to adjust the budget to meet the organization's budget capabilities. This adjustment is typically accomplished through reductions in expenditures. Open-ended budgeting is still done, but it has fallen into disfavor in an era of accountability and limited budget growth. A *fixed ceiling budget* normally places a limit on the growth of a budget. A fixed growth assumes that previous budgets have been adequate and that a minimal growth will continue to meet needs. Such budgets fail to take into account changing needs of the organization. The format reacts to available funds, which suggests that either politics or an attitude of sharing proportionately among competing groups is an equitable way to assign budgets. A fixed ceiling budget is still a common approach for many organizations. A budget based on *workload measurement and unit costing* seeks to devise units of work and to determine unit costs. This budget approach attempts to quantify work as performance and output. In sport and leisure service organizations, workload measurement budgets work best with repetitive types of activities.

An *increase/decrease* analysis is a form of fixed ceiling budget that depicts increases and decreases from the previous year's expenditure lines. An *item-by-item control* looks at each budget item and asks if it is essential, desirable, or justified. Alternative budget proposals ask staff members to prepare a basic budget supplemented by an outline for alternative budget levels. *Alternative budgets* provide rationales for different budget proposals and detailed budget information. Almost all budget preparations go through some form of alternative budget preparation, but rarely in a formally requested manner. Such an approach requires a considerable amount of time and effort on the part of the budget preparers and suggests little reason for the additional work.

Factorial estimating looks at past expenditures and then factors what it believes will be future expenditures. More specifically, it looks at operating and revenues in a detailed format over a period of years and attempts to estimate or forecast what future expenditures will be. The reliance upon historical data is appropriate for most sport and leisure service organizations, but those organizations that rely wholly upon the past to predict the future will find themselves ill prepared to meet the demands and needs of their constituents or legislative body. *Historical analysis* is an almost identical approach, except it typically leaves out personnel-related services.

Multiple preparation philosophies are frequently used in a single budget. Historically based open-ended measurement or work measurement has been the most commonly used budgeting process in determining work program requirements. Personnel needs have used work measurement and historical analysis. An estimation of the cost of supplies, materials, and equipment usually relies upon historical analysis and some workload measurement. Equipment needs have used a fixed ceiling format as the primary method, although in some instances, open-ended budgeting has been used.

Preparing the Departmental Work Plan

The departmental work plan is an integral part of the budget preparation process. It involves identifying the work of the sport and leisure service organization for the planned fiscal year and then attempting to match the proposed budget with the desired work. It usually requires a series of trade-offs between what the organization would like to do and what it can realistically accomplish within the constraints of its potential budget. The department work plan involves at least three components: (1) ongoing functions of the leisure service organization, (2) new or proposed functions of the organization, and (3) special one-time or infrequently reoccurring functions of the organization.

Preparing an annual work plan requires in-depth knowledge of the organization's work processes and their relationship to both the vision and the mission of the organization. Delegating budget preparation and management to the lowest possible level in the organization assumes that those who do the work are best prepared to estimate its costs and effects. The delegation of budget preparation does not eliminate the need for constant oversight and justification at each step of the process. In an era of limited economic growth, it is appropriate for each service or program to participate in a continuous evaluation of how well it meets customer expectations, annual work plans, and the vision and mission of the organization.

To facilitate the process of budgeting for annual work plans, the sport and leisure service organization should do the following:

- Conduct an annual review of each program or service and assess how each one agrees with the organization's vision and mission.

- Annually assess the effectiveness of each program and service in relation to the organization's goals and objectives, the standards established for the program or service, and customer satisfaction.

- Initiate a level-of-performance review to determine that the program or service meets agreed-upon levels of service or satisfaction.

Estimating Personnel Service Requirements

In most sport and leisure service organizations, personnel costs are the single largest expenditure item. They will range from 50 percent to 90 percent of the organization's operating costs. Given this level of funding, the importance of determining personnel costs cannot be underestimated. In the budget process, the purpose of the personnel functions is to determine the type, quantity, and quality of personnel needed to accomplish the work plan of the organization during the fiscal period.

Personnel costs are most frequently figured on a fixed growth as opposed to a fixed ceiling budget. An organization should take several approaches to determining personnel costs. First, it should determine the costs for full-time personnel. Since the bulk of these individuals are already on a fixed salary, the annual allowable percentage of growth is frequently determined by the legislative body. In government and nonprofits, it may be a fixed percentage of a salary base (e.g., cost-of-living raises will be 3.5 percent for the next fiscal year). This has been and continues to be the most common type of approach taken to salary adjustments. The fixed growth may be based on anticipated available funds, government-determined cost-of-living increases, inflation figures, or what the legislative body negotiates with the employees or their representatives.

Most full-time, salaried employees are compensated within a fixed salary range. Employees are hired at a particular salary within the range. Every year the employee is promoted to the next salary level within the range. Table 9.4 illustrates salary ranges for different positions.

Position Code	Step 1	Step 2	Step 3	Step 4	Step 5
87456	$27,456	$28,692	$29,983	$31,332	$32,742
85543	$33,663	$35,178	$36,761	$38,415	$40,144

Table 9.4. Example salary ranges.

The salary ranges, or steps, as shown in Table 9.4, represent the salary increases an employee will receive after a specified period of time with the organization. A person starting at step 1 of position code 87456 will receive $27,456 in annual wages. Each period, usually of one year, the person can anticipate a salary increase to the next range. In addition, there may be annual cost-of-living increases that would affect each step. The steps in Table 9.4 are based on a 4.5 percent increase. If the legislative body determined that a 3.0 percent cost-of-living increase was appropriate, then the entire step range would increase by 3 percent. An individual at step 2 would receive an increase of 3 percent and have a new annual salary of $29,552. At step 5, the individual has achieved the highest pay possible in that position. Future increases would come from cost-of-living adjustments or a redefinition of the salary range. The number of steps in a salary range will vary from organization to organization. It could consist of as many as 20 or more steps.

Permanent part-time positions may be determined the same way, or they may be based on another approach. Seasonal or temporary part-time positions can be determined in any number of ways. For these positions, most organizations begin with a minimum wage approach and then value each position on the basis of its contribution to the organization, the prevailing wage for a similar position, and the availability of qualified individuals. In one community, when the indoor pool began its fall and winter season, the parks and recreation department could not hire a sufficient number of qualified lifeguards. An analysis of the job market showed that the number of available lifeguards was far diminished from the summer. The agency had erroneously assumed that the summer lifeguard wage would be adequate for the indoor season. What it had failed to take into account was that students, who made up the core of the summer lifeguards, returned to school, thus reducing the market availability by over 60 percent. The parks and recreation agency ultimately increased the wage by $2.00 per hour to attract qualified lifeguards.

Budget preparation is often a process of shared decision making.

Staffing Issues

Determining staffing needs for programs is a function of each budget manager. Information pertaining to the number of personnel, the rate of pay, the length of time to be employed, and the justification for the position need to be given to the budget preparation officer for inclusion in the budget. Tools that are used by budget preparation officers and CEOs to determine staffing needs include reviewing staffing patterns, as identified in detailed organization charts, tables of organization, or manning tables. Additionally, the budget preparation officer needs to look at workload trends in the organization. Organizations should be involved in some type of workload analysis that provides this information. Included in workload trends are new or amended legal requirements affecting the organization's programs and services, newly initiated policies or changes in existing policy regulations, planned changes in the organization, changes in systems and/or procedures, and approved workload consolidations. The CEO must attempt to balance workload demands with available personnel and match these demands with existing commitments. At the disposal of the CEO is his experience over a period of years with staffing patterns. This experience quotient, although not scientifically based, is an important component of the budgeting process. Finally, the CEO has to make certain assumptions about the future. These assumptions are based on existing facts, past history, knowledge of the organization and its members, political implications and realities, and stakeholder expectations.

Personnel costs are collated for all positions and placed in the department's operating budget. If the personnel costs are assigned to different funds within the organization, the positions are appropriately categorized. This process can become complicated, but when properly organized and cross-referenced, it becomes a clear and whole picture.

In most organizations, there will be some *salary savings* every year. A salary savings occurs when one or more positions in the organization remain empty for any period of time. For example, a position paying $2,000 a month that is vacant for three months results in a $6,000 salary savings for the organization. Over a period of time, these vacancies can produce a significant savings for the organization. In some cases, the budget preparation officer may know about these vacancies in advance; in other cases, they will occur during the fiscal year, and adjustments will have to be made in the operating budget. Most budget preparation officers anticipate salary savings and figure them as part of the budget.

For some organizations, overtime is a significant issue. The Fair Labor Standards Act (FLSA) prescribes overtime rules for most organizations. Employees can be identified as exempt from overtime, depending on their position and responsibility, but most employees will more likely be affected by the FLSA overtime rules. Public organizations are particularly challenged by the overtime costs. In a northern community, for example, the parks and recreation department may be tasked to be part of the snow removal process—a responsibility whose cost is almost impossible to predict, but which will always involve overtime. Most organizations set aside a certain amount of the personnel costs for overtime. The organization must determine what is an acceptable level of overtime and how the organization will fund the overtime. In some cases, organizations have adjusted work hours to overcome their overtime costs. In one community, the recreation maintenance crew members modified their hours from mid-December through mid-February so that they would be working six days a week on maintaining outdoor ice rinks. They would typically begin at 4:30 a.m. and work until 11:00 a.m. each day.

Determining Salary Costs

The examples in this section move from a relatively simple cost determination to a more complex cost problem. The programs in Example 1 meet once a week. In Example 2, most of the programs meet once a week, but some meet three times a week. Regardless, the budget manager should adhere to some simple rules. A certain amount of information is always known about any program or activity. It may vary from program to program, but nonetheless, this is a staring point for budget construction. It may include salaries, facility rental costs, supplies, and type of program. It is also essential to determine what information needs to be known. For a piece of information that needs to be known, the question that needs to be asked is "How can it be learned or secured?"

Example 1: Simple Class Budget

Known information:

- There are 12 classes. All of the classes meet once a week for 8 weeks, and each class period is 1 hour long.

- The cost for the instructor is $9.00 per hour; for the dance coordinator, $2.50 per class; and for the room, $5.00 per hour.

- There are 15 participants per class.

- The program fee is designed to recover costs (it should neither lose nor make money).

To determine what the program manager needs to know, the question that should be asked is "What information is essential?" The reason is that there may be information related to the program that is not essential. Essential information allows the program manager to determine the answer to each unknown piece of information. In this case, the essential and unknown information is as follows:

- Total number of hours classes meet. This is determined by taking 3 known items and multiplying them, as shown below:

> 12 classes x 8 weeks x 1 hour per class = 96 hours

- Total cost of instructors, dance coordinator, and room rental. Multiply the cost of each by the total number of hours:

> 1 instructor x $9.00 per hour x 96 hours = $960
>
> 1 coordinator x $2.50 per hour x 96 hours = $240
>
> 1 hour of room rental x $5.00 per hour x 96 hours = $480

- Total cost of program is determined by adding together the cost figures above. In each case, new information was generated that was used to answer the next question:

> $960 + $240 + $480 = $1,680

Example 2: Class Budget—Expanded

Known information:

- There are still 12 classes, but only 7 of the classes meet once a week for 8 weeks. Five classes meet 3 times a week for 8 weeks. All class periods remain one hour in length.

- The cost for the instructor is $9.00 per hour; for the dance coordinator, $2.50 per hour; and for the room, $5.00 per hour.

- The program has an indirect cost of 12.5%.

- There are 15 participants per class.

- The agency has determined that indirect costs should be charged at a rate of 12.5% added to the total cost of the program.

- The program fee is designed to recover costs (it should neither lose nor make money).

To determine what the program manager needs to know, the question to ask is "What information is essential?" There may be information related to the program that is not essential. Essential information allows the program manager to determine the answer to each unknown piece of information. In this case, the essential and unknown information is as follows:

- Total number of hours classes meet. For the 7 classes that meet once a week, use the same formula as in Example 1. For those meeting 3 times a week, include the "3" as a new variable:

  7 classes x 8 weeks x 1 hour per class = 56 hours

  5 classes x 8 weeks x 3 times per week x 1 hour per class = 120 hours

  56 hours + 120 hours = 176 hours (Total Hours)

- Total cost of instructors, dance coordinator, and room rental. Multiply the cost of each by the total number of hours:

  1 instructor x $9.00 per hour x 176 hours = $1,584

  1 coordinator x $2.50 per hour x 176 hours = $440

  1 hour room rental x $5.00 per hour x 176 hours = $880

- Total cost of program is determined by adding together the cost figures above. In each case, new information was generated that was used to answer the next question:

  $1,584 + $440 + $880 = $2,904

- The indirect cost of the program is figured by multiplying the program cost by the indirect fee:

  $2,904 x .125 = $363

- Total cost of program is arrived at by adding the indirect costs and program costs:

  $2,904 + $385 = $3,267

Contractual Service Requirements

A growing cost in public, nonprofit, and private organizations is that of contractual services. The growth of contractual services is based, in part, on the belief that some functions can be done more effectively and efficiently at a lower cost by an outside vendor. Whole communities have embraced the concept of contracting out services. The City of Indianapolis, Indiana, has been a leader in this movement, leasing its golf courses, selected swimming pools, and community centers to private individuals and nonprofit and commercial organizations. At one point, the city even contracted for the parks and recreation department's CEO. Every organization has some form of contractual arrangement, even if it is only with the copy machine repair person. The level and extent of contractual management is not typically an issue in the budget process. At some policy level, the decision (and action) to become involved in contractual management has already been made.

If the organization has not made the decision about contracting for services, then the budget preparation process may be used to make such a determination. Issues that need to be resolved include the following: comparative costs between the sport and leisure service organization accomplishing the task versus a commercial contractor, presence of qualified contractor personnel, actual cost, impact upon the organization's productivity, and quality of work.

Table 9.5 illustrates the types of services and the major cities involved in privatization or competition.

	Colorado Springs	Indianapolis	Philadelphia	Phoenix	San Jose
Park Maintenance		✗	✗		
Golf Courses		✗	✗	✗	✗
Landscape Maintenance	✗	✗	✗	✗	✗
Tree Trimming	✗	✗			✗
Fleet Maintenance		✗			✗
Animal Control				✗	✗
Building Maintenance	✗	✗	✗	✗	✗
Janitorial Services	✗	✗	✗	✗	✗
Refuse Collection	✗	✗		✗	✗
Security Services	✗	✗	✗	✗	✗

Table 9.5. Examples of service privatized by city.

In San Jose, California, the decision to become involved in public-private competition began in late 1996. The assumption in public-private competition is that the public sector should be competitive with the private sector in both cost and quality. It does not necessarily involve the replacement of public workers with private workers. In San Jose, the effort focused on "maximizing the value of services for the public, rather than on which sector ultimately delivers the service" (San Jose, 1997). The process includes contracting in, as well as contracting out. In fiscal year 1996, San Jose contracted out about 25 percent of its operating budget, or $250 million. In establishing the public-private competition, the city also established criteria for each service it looked at for competition. An important part of the competitive model was to ensure that employees were not threatened by the new process and that they had the opportunity to bid on privatized projects.

Materials, Supplies, and Equipment Costs

Materials and supplies comprise the second-costliest item in most operating budgets. Budget managers need to determine the type, quantity, and quality of material required to carry out the annual work plans. Organizations will take into account issues such as present inventories, cost, any patterns in changing use or provision of services, new programs and services, and the like. The organization usually begins with an assessment of what was purchased the previous year and whether it was sufficient to accomplish the tasks. Program reports, year-end reports, and inventories should provide some of this information. Proposed work plans are compared with the previous year's work plans to determine changes in anticipated needs. If standards have been established for programs or services, or if they exist and are modified, they may affect the need for materials and supplies.

Projected inventories assist in providing another picture of material and supply needs. Many organizations have adopted a just-in-time delivery process in which the supplier provides storage and delivers on call. For example, one park district determined it needed 30,000 pounds of seed for the entire year. In previous years, it had purchased seed on three separate occasions. Consolidating into a single purchase and requiring the supplier to maintain the inventory reduced the cost significantly and eliminated the need for long-term storage requirements. The purchase was negotiated so that payment was made only when seed was delivered. Thirty thousand pounds was the guaranteed purchase at a guaranteed price.

Where purchasing departments are nonexistent, it is incumbent upon the sport and leisure service organization to participate in well-formulated purchasing. The establishment of standing purchase orders with local vendors is a common strategy for maintenance operations. Larger purchases are typically bid to a number of potential vendors. A set of specifications is established for each purchase item and used as a guide for the vendor to make a bid. Careful development of the specifications is essential, as well as an effort to ensure that bias is removed from the purchasing process. There is rarely a requirement that an organization take the low bid, but when not taking the low bid, the organization must demonstrate that the higher bid more closely conforms to the advertised specifications. At what level the organization must go in order to bid is typically determined by statute and also by the legislative/policy body.

Equipment purchases include items that have a longer life and contribute to the operation of the organization. They can include items such as fitness equipment, pitching machines, computers, lawn mowers, trucks, and cars. In almost every situation, the equipment has a specific life span, after which it will need to be replaced. In preparing the equipment portion of the budget, the sport and leisure service organization needs to ensure that there is an inventory of all equipment. The inventory should include date of purchase, classification code of the equipment, description of the item, purchase price, its current location, current condition (which may require an annual inspection), and life expectancy. For some pieces of equipment, the budget preparation officer may desire to establish a replacement schedule. A replacement schedule allows the budget preparation officer to look forward and anticipate major equipment costs for the organization. Some organizations set aside money every year for replacement of equipment into a special capital replacement fund. This strategy reduces the drain on the operating budget for major purchases that all take place in one fiscal year. Equally important is the spreading of major purchases over several years, rather than trying to make all purchases in a single year.

Reviewing Budget Estimates at the Departmental Level

While the CEO must ultimately accept responsibility for the final budget document, it is the formal and informal processes that make up the submitted document. Throughout the process, there is a continuous flow of information up and down the organization, exchanges of detailed data, analyses of decisions regarding the budget, etc. Each budget manager should meet with the budget preparation officer and the CEO and brief them on their section of the budget document. The CEO should provide a completed budget presentation for the sports and leisure service organization's budget managers and then answer questions. This final review assures that all of the issues associated with the budget's preparation have been discussed and the document is ready to be submitted to the legislative or policy-setting body.

Preparing a Simple Activity Budget

The foundation for many budgets in sport and leisure service organizations lies with the activity budget. In constructing a budget for a single activity, some information will be provided in detail, while the budget manager must determine other information. The following case illustrates a budget for a single activity:

The public swimming pool is an outdoor facility that opens the same day that classes are dismissed (June 5) from the public schools and closes the day school resumes (August 27). The aquatic supervisor is paid $13.00 per hour, is a permanent full-time employee, and has a $27,040 annual salary. The salary is wholly charged to the swimming pool budget. A maintenance worker I is paid $9.25 per hour, spends approximately 30 hours a week at the pool from April through September, and has 50 percent of her salary charged against the swimming pool budget ($11,500). Lifeguards are required during open swim, family swim, lap swim, and lessons.

Table 9.6 depicts the activity, the number of guards required for each activity, the number of hours per day guards are required, and the rate of pay for the lifeguards.

In addition to lifeguards, there are two swim team coaches, six learn-to-swim instructors per hour of lessons, one concessions person during lap swim, two concessions persons during open and family swim, and one cashier who collects swim fees and passes. The pool manager is present an average of 10 hours a day, six days a week. When the manager is not present, the head guard or assistant head guard assumes the role of acting manager. The head guard and assistant head guard also work regular pool lifeguard rotations.

Swimming is one of the leading recreation, fitness, and family activities. In recent years, the design of aquatic centers has made them profitable.

Full-time employees (aquatics supervisor and maintenance worker I) have benefits equal to 27 percent of their salary. The aquatics supervisor would have benefits totaling $7,300 (base salary x benefits or 27,040 x .27). The benefits are items such as retirement, medical and dental, life insurance, unemployment, and workers' compensation. For part-time and seasonal employees, the benefits are figured at 9 percent of the base salary.

Activity	No. of Lifeguards	Days per Week	Hours per Day	Salary / per hour
Open Swim	6	7	8	$8.70
Family Swim	4	3	3	$8.70
Lap Swim	2	6	3	$7.90
Lessons	1	4	4	$7.90

Table 9.6. Swimming pool staffing needs.

Using the format identified in the section titled "Determining Salary Costs," several questions can be answered. First, what is known? The information in Tables 9.6 and 9.7 provides detail about positions, rate of pay, hours per week, and number of staff. The information that is still required includes how many hours per season each person works, what the total cost is of each position for the season, what the cost of benefits is, and what the total cost is of the salaries for the program.

The aquatic supervisor has 100 percent of his salary assessed to the pool, plus 27 percent of his benefits. Following the process discussed previously, the known information is the annual salary and the annual benefit percentage. The desired information is the cost of benefits and the total cost of the position. The formula for determining cost would be as follows:

Position	Number	Days per week	Hours per day	Salary / per hour
Swim Team Coach	1	5	3	$12.50
Asst. Swim Team Coach	1	5	3	$9.00
Learn-to-swim instructors	6 per hour	3	4	$8.40
Pool Manager	1	6	10	$9.50
Head Guard	1	6	10	$9.50
Asst. Head Guard	1	6	10	$9.00

Table 9.7. Other staffing.

(salary x benefit percent = benefit cost) + salary = total cost

with the known information . . .

1) salary = $27,040

2) benefit percentage = 27%

resulting in a completed formula that looks like:

($27,040 x 27% = $7,300) + $27,040 = $34,340

When repeated for the lifeguards, the formula becomes a little more complex. The known information expands as shown below. The length of the season is also known and is figured in weeks. Running from June 5 to August 27, the season is 12 weeks long. The number of guards per hour is a key factor. In the case of the aquatic supervisor, there was only one person. Because there are six lifeguards per hour, they must be included in the equation. In this case, the formula for lifeguards for open swim would be as follows:

((salary x hours per day x days per week x number of employees per hour x number of weeks in season = total salary) x benefit percent) = benefit cost + total salary = total cost

with the known information . . .

(1) salary = $8.70 per hour

(2) hours per day = 8

(3) days per week = 7

(4) number of employees per hour = 6

(5) number of weeks in the season = 12

(6) benefit percentage = 9%

> resulting in a completed formula that looks like:
>
> (($8.70 x 8 x 7 x 6 x 12 = $35,078) x 9%) = $3,157 + $35,078
> = total cost of $38,235

In each case, *known information* is used to generate needed information. Pausing to reflect on how to set up the formula is essential. This would be repeated for each position until all costs were determined.

The final example for the head guard involves only one person, but includes hours, days per week, weeks in the season, benefit percentage, and salary. The formula is as follows:

> ((salary x hours per day x days per week x number of weeks in season = total salary) x benefit percent) = benefit cost + total salary = total cost
>
> with the known information . . .
>
> (1) salary = $9.50 per hour
>
> (2) hours per day = 10
>
> (3) days per week = 6
>
> (4) number of weeks in the season = 12
>
> (5) benefit percentage = 9%
>
> resulting in a completed formula that looks like:
>
> (($9.50 x 10 x 6 x 12 = $6,840) x 9%) = $616 + $6,840 = total cost of $7,456

When completed, the total cost of salaries, including benefits, is $7,456.

Additional program costs that the budget manager included are listed below:

Supplies and Equipment			
Pool Chemicals	$3,200.00	First Aid Kits	$125.00
Maintenance Supplies	1,200.00	Flotation Devices	1,870.00
Concession Supplies	9,850.00	Utilities	11,200.00

Summary

Budgeting is an essential management tool in any sport and leisure service organization and requires an understanding of how budgets work, of basic budgeting processes, and of how managers use budgets. The budget cycle, budget calendar, and budget guidelines drive the budgeting process for sport and leisure service organization administrators. A knowledge of funds and how they operate contributes to the ability of managers to allocate appropriate resources. Budget formats are prescribed by the legislative or policy body and determine how they choose to look at budgets. Corresponding budget preparation philosophies suggest an approach to budgeting ranging from fixed ceiling to alternative budget proposals. The 18-month to two-year planning cycle for any budget allows a sport and leisure service organization to plan, approve, implement, and close a budget. The knowledge of estimating budget costs increases with experience, but knowing how to prepare an activity budget is often the foundation for all budget processes in sport and leisure service organizations.

References

Aronson, J. R., and Schwartz, E. 1996. *Management policies in local government finance.* Washington, DC: International City/County Management Association.

Kelsey, C. W., Gray, H. R., and McLean, D. D. 1993. *The budget process in parks and recreation: A case study manual.* Reston, VA: American Alliance for Health, Physical Education, Recreation and Dance.

Listro, J. P. 1998. *Nonprofit organizations account and reporting.* (2nd ed.). Dubuque, IA: Kendall/Hunt Publishing Company.

Rabin, Jack (Ed.). 1992. *Handbook of public budgeting.* New York: Marcel Dekker, Inc.

Reed, B. J., and Swain, J. W. 1997. *Public finance administration.* Thousand Oaks, CA: SAGE Publications.

San Jose, City of. 1997. *New realities update.* San Jose, CA: City of San Jose.

Chapter 10

Budget Formats

Introduction

Budget preparation is only half of the budgeting process. Budgets must be organized into a format for presentation to the legislative/policy body. There are multiple formats an organization can select. Each sport and leisure service organization must determine the format that is appropriate for its needs. A commercial or nonprofit organization may select a format that meets its unique needs. A board of directors or a legislative/policy board may establish a different format consistent with its own needs. A large organization may specify multiple budget formats, each with a different purpose. This chapter looks at the most common formats that organizations use. The example presented at the conclusion of Chapter 9 will be used throughout this chapter to illustrate the different ways that the same budget information can be formatted.

Budget Formats

Budgets can be presented in a variety of formats, but the choice is typically dependent upon the organization's view of how a budget should be formatted. The purpose of budgeting is to secure financial control and to achieve goals, mission, and vision attainment for the organization. Additionally, managerial productivity is seen as an important outcome of budgeting. The type of approach adopted by a sport and leisure service organization is a reflection of how the legislative or policy body best feels the organization should achieve its goals. Different types of budget formats reflect an emphasis upon different goals. For example, an object classification or line item budget focuses on financial control. Program and performance budgets focus on goal attainment. Zero-based budgeting and planning-programming-budgeting systems focus on managerial productivity. The CEO and the budget preparation officer should determine the level of detail presented in any budget format. Six of the most common operating budget formats are presented in this chapter. They are representative of formats found in most sport and leisure service organizations.

Object Classification and Line Item Budgets

The object classification and line item budgets are the most common of all budget formats adhered to by sport and leisure service organizations, and they both share similarities. Both budgets, for example, rely on a coding system for all budget items. In this section, primary emphasis is given to the object classification budget, although the same principles can be used for a line item budget. (Henceforth, only the object classification budget will be used to represent both budgets.) An object classification or a line item budget organizes budgets into predetermined categories. Each line in the budget reflects either an expenditure or a category. For example, "personnel costs" become a major line with sub-classifications. Sub-classifications might include types of personnel (program, maintenance, support, full-time, and part-time) and benefit areas (medical, retirement fund, uniforms, and overtime). The emphasis in the object classification budget is on input rather than measurement. Conformance and compliance with an established budget as a requirement is paramount to understanding how the funds are being used or collected.

Construction of an object classification budget involves four steps. But before initiating the budget construction, specific information must be gathered. The data to be gathered were addressed in Chapter 9 and are partially repeated here. In an object classification budget, the organization commonly uses a *fixed ceiling* approach to allocation. Preparation items include (1) budget letter with guidelines from the legislative authority; (2) allowed budget growth (usually in percent of allowed growth of total budget), if it is a fixed ceiling budget, or some other detail regarding the approach to budget development; (3) list of classification codes (this can run to many pages); (4) personnel salary ranges and steps; (5) specific or unusual budget request issues; and (6) budget forms. Items 1, 2, 4, and 5 will be common to most budget formats.

Step 1: Collect all budget data.

The collection of all budget data from the sport and leisure service organization's budget managers is the first step. The assignment of collecting budget data should be delegated to the lowest possible level. Budget managers should complete as much of the budget process themselves for familiarity purposes. The budget preparation officer will ultimately check all information provided.

Step 2: Identify appropriate classification codes for each budget item.

The classification codes and budget forms will be unique to the object classification budget. The list of lines or classification codes is given to the budget preparation officer and budget managers who must ensure that each item in the budget conforms to the existing codes. These codes can run to many pages and will have definitions to assist the budget manager as she attempts to determine which item fits within a particular code. Examples of expenditure classification codes and definitions appear in Table 10.1.

Step 3: Place items in detailed sub-classifications (object codes).

Assignment of expenditure and revenue items to classification object codes, as depicted in Table 10.1, is followed by placing the same items into more detailed expenditure and revenue object codes (Table 10.2). Recall that the purpose of the object classification budget is to provide financial control. Placing each expenditure and revenue item into a detailed sub-classification allows the CEO and the budget preparation officer to have a clear and detailed understanding of the total budget and where the money is going to be spent. It allows multi-year tracking of revenues and expenditures for comparative and evaluative purposes. The advantage of this type of a budget format lies in the CEO's ability to be aware of subtle, as well as major, shifts in the budget.

Definitions:

100: <u>Personnel Services</u> – Expenditures for direct personnel services including wages, benefits, overtime, special benefits and the like. Includes full-time, part-time and seasonal employees.

200: <u>Contractual Services</u> – Services involving work performance by non-organization employees through a contract or agreement. The work may include the contractor to provide equipment and commodities.

230: <u>Printing Services</u> – Expenses related to printing, copying, reproduction, binding, publication, advertising and the like.

240: <u>Utilities</u> – Charges for heat, water, electricity, telephone, cable television, and other utility based enterprises.

250: <u>Repairs</u> – All repairs for fixed structures. Does not include vehicles, equipment and expendable items.

300: <u>Commodities</u>

310: <u>Materials</u> – Items, more permanent in nature, that may be combined or converted for other uses. Includes lumber, concrete, concrete blocks, paint, and other building materials.

320: <u>Supplies</u> – A commodity consumed, impaired or worn out in an expectedly short period of time. Includes such items as paper, crafts supplies, food, clothing, fuel, oil, grass seed, etc.

400: <u>Encumbered Obligations</u> – Fixed expenses and/or binding contracts created from previous obligations of the legislative authority. Included in this category could be temporary loans, interest on city's debt, grants and subsidies, court ordered payments, and the like.

500: <u>Existing Charges</u> – Provided at the option of legislative authority, it could include costs of insurance, licenses, rent, leases and the like.

600: <u>Debt Payment</u> – Includes the amount of annual payment for reduction on debt incurred by the legislative authority.

Table 10.1. Example object classification codes and definitions.

The amount of detail determines how many object codes the organization will utilize. An organization that is not concerned about budget detail may have few object codes, while an organization trying to gain control of its expenditures may require detailed coding. One parks and recreation director noted that almost 50 percent of the department's expenditures were coded as "miscellaneous." Upon investigation, it became obvious that no one had previously shown a concern about expenditures, nor tried to track them. When it was explained to the organization's members what the goal was—to gain a better understanding of expenditures—and when the director refused to accept miscellaneous classifications, expenditure control and knowledge of expenditures increased significantly.

The object classification codes provided in Tables 10.1 and 10.2 are relatively simple. They can be much more detailed. Figure 10.1 illustrates a more detailed object classification code. In this case, the first two numbers represent the department, such as parks and recreation or convention center. The middle four numbers represent the expenditure classification code, which describes via an object code how the money was spent. This can also be a revenue object code. The last four digits represent the program area (e.g., sports, recreation centers, and office administration) and specific programs. This might include the sports program area and its programs of softball, volleyball, flag football, to name a few. Codes can allow highly detailed analyses of budgets. The code in Figure 10.1 could be interpreted to represent the Parks and Recreation Department [24] purchasing art supplies [5135] for the arts program's [13] pottery classes [24]. Expenditures identified down to the program detail provide budget managers with a very clear picture of costs of programs and allow these managers to make fiscal decisions that are based on relevant information. The object classification budget can function simultaneously with other budget formats.

Expenditure Classification by Objects	
100 Personnel	252 – Repairs to Buildings and
110 – Salaries, Regular	other structures
120 – Salaries, Temporary	253 – Repairs to Playground
130 – Salaries, Seasonal	equipment and surfaces
140 – Salaries, Permanent Part Time	300 Commodities
200 Services: Contractual	310 Materials
210 – Communications	311 – Masonry
211 – Postage	312 – Road Materials
212 – Telephone	313 - Lumber
213 – FedEx, UPS, Other Freight	314 – Paint
214 – In-State Travel	315 – Structural Metals
215 – Out of State Travel	316 – Other Materials
216 – Radio Communications System	330 – Supplies
220 – Subsistence, Care and Support	321 – Office Supplies
221 – Storage and care of vehicles	322 – Program Supplies
230 Printing Services	323 – Cleaning Supplies
231 – Printing	324 – Food Products
232 – Photocopying	325 – Clothing & Dry Goods
233 – Word Processing	326 - Chemicals
234 – Binding	327 – Other Supplies
235 – Photography	400 Encumbered Obligations
236 - Advertising	410 - Rent
237 – Publication of Notices	411 – Buildings and Spaces
238 – Blueprints	412 - Equipment
239 – Graphic Services	420 - Insurance
240 – Utilities	500 Existing Charges
241 – Natural Gas Utilities	510 – Interest on Debt
242 – Propane	520 – Pensions and Retirement
243 – Electrical Utilities, Indoor	530 – Grants and Subsidies
244 – Electrical Utilities, Outdoor	540 - Taxes
245 – Water Service	600 Debt Payment
246 – Sewer Service	610 – Serial Bonds
247 – Telephone Service	620 – Revenue Bonds
250 Repairs	630 – Sinking Fund Installments
251 – Repairs to Equipment	640 – Other Debt Payment

Table 10.2. Example classification codes by object.

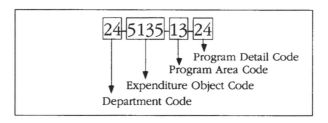

Figure 10.1. Object classification code.

Step 4: Organize the budget.

Work at this stage involves collating the collected budget information, checking and verifying budget requests, organizing data for a budget review, making recommendations regarding budget allocations, and presenting the budget to the legislative body for approval. Table 10.3 illustrates a traditional object classification budget for the aquatics program presented in Chapter 9. This budget would be combined with all other activity budgets in the agency to provide a total budget picture to the legislative body. The budget provided to the legislative body would provide the level of detail seen in Table 10.3, but would also provide summary data representing all of the budget areas within the organization as depicted in Table 10.4.

Boards and commissions deliberate over budget recommendations
made by the professional staff.

A final budget request is submitted to the legislative body, showing all of the proposed expenditure income sources for the organization. The budget request is usually presented as a historical representation showing the proposed fiscal year request, the current fiscal year approved, and the previous fiscal year actual (Tables 10.3 and 10.4). The terms used to present each fiscal year are important. In the case of Tables 10.3 and 10.4, the *last year actual* represents the expenditures for that fiscal year. The fiscal year is complete, and all of the expenditures have been accounted for and/or paid. The *current fiscal year approved* indicates the budget is in process. The legislative body has approved the budget, but because the fiscal year is not complete, there is only an estimate of what the actual budget will look like at the conclusion of the fiscal year. This picture of the budget is incomplete, but has been modified on the basis of anticipated revenues and expenditures. The proposed fiscal year is called *next year requested.* At this point, the legislative body has not approved the proposed budget. Until it is approved, it remains a requested budget.

The object classification budget is the most common of all budget types. It is malleable enough to be used with other budget formats. This flexibility allows the sport and leisure service organization to maintain fiscal control and simultaneously administer the budget in other formats in order to accomplish other objectives.

Object Code	Description	Last Year Actual	This Year Projected	Next Year Requested
100	Personnel			
110	Salaries, Permanent Full-Time	$35,242	$37,383	$38,540
120	Salaries, Temporary	$0	$0	$0
130	Salaries, Part-Time	$67,651	$72,743	$75,774
200	Services: Contractual			
220	Subsistence, Care and Support			
221	Storage and care of vehicles	$0	$0	$0
326	Pool Chemicals	$2,785	$3,000	$3,200
323	Maintenance Supplies	$986	$1,100	$1,200
	Concession Supplies			
327	Snack Bar Supplies	$2,732	$3,200	$3,500
324	Food Service Supplies	$4,905	$5,300	$5,600
323	Cleaning Supplies	$675	$699	$750
	Other Supplies			
322	First Aid Kits	$250	$375	$500
322	Awards: Patches	$185	$200	$225
322	Flotation Devices	$0	$0	$1,870
	Utilities			
241	Natural Gas Utilities	$453	$500	$600
243	Electricity	$454	$500	$650
247	Telephone	$165	$164	$175
	Insurance			
263	Fire & Comprehensive	$856	$1,000	$1,000
267	Boiler	$100	$100	$100
262	Liability	$2,500	$2,500	$3,000
	Marketing			
231	Brochure Costs	$12,356	$14,000	$15,000
231	Tickets/Passes	$450	$400	$450
236	Advertising: Newspaper	$675	$800	$800
283	Television	$862	$1,000	$1,200
	Total	$134,282	$144,964	$154,134

Table 10.3. Partial object classification/line item budget.

Object Code	Description	Last Year Actual	This Year Projected	Next Year Requested
100	Personnel	$102,893	$110,126	$114,314
200	Services, Contractual	3,771	4,100	4,500
	Utilities	1,072	1,164	1,425
	Insurance	3,456	3,600	4,100
	Marketing	14,343	16,200	17,450
300	Supplies & Equipment	8,747	9,974	12,445
	Total	$134,282	$144,964	$154,134

Table 10.4. Summary budget data.

Program Budget

Program budgeting was first introduced during the Kennedy Administration and was called Planning-Program-Budgeting-System (PPBS). Traditional budgeting formats focus on input (personnel, program, and capital costs), but program budgeting focuses on outputs (end results, goals, and objectives). The emphasis of program budgeting is upon effectiveness rather than efficiency or spending. This emphasis represents a major shift in the way budgets have been constructed. The program budget's major advantage was in its ability to cross departmental or divisional boundaries. Program budgeting has fallen into disfavor at the federal level, but has flourished at the state, municipal, nonprofit, and commercial levels. The emphasis upon outcomes and measurement has received a positive reception among administrators and the public alike. Output measurement through goals and objectives, public surveys, satisfaction determination, and benchmarking has contributed to the acceptance of program budgeting.

A program budget takes expenditures and breaks them down into viewable units according to the service provided. For example, the object classification budget looks at the entire budget as a single entity. It provides no understanding of how funds are to be expended. The program budget provides more information to the budget manager and others who have a desire to know how the allocated funds will be expended. The budget is subdivided into program areas, and each program area is reported as a separate part of the budget. For program managers, this separation provides greater authority and accountability as they become budget managers. Their decisions are reflected in their management of their portion of the budget. Figure 10.2 depicts how a program budget format might be organized. A program budget is organized to provide details to the program manager, the administrators, and the legislative/policy body.

The *department* represents the highest level of budget authority and responsibility. At this level, the department or division determines the organization's vision, mission, and major goals. The development of goals and objectives for the sport and leisure service organization and its sub-components should be based upon a strategic planning process. The *program areas* are aimed at specific goals, or in the example of most sport and leisure service organizations, program-specific areas (or populations). *Programs* are designed to meet more specific population needs; they are also referred to as support activities. They emphasize the importance of focusing on who is to benefit from the service or program. *Program elements* represent the basis that budget units use to achieve the goals and objectives of the organization. Consistent with the budgeting process is the development of goals and objectives at each level of the structure. Examples of goals and objectives developed for each level depicted in Figure 10.2 are illustrated in Figure 10.3. In this example, the program area is adult sports, and the program is tennis.

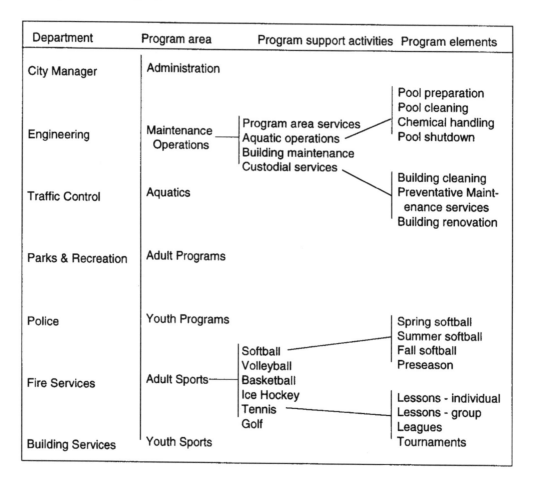

Figure 10.2. Example program budget (adapted from Aronson & Schwartz, 1996).

The development of program budgeting necessitated the rethinking of how budgets were administered. Pushing decision making and administration down to the lowest levels of the organization fostered a new set of concepts and terms. *Cost centers* comprise an independent entity embracing all of the costs of activities and items necessary to achieve a distinct and measurable outcome. Allocation of funds for the cost center may come from several divisions or departments. When expenditures are made, they are charged back to the parent budget authority, but the cost center identification remains consistent. Assuming softball is a cost center, the maintenance division will fund softball field maintenance and preparation and be charged for it. In an object classification budget, it would only appear as an expenditure that's not necessarily tied to a program area. In a program budget, with softball as a cost center, the cost of maintenance and preparation is linked to both the program area and the maintenance division. Maintenance knows how much it is spending overall and how much it is spending just for softball.

Department: Parks and Recreation
 Goal: To provide recreational services and opportunities for leisure experiences
 for all members of the community.

Program area: Adult Sports
 Goal: To provide opportunities for adults to participate in life time sports
 promoting physical and mental well-being.

Programs: Tennis
 Goal: To increase the opportunity for members of the community to be exposed
 and to participate in tennis programs.
 Objective: Provide opportunities for individual lessons
           Provide opportunities for group lessons
           Provide leagues for individual and team participation
           Provide tournaments for local, regional and state participants

Program element: Lessons - individual
 Goal: To provided opportunities for individuals to improve their tennis game
 through individualized instruction
 Output measures: Number of individuals participating in lessons
            Number of individuals returning from previous sessions
             or previous years
            Effectiveness of lessons as measured by participant
             satisfaction survey
            Cost-effectiveness of program

Figure 10.3. Program budget goals and objectives for Figure 10.2.

For the budget manager who may have previously budgeted only for staff and program supplies, he now has a clear picture of the total cost of the program, including salaries, supplies, maintenance, marketing, and administration. The new concept of *responsibility centers* (budget decision points) was also introduced. The term indicates a focus of budget analysis and decision making. A responsibility center manager knows the program budget's cross-functional boundaries within and between organizations. Program managers with cost center responsibilities will make decisions regarding budget allocations within the context of their authority and negotiate with other responsibility center managers for additional resources. For example, if the budget manager for softball determines that maintenance costs need to be increased substantially, she cannot arbitrarily make that decision. Rather, the cost center budget manager must discuss the issue with the functional area budget manager. In this case, the adult sports supervisor will discuss the issue with the maintenance superintendent.

Step 1: Goals and objectives.

Step 1 assumes the organization is already organized around program areas of functions, as illustrated in Figure 10.3. Such an assumption suggests that program managers and functional area budget managers are already talking to one another. The sport and leisure service organization develops goals and objectives for the fiscal year, and these can be a continuation from previous years, or they can be updated, modified, or wholly new each fiscal year. Program managers develop goals and objectives for each level of the program budget, down to program detail. Desired outcomes are determined in advance, as well as decisions about methods of measurement.

Step 2: Provide detailed narrative for each program.

Program areas were identified in step 1. In step 2, the program manager will identify those features of the program that meet specific goals and objectives. The program manager further explains how and why each is important. The narrative relates to the program's goals and objectives.

Step 3: Determine expenditures and revenue for the program.

Using the processes discussed in *preparing a simple activity budget* in Chapter 9, the same budget is adjusted for the program budget format. In those areas where measurements are defined, the expenditures will be tied to specific objectives. Table 10.5 illustrates a completed aquatics program budget. Determining revenue is accomplished the same way; however, it need not be tied to objectives, unless there are specific objectives related to the generation of revenues.

The budget presented in Table 10.5 depicts a program budget with objectives, a narrative, measurement criteria, and income and expenditure expectations. Although each sport and leisure service organization will have its own format for developing a program budget, each will follow a similar pattern. The components remain remarkably similar, with an emphasis on outcomes rather than inputs.

Performance Budget

A performance budget is frequently referred to as a measurement of efficiency. It is most frequently used with recurring tasks, where measurements can be readily developed and applied. Performance budgeting became popular with municipal governments in the early 1950s and remains in use today. It fits well into operations where repetition and measurement can be made easily, such as certain repetitive maintenance functions (e.g., mowing, grounds maintenance, and custodial work). One of the greatest benefits of a performance budget is its ability to provide managers with performance-cost data. Although the development of measurement data is beyond the scope of this book, it requires an assessment of what work needs to be accomplished, what equipment is available to do the work, and capabilities the employees have to accomplish the task. It requires a constant assessment and monitoring of the measurement standards by managers.

Step 1: Identify those components of the budget that fit a performance format.

The budget preparation officer must determine which of the sport and leisure service organization's operations are most conducive to a performance budget. These operations should meet the following criteria: (1) It should be possible for the work to be quantified into measurable work units; (2) it should be possible for the quality of the provided service

Program: **Aquatics**						
Program Description	The Aquatics program is designed to provide recreational opportunities, competitive opportunities, and learn-to-swim lessons to residents					
Performance Objectives						
1. Provide open swim opportunities for the community.						
2. Increase number of program offerings by 5% over previous year.						
3. Achieve a 90% positive satisfaction rating from participants.						

Measurement	Program	Object ive	1999 Actual	2000 Approved	2000 Revised	2001 Projected
Demand						
Estimated participants	Open Swim	1	38,146	45,000	44,700	48,000
	Other Swim	1	9,877	10,000	9,800	11,000
	Learn-to-swim	1	2,300	2,600	2,600	2,800
Estimated Programs		2	36	45	45	47
Workload						
Actual Registrations	Open Swim		38,146	45,000	44,700	48,000
	Other Swim	1	9,877	10,000	9,800	11,000
	Learn-to-swim	1	2,300	2,600	2,600	2,800
Actual programs		1	36	45	45	47
Actual participations	All programs	2	50,323	57,600	57,100	61,800
Total community population		2	110,000	110,000	110,000	112,000
Productivity						
Average cost per participant		1	$2.67	$2.52	$2.54	$2.49
Average cost per participation		1	$2.67	$2.52	$2.54	$2.49
Effectiveness						
Program participation increase/decrease previous year		1	0%	5%	5%	8%
Program offerings increase/decrease previous year		2	0%	25%	25%	5%
Percentage positive rating from participants		3	88%	88%	88%	90%
Percent total population served			38%	39%	39%	42%
Narrative						
The arts program serve as a variety of populations in the community, to include people with physical and mental disabilities, school populations, adults and seniors.						
Resources						
Expenditure Categories:	Personnel		$102,893	$110,126	$110,126	$6,630
	Operations/Maintenance and Supplies		$13,590	$15,038	$15,038	$18,270
	Insurance		$3,456	$3,600	$3,600	$4,100
	Marketing		$14,343	$16,200	$16,200	$17,450
	TOTAL		$134,282	$144,964	$144,964	$154,134
Revenue Funds:	General		$15,600	$15,000	$15,000	$12,000
	Fees & Charges		$105,314	$109,964	$111,465	$119,135
	Donations & Grants		$13,368	$20,000	$18,500	$23,000
	TOTAL		$134,282	$144,964	$144,965	$154,135

Table 10.5. Program budget example.

or activity to be measured; and (3) the performance should be able to hold constant. Examples of work that can be easily quantified include mowing, tree planting, fertilizing, ball diamond preparation, and most grounds maintenance activities, construction activities, and some custodial work.

Step 2: Establish work units.

For each activity that will be measured, *work units* must be established. This is accomplished by measuring current work levels, benchmarking work activities against the same work accomplished by similar organizations, and looking at standards established by various measurement organizations. In the early stages of establishing standards, flexibility is important until an achievable and acceptable standard is determined. Work units are normally measured in performance per hour, although they can be established in other ways. Examples of measurements include square feet per item, cubic yards, acres, and the like. A grass-mowing crew using hand mowers may have a work unit established as .75 acres per hour. The same crew using gang mowers may have a standard of 4.5 acres per hour.

Budget decisions ultimately affect how recreation paricipants are able to utilize and enjoy resources and programs.

Step 3: Determine the cost per work unit to be measured.

The cost per work unit is based upon a number of variables, which include the task to be completed, the capabilities of the employees, the cost of expendable supplies and special equipment, the depreciation of equipment, and travel time and distance. The budget preparation officer looks at all of the variables that affect the work unit and establishes a cost standard. For a mowing crew that travels throughout the city, the cost standard would include travel time between sites, salaries of the mowing crew, cost of gasoline for travel and mowing equipment, maintenance costs of equipment, actual time spent on site mowing, and other associated costs of the task. Assume an 18-acre park has 10 acres of open area suitable for a gang mower; four acres that require hand mowing with a 42-inch mower; and two acres that call for 22-inch hand mowers. Two acres are not mowed. The mowing crew takes an average of 2.5 hours to accomplish the task. The cost of personnel is $26.00 an hour and other costs are figured at $10.00 per hour, with an additional 30 minutes assigned for travel. Three people work on the mowing crew. After a period of assessment and evaluation, the following standards are established:

- Gang mowing at 8 acres per hour

- 42-inch hand mowing at 2.2 acres per hour

- 22-inch hand mowing at .75 acres per hour

Sufficient time is available to accomplish all of the tasks, except the 22-inch hand mowing. Either the standard, the time available for the work, or the equipment must be modified.

Step 4: Determine the frequency with which work must be completed.

Determining costs is, in part, a decision on how frequently particular work needs to be done. Frequency of recurring tasks and of annual tasks is based on need and the level of quality the particular task has assigned to it. Using the mowing example, the standard for cutting is that the grass will be cut when it reaches six inches in height. In a normal year, that would be every 10 days from late April through mid-October. If, however, it rains more than normal, the grass will grow more quickly, and mowing may occur every eight days instead of every 10. This alteration will require a budget adjustment. It will also require a workload adjustment, as the mowing crew will not be able to accomplish other tasks that may have been assigned to them. Just the opposite would occur in a low-rain year, when mowing might only occur on demand, maybe as infrequently as every three weeks. More than likely, the mowing crew's responsibilities would change dramatically, and they might have to water new trees and turf areas to preserve them through a drought. At best, the budget manager must work on what she believes will occur. In those activities not affected by weather, the budget planning can be more accurate, but nonetheless, the budget manager must anticipate that things will not always go as planned.

Step 5: Organize budget.

When all of the performance budget steps are completed, the budget manager or budget preparation officer compiles the budget. Table 10.6 depicts a type of format for a performance budget.

Activity	work unit	cost per work unit	number of work units	frequency	no. times	total cost
softball diamond preparation	per diamond	$9.45	18	daily	98	$16,670
gang mowing	per acre	$4.45	800	10 days	12	$42,720
hand mowing	per acre	$6.50	120	10 days	12	$9,360
tree planting	per tree	$6.25	1,200	once a year	1	$7,500
pool cleaning	per pool	$15.60	3	7 days	15	$702
trash pickup	per day	$17.00	1	daily	120	$2,040
sign installation	per sign	$32.00	40	as required	1	$1,280
Total						$80,272

Table 10.6. Performance budget format.

New Directions in Performance Budgets

In recent years, public agencies have made major advances in quantifying outcomes. While performance budgeting follows the same process previously described, it is also linked to strategic planning. One of the key elements of a performance budget is its collection of adequate performance data, and, while this collection is routinely done in the private sector, it is an approach that is relatively new to the public sector. Existing results have been less than convincing to many budget managers, but processes continue to be refined. The key difference in performance-based budgeting *is the asking of a different set of questions.* In traditional object classification budgeting, budget managers ask what it will take to complete a particular task. In performance budgeting, the first question asked is "What is the outcome to be achieved?" The outcomes become the basis for performance measures. For example, the question might be "How many softball teams will play in the summer?" The outcomes are defined through a modified strategic planning process that considers the critical issues facing the agency, along with the organization's capabilities and input from stakeholders.

Minnesota's state government reported that it had been involved in performance budgets off and on for 25 years, but only recently has the system been reintroduced and begun to show success. Even with the performance mandate for recent budgets, the state determined that many agencies reported existing data in new ways to emphasize performance, although agencies usually did not provide outcome-based rationales when making proposals for new spending initiatives. "It will likely take time for agencies to develop a consensus on appropriate measures of performance and collect reliable supporting data" (Minnesota report on Performance Budgeting). Most public administrators agree that performance budgeting is a growing trend in public and private agencies and that measurement techniques will be refined.

Running Budget

A running budget has become more common among nonprofit organizations and businesses, as they attempt to adjust budgets to changing revenue streams. The running budget reflects more of a way of managing expenditures than it does constructing a budget. The budget can be constructed in any format, but decisions about expenditures are made on a scheduled basis throughout the fiscal year. If revenues exceed expectations, the budget can be adjusted to reflect the increased revenue. If revenues decline, the budget can be reduced to accommodate the decrease in income. There are some distinct disadvantages to this type of budget. First, budget managers never know from day to day exactly what their budget will be. Second, good decision making is hampered when the focus of decisions appears to be on revenue rather than on needs. Third, budget managers may be encouraged to make big purchases early to ensure that their major items are secured. This can lead to a mind-set in the organization that is not conducive to stability or growth.

On the positive side, a running budget allows an organization that experiences negative financial growth to be responsive to that situation by appropriately reducing costs. In addition, the organization does not extend itself beyond its capabilities and also recognizes a responsibility to its legislative body and to its constituents by not incurring debt. This type of budget is most often seen in organizations experiencing or anticipating significant declines in funds available for the operating budget.

Step 1: Construct the operating budget.

Any budget format can be used, whether it be an object classification, line item, program, or performance budget. The principles for construction are similar to those for any of the other budget formats. As suggested, the change comes in the administration of the budget. When the budget preparation is complete, it is submitted to the legislative body for review, modification, and ultimate adoption.

Step 2: Determine frequency of budget reporting.

The essence of the running budget is that it helps the organization to know always the status of its expenditures and revenues and to make adjustments in authorized expeditures. Adjusting expenditures at multiple times during the fiscal year allows the organization to adjust its budget when revenues are uncertain. Adjustments can occur on a daily, weekly, bi-weekly, monthly, or quarterly basis. The decision of frequency will be determined in great part by the anticipated variance in revenues and how often revenues are received. A historical analysis provides a great deal of information for making this decision. If it is a membership-based organization, and membership dues are received on a scheduled basis, anticipated revenues might be predetermined. If, for example, dues statements are sent out quarterly, then the organization can project on a quarterly basis its progress towards achieving its revenue goals. Under these circumstances, it may only be necessary to do a budget adjustment on a quarterly basis.

Step 3: Establish spending limits.

Establishing spending limits is a common tool of budget preparation officers as they attempt to lighten the impact of concentrated spending by the organization. In a running budget, it is particularly important. Each part of the organization will need to negotiate levels of spending in any given time period. Arbitrarily allowing the different parts of the organization to spend one-fourth of their budget per quarter does not take into account the special needs of the different parts of the organization. The administrative branch might easily spend one-fourth of its budget each quarter, but the convention division might spend 60 percent of its budget in the second quarter and the other 40 percent over the next three quarters. Creating an acceptable balance of spending across the different parts of the organization requires a thorough understanding of the budget process. Of necessity, it must be negotiated with the budget managers throughout the organization.

Step 4: Determine how often the budget will be adjusted.

Making budget adjustments based on actual revenue and expenditures is the heart of the running budget process. On the basis of the same criteria discussed in step 2, the legislative/policy body must determine how often the budget will be adjusted. Typically, budget adjustments will be made in both the revenue and expenditure portions of the operating budget. A quarterly basis is the most frequently accepted adjustment period; however, in a highly volatile budget situation, adjustments can be made more frequently. Historical and current information must be provided to the legislative body, along with recommendations for adjustment. A clear rationale should be made for the adjustment, along with a discussion of how the adjustments will affect programs, services, and outcomes.

Zero-Based Budgeting

A zero-based budget is so named because it assumes that the organization starts each fiscal year as if it doesn't have an existing budget. While this isn't entirely true, its purpose is to allow the sport and leisure service organization to look at everything it does and value its importance to the organization and its stakeholders. It allows the organization to look at all of its operations, activities, and functions and to justify each one. In doing so, it promotes the reallocation of funds from lower priorities to higher priorities. The zero-based budget is an effort to be responsive to changing needs of the organization and of those it serves. This budget format is designed to facilitate competition among units and functions. Figure 10.4 illustrates the zero-based budgeting approach.

Zero-based budgeting is a private-sector budget format developed by Texas Instruments. Jimmy Carter adapted this budget process for Georgia's state government, and when he became president, it was brought to the federal level. There have been some concerns about its use at the state level and its ability to deal with ongoing, legislatively funded programs at that level. It has essentially disappeared at the federal level, but remains a frequently used format at the local level and in commercial enterprise.

Assumptions of Zero-Based Budgeting

Several assumptions are made about an organization's capability to implement zero-based budgeting. First, it is assumed that the organization can clearly define goals and objectives for the entire organization. This is a sometimes daunting task that requires considerable attention at each level of the organization. Second, it is assumed that there is adequate budget preparation time. Zero-based budgeting is a time-consuming task. If the organizational members do not have time to contribute to it, then it should not be embarked upon. Third, there will be an impact upon the morale of the organization as a result of increased competition for available budget funds. Fourth, zero-based budgeting is internally focused and does not always take into account external needs or requirements. Fifth, zero-based budgeting assumes a significant cost in terms of time, money, and effort as the initial transition is made. There will be ongoing costs for time and effort as the process progresses.

Step 1: Defining goals and objectives and decision units

Program and budget goals and objectives are established and decision units are defined at the program/service level. The development of measurable goals and objectives is based upon outcomes and user/customer defined expectations. Great care must be taken in developing these goals so that effective measurement can occur. Goals are developed at multiple levels and assumed to be part of a top-down process. The organization's goals are developed at the CEO level jointly with the legislative or policy body. These goals become the guiding or overarching goals of the organization. All other goals and objectives developed need to be consistent with these goals. Ultimate measurement of the effectiveness and appropriateness of programs and services will be based on these goals. At each descending level, goals are developed to provide direction and to ensure consistency.

A *decision unit* is a point at which budget and programming decisions are made—ideally, at the lowest reasonable level in the organization. In aquatics, for instance, the decision unit may not be the whole aquatics program, but, rather, could be divided into learn-to-swim, swim club, adult lessons, and youth lessons. At a later analysis level, these could be com-

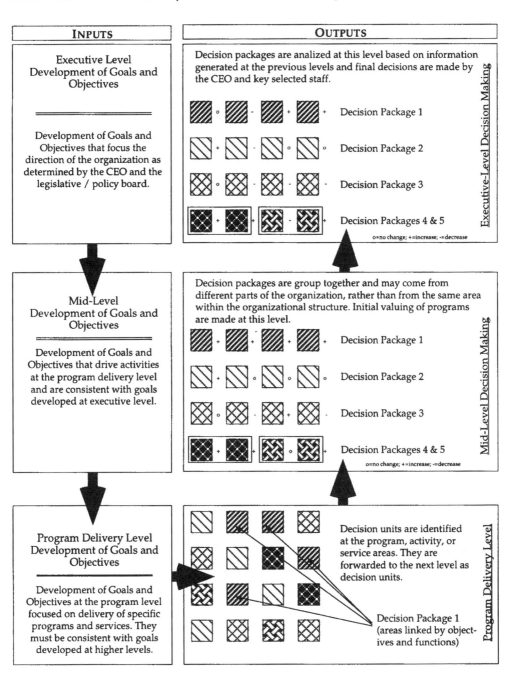

Figure 10.4. The zero-based budgeting process.

bined or remain separate. Budget requests cannot be based on previously experienced levels of expenditures. To do so reduces the effectiveness and purpose of zero-based budgeting. Table 10.7 depicts an example decision unit worksheet without the fiscal information.

The decision units do not need to be consistent with the organizational structure, but frequently are. In a YMCA, the initial decision unit would likely be at the program-manager level. If a program manager had responsibility for multiple program areas, however, the decision unit could be modified. It would seem logical that, wherever possible, the decision unit and organizational structure would be consistent.

Step 2: Decision assessment and analysis

Step 2 involves analyzing and assessing each decision unit within the framework as a *decision package.* The decision package becomes the building block of zero-based budgeting. The decision package becomes a cluster of decision units related to the accomplishment of the unit's goals and objectives. As the budget process moves up the organization, decision packages can be grouped according to their commonality of objectives. This grouping could result in decision units not remaining within the structure of the organization.

Managers at the program-delivery level must look at alternative means of achieving objectives, as well as determining appropriate levels of service and use of resources. The notion of zero-based budgeting is meant to encourage managers to focus their energies on those

Program Area: Learn-to-Swim	Division: Aquatics	Fiscal Year: 2001
Level of Services Currently Provided	Justification for current/expanded level of service	Funding Recommendation(s)
• Lessons offered throughout the year with an emphasis on summer • Lessons offered for beginners through advanced swimmers • Lessons offered to pre-school through senior citizen • Summer services offered at 11 community pools 3 times a week • Academic year services offered at 3 indoor pools after school and evening for youth and during day as well as evening for adults • Currently meet Red Cross learn-to-swim guidelines	The learn-to-swim program has been offered for over 40 years by the department. Each year more than 5,000 youth and adults are served by the program. This is the only community-wide program provided. The school district does not provide learn-to-swim and the YMCA caters to a smaller number of individuals. The program has consistently paid for itself and has contributed to a positive cash flow in the aquatics division.	It is recommended that funding be retained at the current level. Any reduction in funding would result in a degradation of a program that has high community visibility and provides a recognized service to the community. Revenue levels could be increased if fees are increased. A study to determine the impact of a fee increase would be recommended.

Table 10.7. Decision unit worksheet example.

activities that are perceived as most critical to the organization's mission and vision. Activities that do not directly contribute to the vision and mission are either eliminated or receive reduced levels of funding. Such decisions encourage managers to set up levels of service and to seek alternative funding.

Included in the decision process are variables such as workload, performance measures, cost-benefit associated with each level of service, revenue, and expenditures. Each decision package can receive one of four actions: (1) increased resources, (2) maintenance of current resources, (3) reduced resources, or (4) elimination of resources. Additionally, decision makers are afforded alternatives to accomplish each decision unit. The alternatives allow decision makers to determine the most appropriate approaches for the delivery and level of services.

Step 3: Ranking decision packages

Once all of the data have been generated, the ranking of decision packages occurs at predetermined levels. Decisions are based on consistency with the organization's goals and objectives, determined cost-effectiveness, how well each decision package meets the needs of the users, availability of funds, and any predetermined policy guidelines. Rankings of decision units are made and funds are allocated to the decision units. Once funds are allocated to decision units, they are returned to the appropriate organizational level for budget action.

If a decision unit does not receive the level of funding necessary for sustaining it, the program manager will already have created alternatives for funding at reduced or increased levels, either for different delivery approaches, or for no funding at all. The decision process will put such alternative approaches into action.

Step 4: Budget request formulated

The budget format may follow any of the preexisting budget formats previously discussed. It is submitted through normal processes to the budget preparation officer and the CEO for final submission to the policy or legislative body.

Advantages and Disadvantages of Zero-Based Budgeting

There are several advantages to using a zero-based budgeting format. First, in zero-based budgeting, all programs start out on equal footing at the beginning of the process—no single program is favored over another. Programs, services, and functions all have the same opportunity to receive funding. Second, budget decision makers will find that more detailed information is generated than it is with other budget formats. When implemented properly, there is a systematic and well-conceived allocation process. Third, the goals of the organization and its individual and collective activities are under constant review and prioritization. As such, individuals who work in this format are more actively engaged in goal setting, goal attainment, and goal negotiation. Fourth, this budget format provides service level options where none may have existed before. It requires that program managers look at alternative program and service delivery methods and at what level each program or service should be delivered. Finally, it has been suggested that zero-based budgeting eliminates waste in the organization by eliminating or reducing funding for programs that are not meeting the needs of the organization or its clientele.

A number of disadvantages have been suggested for zero-based budgeting. Most significant among the reported disadvantages is that it has not lived up to its promises. In instance after instance, there were high levels of budget pre-activity as individuals and groups attempted to influence the decision making—sometimes with high levels of influence in the outcomes. The results provided outcomes similar to the pre-zero-based budgeting format and also what appeared to be no perceptible change in the decision making. The second major disadvantage of zero-based budgeting concerns information overload. Decision making is ultimately top-down in zero-based budgeting, and everything generated at the lower levels is designed to aid the decision maker. One governor found himself with 11,000 decision packages, far more than any management scientist would recommend and more than can be effectively dealt with by any one individual.

Modified Zero-Based Budgeting

While zero-based budgeting, as a single budget format for an organization, has fallen out of favor, it remains in use in a modified form as a supplemental format in many organizations. For example, in Phoenix, Arizona, city departments submit an estimate (called the base) of the costs associated with providing their current levels of service for the following year. City budget and research staff review the base budget submissions to ensure that only that funding necessary for current service levels is included in the department's base. The review is called a "technical review" because of its nonprogrammatic line-item-by-item review of a department's budget. A department's base funding may differ from its current-year funding for a variety of reasons. For example, an increase or a decrease in utilities would be reflected in the base.

In addition to base budget submissions, departments submit 5 percent to 10 percent of their following year's base budget for potential elimination. These submissions are called "base reductions," and they represent the department's lowest-priority activities. At the same time, departments are also asked to submit any requests for new, restored, or expanded programs, which are called "supplemental budget requests."

The base reductions and supplemental requests include all costs associated with a specific program or service, such as the cost of operating a new swimming pool. Costs for pool operation would include those associated with personnel, chemicals, building maintenance, supplies, and utilities.

When the base reductions and supplemental requests are submitted, they are ranked together according to the department's priorities. The department's ranking indicates whether it would be possible to make a base reduction in order to add a new program. The ranking also indicates which supplemental programs and base reductions are most critical to the department.

Budget Presentation

The budget presentation is the culmination of the budget preparation process. In sport and leisure service organizations, the CEO presents the proposed budget to the legislative/policy body. Budget proposals usually include a cover letter from the CEO, a budget summary, a detailed budget, budget explanations, and a capital budget. The larger the organization and the more complex the budget, the longer the budget presentation. The budget presentation may involve multiple constituencies including a board, public hearings, other citizen participation, and the legislative authority.

The desired outcome of any budget presentation is the adoption of the budget by the legislative body. This usually occurs after an exhaustive review of the budget proposal by the legislative body. The legislative body can make adjustments to the budget to reflect special interests or concerns. After adoption of the budget, the sport and leisure service organization can begin its administration with the commencement of the fiscal year.

Summary

Budget formats allow sport and leisure service organization managers and administrators to view a budget from a particular perspective. These formats may be combined for differing purposes. The object classification budget is the most common of all budget formats for sport and leisure service organizations. Other common and effective budget formats include the program budget, the performance budget, the running budget, and the zero-based budget.

References

Aronson, J. R., and Schwartz, E. 1996. *Management policies in local government finance.* Washington, DC: International City/County Management Association.

Kelsey, C. W., Gray, H. R., and McLean, D. D. 1993. *The budget process in parks and recreation: A case study manual.* Reston, VA: American Alliance for Health, Physical Education, Recreation and Dance.

Listro, J. P. 1998. *Nonprofit organizations account and reporting.* (2nd ed.). Dubuque, IA: Kendall/Hunt Publishing Company

Rabin, Jack (Ed.) 1992. *Handbook of public budgeting.* New York: Marcel Dekker, Inc.

Reed, B. J., and Swain, J. W. 1997. *Public finance administration.* Thousand Oaks, CA: Sage Publications.

Section D

Long-Term Financial Planning

The final section of this book on financial management for sport and leisure service organizations addresses the need for financial managers to be able to plan for new enterprises and/or expand existing activities. The business plan is an important long-term planning document that can be instrumental in generating sufficient funds to implement its design. Chapter 11 describes each element of the business plan and explains how the information contained therein is used by the plan developer, suppliers, investors, and creditors. The business plan provides essential support for and documentation of claims and analyses that are used in generating resources needed for capital development. Capital budgeting in general and as it applies to the public, private nonprofit, and commercial sport and leisure service enterprise is discussed in Chapter 12.

Chapter 11

Business Planning

Introduction

The oft-repeated advice to sport and leisure service managers to develop and follow business plans is too commonly relegated to the "nice concept, but not for me" file. For some managers, this ignorance (the act of ignoring the advice) is based on ignorance (a lack of understanding or knowledge). Business plans, it is erroneously believed, are for high-risk, high-volume production companies which depend on major investments and have a high degree of accountability to investors. Just as erroneously, some sport and leisure service managers believe that business plans are master planning documents that establish general directions only for the entire organization and are of little direct relevance to specific programs or events. The business plan is an effective tool for the management of sport and leisure service organizations. Failure to develop and follow business plans at a variety of levels of operation is a serious management flaw, which this chapter is designed to help overcome.

A business plan is a written document which describes all aspects of an enterprise. An enterprise could be a program, service, event, or activity. The business plan differs from a program plan in its inclusion of detailed analyses of resource opportunities, requirements, and management functions. It is especially concerned with (but not limited to) the financial elements of the sport or leisure enterprise. It is, in effect, the management "game plan."

The business plan is a proven and effective tool for facilitating an internal evaluation of existing or proposed programs or services. It helps those who have dreams and aspirations to objectively determine the desirability and feasibility of their ideas. It helps to identify and consider all conditions that relate to the potential success of an enterprise. Business planning, like other types of planning, forces a manager to seriously consider everything that is necessary for the success of the enterprise. It identifies foreseeable problems and expresses specific commitments to the resolution of those problems. It also identifies available resources and articulates the intended application of those resources to the achievement of stated objectives.

Beyond serving this internal evaluation function, the business plan also helps to meet the information and documentation requirements of external providers of required operational resources. The plan states the objectives to be met by the enterprise and then outlines the chosen approach to meeting those objectives. In so doing, it allows investors, lenders, donors, regulators, suppliers, employees, and customers to develop confidence in the enterprise and, thereby, justify extending credit, permission, patronage, or other support that is needed for success. Readers of the business plan will view it from different perspectives and focus on those elements that are relevant to their interests. Bankers, for example, will read business plans and pay particular attention to descriptions of fixed assets and available collateral. This information helps to determine how well their loans are protected and how ably the borrower can repay loans on schedule and at the agreed-upon rate of interest. Suppliers, such as the owner of a sports stadium, will focus on market and competitive analyses and expect the business plan to demonstrate a reasonable expectation of corporate viability and longevity before entering into a long-term lease agreement with, for example, a minor league baseball team. Furthermore, prospective major charitable donors will study the management and product/service elements of the business plan of a nonprofit youth-serving agency to learn about how their philanthropic support would be used.

Format of the Business Plan

The following paragraphs describe the essential elements of and a commonly used format for effective business plans. Note that such documents do provide for the demonstration of creativity in presentation, and there is a wide variety of styles used in business plans for sport and leisure enterprises.

Title Page

The title page or cover page is used to identify the plan at a glance. Obviously, the name of the enterprise should be boldly displayed. Also, the name, address, and telephone number of the plan's author (or corporate agent for whom the plan was prepared) should be included on the title page. The aesthetic aspects of the cover page do deserve attention, but inordinate energy and resources should not be dedicated to this part of what is really a rather technical document. The entire business plan should be professional in its presentation, both visually and substantively, and the cover page is a good place to demonstrate this standard.

Figure 11.1. Sample business plan cover page.

Inasmuch as business plans articulate ideas that may provide a competitive advantage or should more appropriately be unveiled in a controlled setting, the title page should, where applicable, include a clear notice of the confidential nature of the document. If the business plan is a confidential or restricted-distribution document, then the restrictions should be clearly stated either on the cover or very early in the document.

Front Matter

Included in the front matter are all those parts of the plan that are organized for ease of reading. Following the title page, a transmittal letter or preface officially introduces the plan to the reader. This brief section (usually less than one page of text) can also be used to "hook" the reader by highlighting some major points of the plan that would be of particular interest. The preface is followed by a table of contents, which offers the reader an outline of the plan by listing all the headings and subheadings. In addition to its value as an overview of the contents of the plan, this table provides references to the locations of various sections in the plan. The front matter might also include a table of tables or a table of figures to further assist the reader in finding key information within the body of the business plan.

Executive Summary

The executive summary is a concise review of plan highlights that enables the reader to quickly get a sense of the nature of the sport or leisure enterprise and the resource needs of its management team. It must be brief enough (two to three pages) that even the busiest person could find time to read it, and it should be crafted in such a way as to capture the reader's interest and motivate further exploration and consideration of the plan. Although the executive summary is positioned at the beginning of the business-plan document, its writing should be done after the main body of the plan has been completed. Some business managers have also appended to the Executive Summary a "Fact Sheet," which states, in number form, the following:

1. the name of the sport or leisure organization and the program or enterprise covered by the plan,

2. the address and telephone number of the organization representative responsible for the program or enterprise,

3. the type of industry (Standard Industrial Classification) in which the organization operates,

4. the form of agency organization (government agency, proprietorship, partnership, or corporation),

5. the principal product(s) or service line(s) included in the plan,

6. any registered patents, trademarks, or service marks affected by the plan,

7. the number and names of founders, partners, corporate commissioners, and shareholders,

8. the length of time the enterprise and the organization have been operating as such,

9. the current and/or projected market share,

10. the funds invested in the enterprise to date and their source,

11. any additional financing required,

12. proposed terms and payback period for required financing,

13. the total value or net worth of the organization, and

14. the names of business advisors (legal counsel, accountant, others).

The Enterprise

The first section of the body of the business plan is designed to provide the reader with a context in which to consider all the information that follows. This important part of the business plan effectively familiarizes the reader with the history of the enterprise and the organization, provides insight into the current situation, and speculates about the future of the enterprise. Historical information is presented in the form of a narrative about how, when, and why the enterprise was or will be started, as well as an identification of the key individuals directing the activity and a description of the principal products or services to be offered. If the business plan has been developed for an existing activity, a discussion of the success experienced thus far should be included. The description of current conditions is limited to relevant circumstances, such as market opportunities, production capabilities, and competition, while speculation about the future takes the form of vision statements and articulated goals, objectives, and strategies.

The Industry

The preparation of this second section of the body of the document provides an opportunity for careful examination and description of the nature and scope of the industry in which the enterprise will operate. Since it is likely that at least one of the readers of the business plan has little familiarity with the industry or field, this part of the business plan is important because it brings all readers up to the same high level of understanding and awareness that the plan's author has of the environment in which the plan will be implemented. Other readers who are in the industry may already have that understanding, but, nonetheless, will welcome the author's demonstration of environmental consciousness.

The principal characteristics of the industry to be described in the business plan include its size, sales/participation levels, and performance standards. For example, the business plan of a public learn-to-swim program would include a description of the number of such programs offered in the community, region, state, and country. In addition, the total number of program participants, the time of year that courses are typically offered, and the number of badges awarded at each level of instruction would be useful information to offer.

This analysis of the industry will also identify the major participants in the industry and describe their market niches, market shares, strengths and advantages, and weaknesses or disadvantages. The manager of the public swimming program might, for example, explain that aquatic instructional programs in the area are offered by several agencies, including the YMCA, the Boys and Girls Club, and the Community School Corporation. She would then point out that the Boys and Girls Club and the schools do not offer summer programs, and the YMCA has a recreational orientation for its family-based membership. The public agency is targeting young adolescents in the summer season for a highly structured program of aquatic safety training. It will compete with the YMCA to some degree, but it has a competitive advantage through pricing and location.

Further understanding of the industry is promoted by a discussion of industry trends. This requires a careful study of past performances in light of past conditions, as well as speculation about future successes based on an educated guess as to how the relevant operating environment will be. Fortunately, many elements of the sport and leisure service industry are closely monitored, and trend analyses are readily available. For example, the trends in aquatic programming are discussed in a variety of publications such as the regular *Parks and Recreation* magazine special issues on aquatics. The business plan for the learn-to-swim program might emphasize and detail an industry-wide observation that interest in such programs is increasing.

Product/Service Offering

In describing the product or service that will be delivered to consumers, the business plan should focus on its unique features and emphasize its particular advantages. If a novel concept is being introduced, more detail will be required in its description than would be in the description of a product or service with which the reader is already very familiar. In this section of the business plan document, it may be sufficient to describe a proposed three-on-three basketball tournament with just a scant reference to the rules of play and play-down structure and a slightly more descriptive account of the scheduling, setting, and game format to be applied. Conversely, a proposed ice-sculpturing competition and winter festival would warrant extensive explanation of the purpose of the event, nature of the activity, schedule of events, qualifications for participation, warm weather alternatives, theme guidelines, site selection, security measures, etc. This is the section of the business plan that is used to ensure that its readers know exactly what the program, service, good, or event is that they are to consider while examining the other important information presented later in the plan.

If the sport or leisure product is not in the public domain and is protected by copyright, patent, or other proprietary rights, the nature of that protection should be described in this section. Any contract releases received or awarded should also be identified. It is important for sport and leisure service managers to assure the readers of their business plan that the products they "sell" are rightfully theirs to produce or distribute. For example, a sports merchandiser's business plan should state that his invention, the portable heat-generating arena cushion, is patented. If the cushion is to be adorned with the logo of a professional hockey team, the merchandiser will also need to articulate the rights he has to use the logo, as stated in the copyright permission or license agreement.

This part of the business plan also provides an opportunity to discuss the ways in which the product or service under consideration contributes to the realization of organizational objectives. It should include an estimate of the potential for this enterprise to grow, or, if it is a program within a larger set of programs and services, its contribution to the effectiveness, stability, profitability, and growth of the sport and leisure organization should be described.

Market Analysis

In the previous section of the business plan, the product was described. Of course, a well-defined product is of little value to the sport and leisure service organization if there are no consumers of that product. Potential consumers constitute the market, and understanding the market is vital to the success of the sport or leisure enterprise.

The business plan describes the relatively homogenous group(s) of individuals that might be customers, clients, program participants, or service recipients. This description should clearly establish that the target market is (1) large enough to warrant the offering of a program or service; (2) sufficiently distinct to guide product development, distribution, pricing, and promotion decisions; and (3) accessible to the sport or leisure service organization. It may be that the target market is made up of several meaningful market segments; if so, each segment should be described separately. Readers of the business plan will be interested in knowing who and where the market is, what makes individuals in the target market good customer/client candidates, and how successful the organization has been in the past in serving their needs.

It is likely that there will be some form of competition for the attention and resources of the target market. Significant forms of competition include the following:

- other sport and leisure services offered by the organization,

- services and products offered by other sport and leisure organizations with access to the same market(s),

- other discretionary activities available to the target market, and

- market inertia.

The market analysis includes an assessment of the strengths, weaknesses, advantages, and disadvantages of all major competitors, along with a statement of how the sport and leisure service organization plans to address the competitive challenge.

Based on the leisure service organization's understanding of the market's needs, constraints, and opportunities, as well as an awareness of the competition it faces in the marketplace, it is also expected that this section of the business plan will include a realistic and defensible estimate of the share of the market that can be attracted at different stages of the enterprise's development. It is understood that estimates are nothing more than educated guesses based on relevant information and certain assumptions. The assumptions, therefore, should also be stated.

Marketing Plan

Marketing plans are usually separate, extensive documents that relate market conditions to strategic decisions about product development, sales and distribution, pricing, and promotion. The business plan incorporates a synopsis of the marketing plan and provides the reader with a clear sense of how the organization will manage the marketing of its sport or leisure product throughout that product's lifetime. Since some elements of a full marketing plan are addressed in the preceding sections of the business plan, this section will focus on pricing, distribution, and promotion matters:

Pricing. The business plan should discuss the price that will be set for the sport and leisure service products of the organization. In addition, the following questions (among others) should be answered:

- How are these prices determined?

- What cost-recovery ratio(s) do these prices reflect?

- How do they compare to those charged by competitors?

- How will these prices contribute to achievement of the organization's financial goals?

- What will be the impact of price changes on consumer responsiveness?

Distribution. How, when, and where the sports or leisure service will be delivered to the consumer is also of great interest to the reader of the business plan. This section would normally include descriptions of the service area, season(s) of operation, schedule of marketable events, sales force, and locations of service delivery.

Promotion. The promotions mix (which might include advertising, publicity, personal selling, public relations, and/or sales promotions) should be described in order for the reader to judge the likelihood of the sport or leisure service organization reaching its target market and effectively facilitating a desired exchange. The promotions budget should be outlined, along with a process for assessing the impact of the various strategies employed in the promotional plan. Financially oriented readers would be interested in seeing an estimate of the conversion ratio. The conversion ratio is simply an estimate of the consumption (sales revenue or participation) directly resulting from promotion activities in relation to the costs of implementing those promotional activities. For example, the conversion ratio for a $2,500 advertising campaign that increased sales of karate lessons by $12,500 is a respectable 5:1.

Development Plan

If the product around which the enterprise is being established is not fully developed at the time of the business plan's preparation, then this section may be used to report on the status of the product's development. All costs associated with getting the product into a marketable form should be identified, along with development schedules.

The improvement, refinement, or expansion of existing or market-ready products may also be considered in this section. Again, development schedules and associated costs should be identified.

Production/Operations Plan

In the production of sport and leisure services, there are certain aspects of operation that contribute significantly to the success of the enterprise. They include location, facilities and equipment, and labor.

For most businesses, including sport and leisure service enterprises, the three most important details are said to be "location, location, location." Consider, for example, the obvious folly of establishing an alpine ski shop in the plains of west Texas, or a mountaineering school in Saskatchewan. A less obvious but equally disastrous mistake might occur in offering a public recreation program at a neighborhood park which, unbeknownst to the recreation agency, has become a place of clandestine drug distribution. Such mistakes do sometimes occur quite innocently, but the opportunity exists in this section of the business plan to show that every reasonable care was exercised in selecting a location that will contribute to the realization of business goals.

Any facilities and/or major equipment that is required to operate the sport or leisure service should be described in the business plan. Sometimes simple floor plans or photographs of buildings and rooms are included to help the reader to visualize those physical needs. Recognizing that not all buildings or equipment must be owned by the organization in order for them to be used in production or service delivery, a listing of leased and purchased items should be presented, along with the costs of such properties.

In general terms, the labor requirements should be described. Especially in the delivery of sport and leisure services, personnel are key to the success of the enterprise, and the labor needs of the organization deserve careful scrutiny. In this section of the business plan, the number of employees and their general job duties should be discussed. Sometimes, business plans also describe the qualification requirements of employees, their availability (i.e., the number of qualified people in the area that could be hired), compensation and benefits programs, and union affiliations.

Management Team

Even with a good product and a meaningful, identifiable, and accessible target market, a sport or leisure service or program can experience limited success because of managers who are not well suited to the enterprise. The business plan provides an opportunity to identify the management team and expound on that team's qualifications for directing the program or service. For many readers of the business plan, this information is as important, or even more important, than the details of the program, market, or financial structure. They believe that the right person managing the enterprise will make sure that the product is good and the financial aspects of the activity are sound.

An organizational chart focusing on the management structure could be used to illustrate hierarchies and functional responsibilities. Whether in chart form or as a narrative, the names of each member of the management team or program leadership staff should be listed, along with brief résumés and annotated job descriptions for each person. More complete résumés and job descriptions can be appended to the business plan if necessary or desirable. The purpose of providing this information is to help readers to develop confidence in the management and operation of the enterprise.

It is also customary to discuss the compensation package (salaries, benefits, other contract terms, etc.) that each manager will receive, although such disclosure is often unnecessary when the business plan is used as a planning and evaluation tool for programs and services that are just one part of a larger set of activities conducted by the sport or leisure service organization. It should be noted that, if the manager is already on staff and is compensated in a manner consistent with his previous position, declaring the manager's compensation for this enterprise may be a contractual violation or, in some other respect, considered to be inappropriate. If the manager is also the owner, a partner, or a shareholder in the organization, the level of ownership needs to be reported, as do any incentive stock options that may be offered.

In concluding this section, it is appropriate and desirable to list other individuals who are not a direct part of the management team, but may influence it significantly. This list includes consultants, professional mentors, advisors, accountants, bankers, and lawyers. This listing should also indicate the amount of compensation (retainers, consulting fees, stipends, honoraria, etc.) received by these influential advisors for their professional service to the sport or leisure service organization.

Financial Plan

One of the main reasons for going through all the work to develop a business plan is to demonstrate the advisability of investment in the particular sport or leisure service enterprise. Therefore, it is essential that the plan clearly indicates the level of financial investment that is required. Not only must the business plan state how much money or credit is needed, but it should also describe the type of funding that is needed. For example, the proponent of a new guide fishing enterprise may need $450,000 to acquire equipment, licenses, advertising, etc., but would like to have only $150,000 as debt (i.e., borrowed money) and the remaining $300,000 as equity (i.e., shared ownership). In order to justify the confidence of a lender or an equity investor, the author of the business plan should discuss and include (either in this section or as an appendix) the following financial documents (see Chapter 8 for examples):

1. Current Financial Statements (if the enterprise is already in operation)

    Profit and loss statements and balance sheets for the current and preceding two years should be provided.

2. Financial Projections (for new enterprises)

    Profit and loss forecasts, pro forma balance sheets, projected cash flow statements, and a break-even analysis for the sport or leisure event (or first three years of an ongoing operation) should be provided. Since these are projections and, as such, are subject to the limitations of current knowledge and optimistic expectations of future conditions, effort should be exercised in protecting decision makers from the enthusiasm of the enterprise proponent. It is generally considered wise to be as realistic as possible in making financial projections and then temper that realism with conservatism when estimating income. Conversely, realistic expenditure projections should be tempered with liberalism. In other words, estimate low for revenue and high for expenses.

3. Ratio Analysis

> Ratios are quantitative indicators of financial strength and operating success. Different readers of the business plan will focus on the ratios that interest them most. For example, lenders will be most concerned with ratios that indicate the degree of risk associated with extending credit to the sports or leisure service organization, and potential equity investors will be more concerned with return-on-investment indicators. Not surprisingly, there are many ratios that could be calculated and reported in this section of the business plan. Those that are of greatest utility in the development of a business plan for a sports and leisure service enterprise are briefly described here. Ratios of four general types are discussed. Liquidity ratios (also called solvency ratios) indicate the ability of a sports or leisure business to meet its short-term obligations. Activity ratios (also called efficiency ratios) are quantitative indicators of the ability of the business to expediently and efficiently exchange its products for financial resources. Profitability ratios show how successful the business has been during a certain period of time (usually a year) in terms of investment returns. Debt/Coverage/Leverage ratios measure the long-term solvency of the business. Examples of the commonly used ratios are as follows:

a. Liquidity Ratios

Quick Ratio. Used to estimate the ability of a business to meet its short-term financial obligations without selling off its inventory.

Quick = (Current Assets-Inventories)/Current Liabilities

Current Ratio. Used to estimate the ability of a business to meet its short-term financial obligations (assuming ability to dispose of inventory at full value). Sometimes called the banker's ratio.

Current = Current Assets/Current Liabilities

Debt to Net Worth Ratio. Used to compare the total financial obligations of the business to the investment of its owners. This is used by lenders as a measure of risk involved in extending credit to the business.

Debt to Net Worth = Current and Long-Term Liabilities/Net Worth

Current Liability to Net Worth Ratio. Another measure of the short-term risk associated with lending to the business.

Current Liability to Net Worth = Current Liabilities/Net Worth

Current Liability to Inventory Ratio. Used to estimate the ability of a business to meet its short-term financial obligations without disposing of its assets (other than inventory).

Current Liability to Inventory = Current Liability/Inventory

b. Activity Ratios

Average Collection Period. This is not a ratio, but is often included in the ratio analysis. It shows the average time (in days) to receive payment for products delivered.

Avg. Coll. Period = (Accounts Receivables/Sales) x 365 days

Sales to Inventory Ratio. Used to indicate the inventory turnover rate. Low numbers may indicate an overstock situation.

Sales to Inventory = Cost of Goods Sold/Average Inventory

Assets to Sales Ratio. This ratio is used in determinations of how well the assets are being utilized.

Assets to Sales = Total Assets/Total Sales

c. Profitability Ratios.

Return on Sales. This ratio is used only when comparing with similar businesses or with performance over a period of time. It indicates ability to generate profits from sales.

Return on Sales = Net Income/Net Sales

Return on Assets. Sometimes called the productive ratio, this index is useful for comparisons with other enterprises and with gauging the effectiveness of asset utilization.

Return on Assets = Net Profit after Taxes/Total Assets

Return on Net Worth. This ratio measures the ultimate profitability of the enterprise from the perspective of stockholders/owners. It indicates ability to earn adequate profits and should be higher than conservative (safe) investment rates.

Return on Net Worth = Net Profits after Taxes/Equity

d. Debt/Coverage/Leverage Ratios

Equity Ratio. This ratio indicates the extent of the owner's investment in the enterprise.

Equity Ratio = Equity/Total Assets

Debt to Total Asset Ratio. This ratio indicates the extent of the enterprise's borrowing.

Debt to Total Asset Ratio = Total Liabilities/Total Assets

The ratios that are calculated are instructive in themselves, but they also provide very specific information that allows the readers of the business plan to compare the current or expected financial condition of the enterprise with others in a similar class of ventures. In ratio analysis, comparisons are made between the enterprise in question and the class of businesses represented by an appropriate Standard Industrial Code (SIC). Unfortunately, but understandably, not all sport and leisure enterprises fit neatly into existing SICs. This means that ratio analysis can only provide a comparison between the proposed enterprise and others in an industrial classification that is judged to most closely resemble it. Table 11.1 lists most of the sport and leisure service–related SICs used in the United States prior to 1998.

Table 11.1. Sample enterprises from selected Standard Industrial Codes (OSHA, 1998).

4724 Travel Agencies
4725 Tour Operators
7389 Business Services
 artist's agents
 author's agents
 convention bureaus
 float decoration
 fundraising
 hotel reservation
 promoters of home shows
 promoters of flower shows
 tourist information bureau
 trade show arrangement
7911 Dance Studios
 dance instructors
 ballroom operation
 discotheques (non-alcohol)
 dance studios / schools
7922 Theatrical Prod.
 agents for entertainers
 booking agencies
 burlesque companies
 casting agencies
 concert management
 opera companies
 summer theaters
7992 Public Golf Courses
 golf club (non-membership)
 golf course operation
7993 Coin-Op Amusement
 juke box operation
 video game arcades
 gambling machines
 mechanical games
 pinball machine operation
 music distribution systems
7996 Amusement Parks
 amusement centers/parks
 kiddie parks
 piers, amusement
 theme parks, amusement

7011 Hotels and Motels
 bed and breakfast inns
 cabins and cottages
 casino hotels
 hostels
 hotels, inns, lodges
 motels
 resorts
 ski lodges
 tourist cabins
7929 Entertainers
 actors/actresses
 concert artists
 musicians
 magicians
 drum and bugle corps
 performing artists
 orchestras
 dance bands
7933 Bowling Centers
 ten pin centers
 candle pin centers
 duck pin centers
7991 Fitness Facilities
 health clubs
 spas
 gyms
7997 Membership Clubs
 aviation clubs
 beach clubs
 bowling leagues
 hunting clubs
 bridge clubs
 soccer clubs
 swimming clubs
 tennis clubs
 yacht clubs
 boating clubs
 bathing beaches (memb.)
 riding clubs
 rec. & sports clubs

7032 Camps - Sport/Rec.
 boys/girls camps
 dude ranches
 fishing camps
 hunting camps
 nudist camps
 summer camps
7033 RV Parks & Camps
 campgrounds
 RV parks
7941 Pro. Sports
 arena operations
 athletic field operation
 pro sport club / team
 athlete's manager
 stadium
 sport promotion
7948 Racing
 dog racing
 dragstrip operation
 horses, racing
 horses, training
 speedway operation
 auto/motorcycle racing
 jockeys
 race car drivers & owners
 racing stable operation
7999 Misc. Amuse. & Rec.
 amusement rides
 basketball instruct. school
 canoe rental
 carnival operation
 cave tour operation
 judo instruction
 lifeguard service
 river rafting, operation
 roller skating rink
 sporting goods rental
 swimming pools
 tourist attraction (natural)
 waterslides

In reviewing the list presented in Table 11.1, the difficulty in classifying an enterprise such as a resort-based recreation program becomes readily apparent. Should it be included in SIC#7011 (Hotels and Motels), where lodging and other major business activities strongly influence ratios, or might it more appropriately be included in SIC#7997 (Membership Clubs) because being a guest at the resort is, in fact, like having membership privileges in the exclusive resort recreation club setting? Perhaps the fitness orientation of the program makes it best suited to SIC#7991 (Fitness Facilities), or SIC#7999 (Miscellaneous Amusement and Recreation).

As noted earlier, this system of classification was used in the United States until 1997, when it was replaced by the North American Industrial Classification System (NAICS). The change brought into alignment the classification systems used in Canada, the United States, and Mexico. NAICS categories of relevance to sport and leisure services are identified in Table 11.2.

4511 Sporting Goods, Hobby and Music Instr.
  sport goods stores
  hobby, toy game stores
  music instr. stores
  sewing, needlework stores
4512 Book, Periodical and Music Stores
  book stores
  recorded music stores
4811 Sched. Air Transp.
  passenger transport (air)
4821 Rail Transport.
4871-9 Scenic and Sight-seeing Transport
  land transport
  water transport
  other transport
5121 Motion Picture and Video Industries
  production
  distribution
  exhibition
5141 Information Serv.
  libraries
5322 Consumer Goods Rental
  Video tape & disc

5615 Travel Arrange.
  travel agencies
  tour operators
  convention/visitor bureau
7111 Performing Arts
  dance companies
  musical groups
  theater companies
7112 Spectator Sports
  sports teams and clubs
  racetracks
7113 Arts/Sports Promoters
  with facilities
  without facilities
7114 Agents and Mngers
  for artists
  for athletes
7115 Independent Artists
  writers
  performers
7121 Museums, Historical Sites and Similar Inst.
  museums
  historical sites
  zoos
  nature parks

7131 Amusement Parks and Arcades
  theme parks
  amusement arcades
7132 Gambling
  casinos
7139 Other Amusement and Recreation
  golf/country clubs
  skiing facilities
  marinas
  fitness/rec. sports
  bowling centers
  other recreation
7211 Traveler Accomm.
  hotels and motels
  casino hotels
7212 RV Parks/Camps
  RV campgrounds
  RV camps
7213 Rooming & Boarding Houses
7221 Full Service restaurants
7222 Lim. Serv. Restaur.
7223 Special Food Serv.
7224 Drinking Places (alcoholic beverages)

Table 11.2. Sample enterprises from selected North American Industrial Classifications (U.S. Census Bureau, 1998).

Once the appropriate comparative industrial classification has been selected, a variety of publications can be referred to in order to find the industry standard for each ratio. The most popular publications of this type are the following:

- Robert Morris and Associates' Annual Statement Studies

- Dun and Bradstreet's Industry Norms and Key Business Ratios

- Leo Troy's Almanac of Business and Industrial Financial Ratios

- The Financial Survey of Canadian Business Performance

Ratios reported in these publications are often given for businesses that differ in sales output, asset value, or place within the range of reported ratio values. These reports recognize that, although they may reside in the same industrial classification, businesses vary greatly in their productivity, efficiency, and profitability.

Reporting the results of the ratio analysis is simply a matter of tabulating the calculated ratios for the enterprise and for the comparative industrial class, as well as providing commentary to explain major differences between those ratio figures. For example, consider the following:

HomeFun Recreational Services

Ratio Analysis

Current Ratio = 2.0
Industry Standard = 1.2

> Our ratio is much higher than the industry because we do not need to maintain large i and our short term obligations are incurr of service delivery. By policy, we maint reserve equivalent to 3 months operating

Debt to Equity Ratio = .83
Industry Standard = .87

> Consistent with industry standard.

Return on Sales Ratio = .05
Industry Standard = .07

> Our lower ratio reflects temporary inef normal at start-up. Three year plan pro on is ratio th ore

---

Figure 11.2. Sample format for reporting results of ratio analysis.

In reviewing the industry standards, it may seem that the statistics given are an indication of "what should be." In fact, they are merely measures of "what is." They reflect the current conditions of the entire industrial class and are, therefore, very useful benchmarks. However, a particular enterprise at a particular stage of its development may have quite different ratios, and what is most important is that the manager of that enterprise understands what the ratios and the comparisons are saying to the readers of the business plan. Table 11.3 displays selected ratios for three SIC classes of sport and leisure service business in 1996. Again, these are indicators of how things were, not necessarily how things should have been.

	SIC#7900 Amusement/Recreation	SIC#7991 Fitness Facil.	SIC#7992 Public Golf Course
Liquidity (Solvency):			
Quick (times)	1.0	0.7	0.7
Current (times)	1.4	1.1	1.4
Debt to Net Worth (%)	55.2	103.2	72.8
Current Liability to Net Worth (%)	22.4	34.6	18.8
Current Liability to Inventory (%)	389.2	379.0	274.5
Activity (Efficiency):			
Average Collection Period (days)	26.3	23.4	5.1
Sales to Inventory (times)	44.4	91.5	29.3
Assets to Sales (%)	109.0	80.1	120.7
Profitability:			
Return on Sales (%)	3.0	4.6	4.8
Return on Assets (%)	2.5	5.2	3.7
Return on Net Worth (%)	4.8	16.4	10.2
Debt/Coverage/Leverage:			
Equity (%)	55.7	41.5	48.5
Debt to Total Assets (%)	44.3	58.5	51.5

Table 11.3. Comparison of selected ratios* reported for three types of sport and leisure industries (Dun & Bradstreet, 1996).

*Ratios used are median values.

Appendices

Relevant material may be appended to the business plan. In deciding what to include as an appendix, the information needs of the reader must be the primary consideration. Material should not be included for the purpose of making the document thicker. Appended items should be referred to in the body of the plan and may include the following:

- Full résumés of members of the management team

- Management team job descriptions

- Product specifications

- Relevant photographs

- List of prospective customers or sources of customers

- List of possible suppliers

- Consulting reports and market surveys

- Copies of legal documents

- Letters of reference

Summary

The business plan reflects both the dreams and the careful consideration of the sport and leisure service organization. It can cover the entire range of services offered by that organization, or just one program or event. Business plans are just as valuable in public and private nonprofit organizations as they are in the commercial sector because they describe how the resources of the organization will be utilized to achieve its corporate objectives. Such an informative guiding document will naturally be of great interest and is, almost without exception, required by potential investors, suppliers, and creditors. Business plans typically include descriptions of the enterprise and its products and production capabilities. Also included are market descriptions and detailed statements disclosing the financial aspects of the enterprise.

References

Dun and Bradstreet. (Annual). *Industry norms and key business ratios.* Parsippany, NJ: Dun and Bradstreet.

Robert Morris Associates. (Annual). *Annual statement studies.* Philadelphia: RMA.

Troy, Leo. (Annual). *Almanac of business and industrial financial ratios.* Paramus, NJ: Prentice-Hall.

Chapter 12

Capital Budgeting

Introduction

Capital budgeting addresses a sport and leisure service organization's major expenditures for equipment, buildings, and land. For the most part, sport and leisure service organizations operate two budgets—one for operations and another for capital expenditures. Capital budgeting distinguishes itself from concerns with debt to operate daily activities and functions by focusing on debt and investment in capital resources. Capital budgets are generally approved annually at the same time as the operating budget, but annual capital budgets are just a part of a larger Capital Improvement Program (CIP) that may represent a five- to 10-year period of time. The CIP pulls together all of the identified major asset desires and needs of the organization over a predetermined period of time. Although the CIP extends over a period of years, it is reviewed and updated annually. Capital budgeting is conducted in similar ways in the public, private nonprofit, and commercial sectors. In the public and commercial sectors, sport and leisure service organizations may issue bonds for short- or long-term debt, while nonprofit sport and leisure service organizations would more likely use a capital campaign, which is an extension of the fundraising processes discussed in Chapter 7.

Capital Budgeting in the Public Sector

Capital improvement programs and budgets provide some important advantages to organizations. There are several reasons why capital budgets are adopted:

High-cost items could have a negative effect on operating budgets if they are included in an operating budget. Organizations desire a level of stability in their operating budgets that shows minimal fluctuation from year to year and responsiveness to public demand. Removing capital items eliminates major fluctuations in the operating budget and presents a more accurate projection of actual operating costs. For example, a parks and recreation department may have an annual operating budget of $2 million. It constructs a new band shell in a city park at a cost of $450,000. The construction is financed through a short-term debt (three to five years). If this capital expenditure were included in the operating budget, it would increase that budget significantly and give a false picture of the organization's financial health. Placing the same $450,000 in a capital budget tells the observer and budget manager how money is being used. Capital budgets are normally funded from separate capital improvement funds rather than from the operating budget. Some funds and sources may be similar, but other funds, such as general obligation bonds, revenue bonds, and special assessments, are available for capital projects.

Capital budgeting allows for planned growth and spending. It strives to anticipate specific needs of the organization and to budget for those in advance. If land is to be purchased in the future, current planning can anticipate that and set the stage for securing funds and planning for short- and long-term debt.

Capital budgeting provides focus. It allows the organization to put its energy into a few well-conceived capital projects and purchases rather than be distracted through an inefficient "shotgun" approach.

The Capital Budgeting Process

Capital budgeting allows for planning of expenditures that may have a significant impact on the sport and leisure service organization's budget. Capital budgeting is a four-step planning process that involves inventory of capital assets, needs analysis, cost analysis, and financing.

An inventory of capital assets is an essential first step in any capital improvement program. An inventory should include, at minimum, the following: (1) a description of the type of facility, land, or equipment; (2) the purchase price; (3) any improvements that were made; (4) its current condition; (5) the projected replacement cost for equipment; (6) the depreciated value; and (7) the projected end of the useful life.

The inventory allows the sport and leisure service organization to know, at any given point, the status of its capital assets. For example, if vehicles are purchased on a five-year cycle, the inventory can show what year each vehicle was purchased, how many will have to be purchased in the next five years, and any unanticipated need to purchase in advance of the five-year cycle. For a building, the inventory can show the date it was built, the dates and types of renovations made, its current condition, and its current use.

A needs analysis looks at the future needs of the organization and attempts to identify how those needs will be met and what capital investments will be required. For example, if a fitness club owner determined she needed to expand her facilities in the next five years, the needs analysis would be a part of the process of determining the type and size of the expansion. A needs analysis also looks at replacement needs. Most organizations assume a certain life span for the equipment that they purchase and use that consideration as they plan for the eventual replacement of that equipment.

The strategic plan should be a key element in the needs-assessment process. The strategic plan looks three to five years into the future, providing vision, purpose, goals, and objectives. It provides direction to the capital budgeting process. There are a number of factors that influence the outcome of the needs-analysis process. They include demographics; cultural changes; the local, regional, and national economy; legislation that has an impact (such as the Americans with Disabilities Act); community growth or lack thereof; technological obsolescence; disaster planning; and replacement schedules. Each must be taken into account in the needs assessment.

Capital development and construction are important elements of continuing operations and securing of new visitors.

Cost analysis is a decision-making process that helps to pinpoint where to spend available funds for capital improvements. It is not very different from most decision-making processes. The crux of the cost analysis is the determination of where to allocate limited resources in response to seemingly unlimited demands. The inventory and needs analysis set the stage for cost analysis.

Cost analysis provides key information for the prioritization of projects. There is no single method for establishing priorities. Organizations must take into account a number of variables and weigh each of them accordingly. Some of the variables to consider in the prioritization process include the following:

- relationship of the project to future needs;
- legal mandates;
- capital costs versus operating costs;
- costs relative to the benefits of competing costs;
- political costs and benefits;
- external funding potential;
- impact on improved effectiveness and/or efficiency;
- spin-off benefits;
- costs relative to competing costs;
- financial impact on defined stakeholders; and
- relationship of the proposed asset to defined beneficiaries.

A four-part approach to cost analysis is suggested. *Part 1* involves determining the turnkey cost of the project. For a new facility, such as a family aquatic center, the turnkey costs would include costs for services, construction, and fees as identified in Figure 12.1.

The proposed Family Aquatic Center would have a capacity of 4,200 people (4 percent of the population) and be open from Memorial Day through Labor Day (99 days). The facility would include a wave-action pool, zero-depth leisure pool, activity/water play pool, lazy river with zero-depth entry, flume slide, water-play apparatus, and a flo rider. In addition, the 16-acre facility would include parking for 1,000 cars, internal and external landscaping, support facilities, concession operations, a bath house, wet sand play, sand volleyball, and other amenities. The projected cost of the facility, less administrative costs, utility hookups, and access, is $14,700,000.

Land acquisition	Platting fees	Furniture and equipment
Architectural fees	Bringing utilities to the site	Attorney's fees
Engineering fees	Cleaning	Interim construction interest
Debt financing	Construction costs	Landscaping
Contingency fees	Contracting with a project manager	Insurance during construction

---

Figure 12.1. Cost items associated with a capital development project.

While those represented activities may not account for all of the costs, they represent a major share of the anticipated costs. Table 12.1 depicts the projected costs, as presented in a capital budget, for a proposed water playground. The budget includes all of the projected costs of the project.

Part 2 involves estimating the annual operating costs of the project. Operational costs occur after the purchase or after the project is completed and are typically funded from the operating budget. They include the cost of utilities, staffing, insurance, maintenance, equipment repairs, etc. While construction is a major cost to the organization, operating the facility requires a long-term commitment. The operating budget can begin as a "rough estimate" and then be formalized into a more detailed analysis later. Table 12.2 presents a sample operational cost and revenue projection for a family aquatic center. Failure to take the added operational requirements into account could result in serious budget problems. One midwestern community constructed a 50-meter indoor aquatic complex. When it was completed, the leisure service organization discovered that it had not adequately determined its operating costs. In order to cover those unanticipated operating costs, two full-time positions were eliminated.

Item	Size	Estimated Amount	Total
Pre-Construction Work			$3,500
1. Topographic Survey	Allowance	$2,000	
2. Soils Investigation	Allowance	1,500	
Demolition			40,000
1. Demolition of existing bath house and pool	L.S.	40,000	
Earthwork			4,500
1. Cut & fill on site (approx.)	350 cu. Yd.	4,500	
Water Playground			40,000
1. Water play equipment		40,000	
Tee Cup (1)			
Tumble Buckets (1)			
Rain Drop (1)			
Pool Construction			50,000
1. Concrete zero edge pool		50,000	
Water depth 0-18"			
Gals., 28,500			
Bathers, 250 – 300			
Support Elements			231,635
1. Perimeter decks	2804 sq. ft.	16,824	
2. Admission/Mech./Rest rooms	1,296 sq. ft.	142,560	
3. Landscape & restoration	8,360 sq. ft.	25.080	
4. Perimeter fence 6' high, vinyl coated	356 linear feet	7,170	
5. Pool mechanical	L.S.	40,000	
Utilities & Infrastructure			75,000
Construction Sub-total			444,635
Contingency & Fees			102,265
Estimated Project Budget			$546,900

Table 12.1. Projected capital budget costs for a water playground.

Part 3 is a review of the qualitative and quantitative benefits to be derived from the project. In some cases, projects offer a monetary return that may be estimated and compared with their cost. In commercial enterprises, the cost of capital projects is frequently compared to their payback period. In public projects, this may be one of multiple considerations. As part of this step, a cash-flow analysis should be conducted (see sample depicted in Table 12.2). Because the proposed project has not incurred costs or received income, the cash-flow analysis uses projections that are based on communities or facilities of comparable size and with similar services. The study depicted in Table 12.2 is a rough estimate rather than a detailed study that takes into account local variables.

Level	Bather Capacity	Percent Daily Capacity	Average Daily Attendance	Season Attendance	Cost Per User	Projected Operational Costs	Revenue Per User	Projected Revenue
High	4,200	50.87%	2,137	211,517	$10.80	$2,284,389	$12.87	$2,722,230
Low	4,200	51.61%	2,168	214,594	$2.33	$500,005	$3.13	$671,680
Mean	4,200	59.35%	2,493	246,777	$5.88	$1,451,051	$7.93	$1,956,944
Median	4,200	55.52%	2,332	230,852	$6.01	$1,387,421	$7.56	$1,745,242

Table 12.2. Estimated costs and revenue of a family aquatic center.

Public organizations also consider the "social benefits" derived from projects. This is less a concern for commercial sports and leisure service enterprises. That is why, for example, there are no commercial fire stations in most communities. They simply are not profitable, but their social benefit warrants their public cost. Assessment of the qualitative benefits of a capital project should include consideration of the following:

- Congruence with the vision and mission of the organization

- Long-range impact on the organization's strategic plan

- Effect on the organization's image

- Influence on stakeholders, including primary customers

- Compliance with mandatory requirements or policy

Part 4 requires an evaluation of the project and should be conducted when both the project's costs and the detailed operational and revenue budgets are available. There are two analyses that can be conducted that will help in evaluating the project. The first analysis addresses the need to earn back, in a reasonable amount of time, the original money invested in the capital project. This method of evaluation tells the organization how long it will take for the project's newly generated cash flow to pay for the cost of the capital development that generates the increased cash flows. If a new indoor tennis complex adds a fitness center at a cost of $1.6 million, and it generates revenue of $200,000 per year (after paying operating expenses), then the payback period is 8 years. The payback period is calculated by dividing the capital cost by the annual net operating revenue. Note that the payback period assumes a constant value of the dollar throughout the payback period. Is a payback period of 8 years good or bad? That is for the investor to decide. Whether it is good or bad depends on how long the organization wants to wait to recover its capital development investment.

Evaluation of the project can also be facilitated by calculation of the internal rate of return (IRR). This provides another way of describing the investment opportunity cost of the project. The IRR is calculated by equating the initial investment with the present value of the returns and solving for interest rate that validates the equation.

Initial Investment = Annual returns x $((1-(1+i)^{-n})/i)$

Where: i = the interest rate (IRR)

n = the number of years of receiving the return

Table C at the end of this chapter provides values for $((1-(1+i)^{-n})/i)$. Therefore, the formula can be rewritten as:

Initial Investment = Annual returns x T_C

A $1.6 million fitness center addition with a projected life of 10 years that generates a net revenue of $200,000 per year would have an IRR of approximately 4%. This is calculated as shown below:

$1,600,000 = $200,000 T_C

T_C = 8.00

From Table C, when n=10 years and the tabulated value is 8.00, i= approximately .04.

Once the calculations of the two methods are made, projects can be ranked. The payback method is the more common approach in this early judgment phase. If the IRR is calculated, then that figure should be compared to the organization's cost of borrowing. If the IRR is lower than the cost of borrowing, then the project may not be advisable. If, for example, the cost of borrowing the $1.6 million was 12%, then the tennis complex in the above example would not be built. However, a 3.0% interest rate for borrowing capital funds would greatly improve the chances of the tennis center project being approved.

There are two major approaches to financing any capital project in the public sector. They are referred to as pay-as-you-go and pay-as-you-use. The pay-as-you-go approach is the most conservative. It requires all the money needed for the project to be available before it is started. The advantage of this method is the avoidance of debt (and the costs of debt servicing). With the entire cost of the project being paid for in advance, there is no concern for the payback period. A disadvantage to pay-as-you-go is, however, that many of those who were taxed while building up the cash fund for the project may not ever benefit from its use.

The pay-as-you-use approach incurs debt for the capital project. Pay-as-you-use allows for the cost of the project to be paid while it is being used from revenues generated by the project or from funds generated through taxes, special levies, fees and charges for services, or other approaches. The argument in support of the pay-as-you-use approach is that those who benefit from the capital asset will be the ones who pay for it.

Capital Improvement Revenue Sources

Capital improvements usually require different sources of income than what is used for general operations. Table 12.3 illustrates some of the sources of income used for public capital improvement funding. While some public agencies may use the general fund to provide the necessary revenue for capital improvements, the nature and size of many capital improvements frequently make it inadvisable to rely on this fund. Most capital improvements involve taking on short-term debt and, in some cases, long-term debt. One of the reasons for taking on debt is that taxpayers and others who will contribute to the cost will not have to suffer a significant financial burden over a short period of time. A $10 million recreation center paid for over 15 years places considerably less annual burden on taxpayers than does the same recreation center paid for in 3 years. It places the debt into a longer payback period, allowing the agency to structure the debt so it has minimal impact on those who will assist in retiring it. While Table 12.3 demonstrates most of the commonly accepted ways of financing debt, it is not all inclusive.

Financing Source	Provides Funds	Repayment	Advantages	Disadvantages
General Obligation Bonds (GOB)	Immediately	By all taxpayers over a 5 to 30 year period	• Funds available immediately • Payments tied to benefits received • Potentially lowers interest costs	• Increased property taxes • Competes with other local services for limited resources • Separates payment from benefit
Revenue Bonds	Immediately	By users over 5 to 30 years	• Funds available immediately • Payment linked to benefits • Payment may be linked to those who use	• Increases rates or fees • Interest costs potentially higher than GOB
Tax Increment Financing Bonds	Immediately	By all taxpayers within defined boundaries	• Ties benefit to specific geographic area • Reduces impact upon overall capital budget • Reduces competition for limited resources	• Revenues dependent upon willingness and ability of individuals in area to make payments • Revenues dependent upon growth in assessed value
Bond Banks	Varies	By all taxpayers over a 5 to 30 year period	• Particularly helpful for small communities • Lowers cost of issuance	• Bond issuance may be delayed until enough communities apply
Certificates of Participation	Immediate use of land area	By all taxpayers over a defined period of time	• Allows land purchase over a period of time • Payments made on an annual basis • Is not recorded as formal debt • Does not impact on community's debt limit	• Hides debt of community to bond appraisers • Does not require a public vote, allowing for less public control
Lease Purchase and Certificates	Immediate use of facility or equipment	By all taxpayers over a 5 to 10 year period	• Provides a means of purchasing without issuing debt	• High interest rates • Payments may not be related to benefits
Real Estate Transfer Tax	Immediately	By individuals purchasing or transferring real property	• Provides a continuous source of income every time property is sold • Places burden for development and renovation on real estate purchases	• Unfairly taxes purchasing and selling home-owners for benefits received by entire community
Impact or Dedication Fees	Immediately	By those making a purchase of new property sold for the first time or by developer	• Allows for new residents in fast growing areas to pay for improvements, rather than whole community • Easy to administer and collect • Promotes growth management	• Only a one-time tax and does not promote long-term maintenance funds • Unfairly taxes developer and new owner for benefits received by entire community
Mitigation Financing	Immediately	By those developing property	• Places burden upon developer to provide open space in new development • Takes burden off taxpayer for infrastructure development • Provides local government with flexibility in land acquisition	• Places unfair burden on developer • Allows developer to provide land within development or in another location
Revolving Loans	Immediately	By rate payers over 12.20 years	• Makes funds available immediately • Ties payment to benefits received • Potentially lowers interest costs	• Increased rates or fees and charges • Reporting and administration may be cumbersome • May not be consistent with agency priorities

(Adapted from the Urban Park Institute and the Trust for Public Land)

Table 12.3. Revenue sources used by public agencies.

Bonds

The traditional source of capital improvement revenue for governments is bonding. In 1997 there were $1.3 trillion in municipal bonds outstanding and, at the same time, $2.5 billion in bonds had been issued for state parks across the United States. Bonding allows organizations to borrow large sums of money without a significant impact upon the community's taxing ability. Bonding provides immediate funding to a state, county, or community at a level it could not achieve in any other way. A bond comes in many forms, but there are two ways of classifying bonds. The first is according to the sources of revenue for repayment by the government, and the second is according to the method of retirement of the bond. They are named, respectively, *serial bonds* and *term bonds.*

Serial bonds allow public sports and leisure service organizations to make regular payments, usually annually, on both principal and interest for the life of the bond. A serial bond is similar to installment buying; however, governments typically pay a much smaller interest rate because their bonds are guaranteed by the taxing power of the legislative body. *Straight serial bonds* make annual equal payments of principal until the bond maturity is paid. Since the principal payments are made equal, the interest paid is much higher at the beginning of the period and much lower towards the end. This approach to bond payment suggests that the highest payments are made when the facility is new and has the greatest opportunity for revenue generation. The overall value of the payments by the government gradually diminishes over the life of the bond, even though the principal payment remains the same. Tables 12.4 and 12.5 depict the difference between payments on a serial and straight serial bond when interest is set at 4% and the amount received from the bond is $8 million.

Serial annuity bonds provide for an equal payment each year until the debt is paid. In the early years of a bond, the bulk of the payment is to cover interest charges. In the later years, the bulk of the payment is to reduce the principal.

A *term bond* is paid off with a single payment at the end of the loan period. The public agency must establish a sinking fund where monies are deposited over the life of the bond. The interest generated from the funds received from the bond and the annual deposits guarantees payment at the end of the borrowing period. This is a situation where the future value of a sum must be calculated in order to determine how much to allocate to the sinking fund each year. The term *bond* has fallen into disfavor because of the difficulty of managing the fund and attempting to project interest payments. Most states have legislatively abandoned the use of sinking fund bonds.

The second major method of classifying bonds is by the sources of revenue that will be used to repay the debt. Public park and recreation agencies have undertaken a variety of different methods to approach bonding.

The most common bonding method used by public agencies is the *General Obligation Bond (GOB)*. GOBs are issued by a public agency with the expectation of providing benefits to the entire community. Almost every community, has issued some type of GOB. Because the benefits of GOBs are to the entire community, the retirement of the debt is also spread across the entire community. Retirement of debt is most frequently accomplished through increases in real property taxes. General obligation bonds are particularly

Year	1	2	3	4	5	6	7	8	9	10	Total
Principle Paid	666,328	692,981	720,700	749,528	779,509	810,689	843,117	876,842	911,915	943,392	8,000,000
Interest Paid	320,000	293,347	265,628	236,800	206,819	175,638	143,211	109,486	74,412	0	1,825,340
Total Paid	986,328	986,328	986,328	986,328	986,328	986,328	986,328	986,328	986,328	943,392	9,820,340
Principle Balance	7,333,672	6,640,692	5,919,992	5,170,464	4,390,955	3,580,266	2,737,149	1,860,307	948,392	5,000	

Table 12.4. Cost of an $8 million serial bond on interest rate of 4.0% (numbers in $).

Year	1	2	3	4	5	6	7	8	9	10	Total
Principle Paid	800,000	800,000	800,000	800,000	800,000	800,000	800,000	800,000	800,000	800,000	8,000,000
Interest Paid	320,000	288,000	256,000	224,000	192,000	160,000	128,000	96,000	64,000	32,000	1,760,000
Total Paid	1,120,000	1,088,000	1,056,000	1,024,000	992,000	960,000	928,000	896,000	864,000	832,000	9,760,000
Principle Balance	7,200,000	6,400,000	5,600,000	4,800,000	4,000,000	3,200,000	2,400,000	1,600,000	800,000	0	

Table 12.5. Cost of an $8 million straight serial bond on interest rate of 4.0% (numbers in $).

attractive to investors because they are exempt from federal income tax. In some instances they may be exempt from state and local taxes. Further, GOBs are insured by the full faith and credit of the city, county, or state. This makes them a very secure source of income for an investor, even if the interest rates are not high. The major opposition to GOBs is the increase of property taxes. In public parks and recreation, this has been a particular challenge over the years. However, more recently the level of bonding has increased significantly, as well as a general public acceptance of the value of parks and recreation. The National Trust for Public Land reported that, between 1987 and 1997, bond sales increased from $270 million to $1.37 billion. Figure 12.2 depicts the growth over the 10-year period.

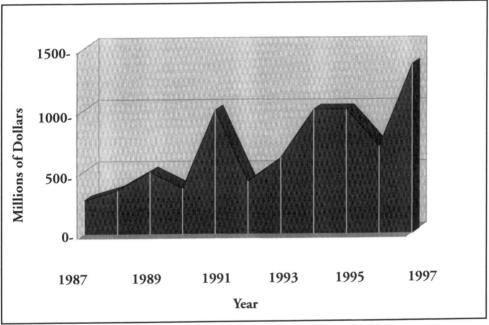

(The Trust for Public Land)

Figure 12.2. Parks and recreation bonds, 1987-1997.

Revenue bonds have received increased attention and emphasis over the last 25 years. Revenue bonds are used to finance a revenue-producing facility with the anticipation that revenues from the facility will wholly retire the bond. Increasingly, facilities such as aquatic parks, golf courses, artificial ice arenas, and recreation centers have been financed through this method. A major challenge of the use of revenue bonds is to ensure that there is sufficient revenue to both retire the debt, operate, and maintain the facility. In some cases subsidization has been used to finance operations and capital improvements. In most cases, however, the emphasis has been upon the facility generating sufficient revenue to cover both operating and debt retirement expenses.

Certificates of participation are authorized in about 25 states and allow public entities to purchase land and pay for it over a period of time. When a willing seller and a public agency enter into a certificate of participation, the public agency agrees to pay a specific price for the land and to make annual payments for a designated period. A certificate of participation does not require a public referendum and, most important, is not counted against the organization's debt limit.

Tax increment financing bonds (TIFs) allow public organizations to secure financing for projects that are enclosed within a political boundary. Commonly used to finance public improvements in development areas (sometimes called redevelopment districts), TIFs have been used to support park and recreation developments. They are most common in urban areas, but have been used in some rural areas. Implementation of a TIF plan freezes the assessed valuation of real property within the designated area. It does not freeze the tax rate. Taxes are collected on the property at the base level while investments are made by public agencies, and new businesses are attracted and property values thereby increase. Project costs or bond costs are paid for from additional sales tax revenues, personal income tax revenues, and the increased assessed value of the property. Bonds issued from TIF districts are paid for only on the projected increase of the value of the property, not on the full faith and credit of the city. TIF districts are common throughout the United States and may provide opportunities for the purchase and development of new park land, as well as renovation of existing parks.

Bond banks are usually organized at the state level for the purpose of allowing government entities which might not have sufficient borrowing power or debt rating to secure an acceptable interest rate. Bond banks allow multiple governmental entities to pool their bond requests into a single bond sale. By pooling their resources, smaller governmental agencies can issue a larger bond and secure a more advantageous interest rate. The public entities desiring the bonds are not purchasing them directly from the bond market, but from a bond bank typically established by a state. The Maine Bond Bank was established by the legislature in 1972 to provide a unique financing program, allowing Maine towns, cities, counties, school systems, water districts, sewer districts, or other governmental entities access to national money markets for their public-purpose borrowing needs. The Maine Bond Bank retains a high investment rating and is able to secure bonds at a low interest rate and then purchase bonds from public agencies. Local agencies submit an application to the bond bank, and it is evaluated on the purpose of the bond, estimated cost, construction schedule, state and local valuation, tax levy or user charges, demographic trends, recent financial and debt history, and economic stability. The local agency is able to sell bonds to the bond banks at their lower interest rates.

Other Capital Improvement Revenue Sources

Lease purchases and certificates are becoming more common among public sport and leisure service organizations as a method of financing projects. This alternative allows a public agency to join with private sources to finance major projects. In most cases, a nonprofit holding corporation is created. This nonprofit holding corporation can purchase, develop, and operate the property. Usually, however, the nonprofit will purchase and develop the property and lease it to the public entity which will operate it. The lease is an annual or multi-year lease with an automatic renewal and an option for the public agency to purchase the developed land at any time. The leasing organization makes the lease payments from revenue generated from use of the property. Then the nonprofit holding corporation uses the lease payment to retire the principal and interest. When the debt for the property is paid, it can then be given to the public agency, and the nonprofit holding corporation can be dissolved. The nonprofit corporation has no taxing power, but it can help the public agency to avoid a risky and expensive requirement to hold a public referendum on the capital project. In many ways, a lease purchase and certificate program is similar to issuing revenue bonds.

Real estate transfer tax is levied on the sale of certain classes of property, such as residential, commercial, and industrial. The tax generally increases with the size and value of the property being transferred (sold). Tax rates are controlled by state legislatures, but the revenues from this source of income are generally collected at the county level. It has become a particularly acceptable form of income for public agencies to accommodate the needs that urban growth places upon community services. The allocation of these taxes for natural resources development has become more commonplace. Florida and Maryland were pioneers in requiring that a portion of these taxes be used for park and recreation acquisition and development. Real estate transfer taxes are a fairly reliable source of income, since they are imposed each time property is transferred.

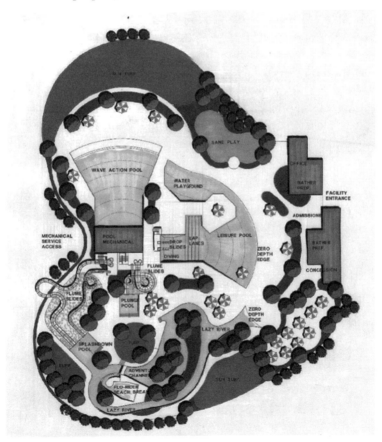

**Capital campaigns are usually based on well-thought-out
and preliminarily designed facilities.**

Impact or dedication fees are assessed by local governments in connection with new housing and commercial developments. Their purpose is to defray the cost of providing new or expanded public facilities that are necessary to serve the development. The fees typically require cash payments in advance of the completion of development, are based on a methodology and calculation derived from the cost of the facility and the nature and size of the development, and are used to finance improvements away from, but of benefit to the development. Local governments throughout the country are increasingly using impact fees to shift more of the costs of financing public facilities from the general taxpayer to the beneficiaries of those new facilities.

The impact or dedication fees supplement local government resources that otherwise have decreased because of diminished state and federal transfers of funds. Local governments have also used impact fees to delay or serve as a substitute for general property tax increases. Impact fees, when based on a comprehensive plan and used in conjunction with a sound capital improvement plan, can be an effective tool for ensuring adequate infrastructure to accommodate growth where and when it is anticipated. In Noblesville, Indiana, the Parks and Recreation Department receives an average of $100 for every new home built. During the late 1990s, this contributed about $100,000 annually to its budget.

Revolving loans allow an organization to secure a specified amount of money for a specified period of time. A line of credit is authorized, and the sport and leisure service organization can then draw off of the line of credit to finance specific projects or equipment purchases. Revolving loans usually carry a higher interest rate than other financial resources. Their value lies in the ability of the organization to have immediate access to a level of funds without requiring voter approval. Revolving funds have been successfully used with smaller, short-term project, where payment will be made from a secure source. It is not generally considered an effective method for financing major projects.

The development of signage in parks allows patrons to find
their way easily throughout the system.

The mitigation land bank has long been a source of development resources for public leisure service organizations. The bank allows developers to either dedicate land in a development for open space preservation or to identify off-site locations they will dedicate. The administering public agency and the developer work together to identify suitable land. The governmental entity may have the authority to create a land bank where developers can substitute money or land in another area of the community for land they are developing. In one Iowa community, the parks and recreation department worked with local developers to acquire a greenbelt along a stream in the community, preserving it for future generations. The use of the land bank is particularly useful when the developer has failed to meet the requirements of land dedication during the development phase of the project.

Capital Budgeting in the Commercial Sector

Capital budgeting in the commercial sector is a little different from that in the public or private nonprofit sectors. There are some key differences that need to be understood. Commercial sport and leisure service organizations bond for one of four reasons. Investments in new equipment to replace old, worn out, or damaged equipment are called *replacement projects. Cost reduction projects* focus on replacing existing equipment with new equipment that may operate more efficiently, be more state of the art, or be required to keep up with customer expectations. When investments are required to comply with safety and/or environmental regulations, they are called *safety/environmental projects*. Finally, *expansion projects* call for the expansion of existing services and resources.

All sport and leisure service organizations should have a long-range plan or a capital project that corresponds with the vision. Essential components of a capital project proposal include market forecasts, revenue projections, acquisition and construction cost estimates, anticipated operating expenses, and expected profit. The collected information allows the organization to have a better understanding of the long-term financial implications of the proposed capital expenditure. Although public and nonprofit sport and leisure service organizations may emphasize the merit approach to a capital project, a commercial sport and leisure service organization must emphasize the profit approach.

The capital budgeting process involves project evaluation and decision making. These are typically approached from an accounting perspective, with emphasis on the *net present value, cash flow,* and *payback period.*

Decision Processes

Several different decision tools are used by commercial sport and leisure service organizations to determine the potential contribution of a capital project to the financial health of the organization. One common method is to determine the *present value* of the returns generated by the project and compare that value to the investment amount. The net present value (NPV) is the difference between the present value of returns and the initial investment. In the decision-making process for a capital project, the investor wants to know if additional value is created by undertaking the project. If the NPV is positive, it means that the present value of the investment and, therefore, the project will add value to the firm and also increase the wealth of the owners.

To determine NPV, the organization must anticipate the future *cash flow*. Cash flow represents earnings before depreciation, amortization, and non-cash charges. For example, a fitness center invests $100,000 in new fitness equipment, supplementing what it already has. It is estimated that, as a result of the investment, an additional cash flow of $22,000 will be realized each year for the next five years. The expected market interest rate during those five years is 8 percent.

If returns are equal (i.e., the same amount each year), the NPV can be calculated by applying the formula:

$$NPV = RT_C - C$$

Where: R = annual returns

                C = the initial investment, and

                $T_C = (1 - (1 + i)^{-n}/i)$ or the corresponding value found in
                        Table C at the end of this chapter

In this example, NPV = $22,000 T_C – $100,000

                = $22,000 (3.993) – $100,000

                = – $12,154

The NPV is negative; therefore, the investment is not advisable.

If the annual returns are unequal (which is a more likely scenario), a different way of calculating NPV must be used. If, for example, the $100,000 5-year investment in a market where 8 percent interest is expected yields cash flows of $30,000 in year 1, $29,000 in year 2, $26,000 in year 3, $25,000 in year 4, and $18,000 in year 5, then the present values can be calculated by multiplying each year's returns by an appropriate interest factor to determine the present values. The present values are then summed, and the initial investment is subtracted from the total present value of the returns. This results in a calculated NPV. The interest factor to be used is found in Table B (see Chapter 1). Table 12.6 shows present values for the preceding example:

Year	Cash Flow	T_B	Present Value
1	30,000	.926	27,780
2	29,000	.857	24,853
3	26,000	.794	20,644
4	25,000	.735	18,375
5	18,000	.681	12,258
Total			103,910

Table 12.6. Sample data for NPV decision using unequal returns (8% interest).

The cash flows described above and shown in Table 12.6 have a combined present value that is greater than the initial investment. According to the NPV decision rule, this is a good investment.

Figure 12.3 illustrates how NPV is calculated using a timeline. The timeline illustrates the increased revenue at the end of each year, beginning with the $100,000 investment and a market interest rate of 10 percent. In this example, returns during each of the five years are $38,000, $47,000, $58,000, $70,000, and $79,000.

NPV takes into account the *time value of money*. The time value of money suggests that a dollar today is worth more than a dollar in the future, because the dollar received today can earn interest up until the time the future dollar is received. To account for the time value of money, the interest factor from Table B is used to determine the present value.

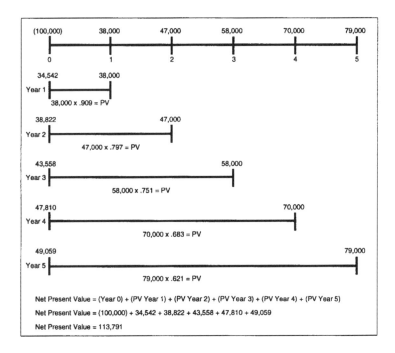

Figure 12.3. Net present value timeline.

Another approach to decision making is to determine the *payback period*. The payback period is the length of time it takes to recover the initial cost of a project. Payback is usually measured in years. The shorter the payback period, the better the investment. The formula for determining the payback period is illustrated below. This formula is used when the return on the project is expected to be consistent from year to year. If a project cost $100,000, and it expected a $22,000 return each year, it would take 4.5 years to pay for the project.

Cost of Project/Annual Cash Flow = Payback Period

$100/000/$22,000 = 4.5 years

When the return varies each year, as in Table 12.6, simply add up the expected returns for each succeeding year, until the total cost of the project is equaled. In this case, the payback period would be achieved early in the third year.

There are some disadvantages to the payback period approach to evaluating capital projects. A payback period approach assumes that cash inflows (or revenue) will exceed cash outflows (or expenses). Second, a payback calculation does not usually consider the time value of money. In a payback model, the interest the money could achieve is not considered.

Income Sources of Commercial Capital Projects

The same two approaches to financing capital projects in the public sector are also used in the commercial and nonprofit sectors. They are referred to as pay-as-you-go and pay-as-you-use. It was noted earlier in this chapter that the pay-as-you-go approach assumes the availability of all the money needed for the project before it is started. The pay-as-you-use approach incurs debt for the capital investment that is paid off during the use of the asset.

Corporate bonds are another common method of securing funds for capital projects. A corporate bond involves lending money to a public corporation. In return, the lender is promised a fixed rate of return on the investment, with the loan to be repaid in full at a future date. Corporate bonds are usually issued in multiples of $1,000 or $5,000. Bonds are sold with different *maturity* dates. Maturity tells the investors when they can expect to get their principal back and how long they will receive interest payments. Corporate bonds are divided into three groups: short-term notes, which mature in 1 to 4 years; medium-term bonds, which mature in 5 to 12 years; and long-term bonds, which extend beyond 12 years before maturing.

There are three types of corporate bonds. *Mortgage bonds* issue bonds backed by real estate and/or other physical assets. Just as with a home that is mortgaged, if the corporation defaults on the bond, the real estate and/or physical assets are sold to pay the mortgage bond. *Equipment trust certificates* are similar to automobile loans. Traditionally, the corporation provides 20 percent of the cost of the capital project. The balance is then paid off over the next 15 years. When it is paid off, the trustee provides the corporation with a clear title. The final type of corporate bond is an *income bond*. Income bonds only pay interest if earned, and to the extent it was earned. There is no set time when the bonds must be paid off. Usually, such bonds are issued by firms in bankruptcy. Additionally, the bond holders are frequently the creditors of the bankrupt firm.

Summary

Capital budgeting is an essential process for most organizations; it stands alone, in planning purposes, from the operating budget. Its focus is on long-term purchases of equipment, land, or facilities. Capital budgeting allows an organization to systematically address long-term needs and to plan financially for those needs.

References

Aronson, J. R., and Schwartz, E. 1996. *Management policies in local government finance.* Washington, DC: International City/County Management Association.

Kelsey, C. W., Gray, H. R., and McLean, D. D. 1993. *The budget process in parks and recreation: A case study manual.* Reston, VA: American Alliance for Health, Physical Education, Recreation and Dance.

Listro, J. P., 1991. *Nonprofit organizations account and reporting* (2nd ed.). Dubuque, IA: Kendall/Hunt Publishing Company.

Rabin, Jack (Ed.). 1992. *Handbook of public budgeting.* New York: Marcel Dekker, Inc.

Reed, B. J., and Swain, J. W. 1997. *Public finance administration.* Thousand Oaks, CA: SAGE Publications.

n/i	2%	3%	4%	5%	6%	7%	8%	9%	10%	12%	15%
1	0.980	0.971	0.962	0.952	0.943	0.935	0.926	0.917	0.909	0.893	0.870
2	1.942	1.913	1.886	1.859	1.833	1.808	1.783	1.759	1.736	1.690	1.626
3	2.884	2.829	2.775	2.723	2.673	2.624	2.577	2.531	2.487	2.402	2.283
4	3.808	3.717	3.630	3.546	3.465	3.387	3.312	3.240	3.170	3.037	2.855
5	4.713	4.580	4.452	4.329	4.212	4.100	3.993	3.890	3.791	3.605	3.352
6	5.601	5.417	5.242	5.076	4.917	4.767	4.623	4.486	4.355	4.111	3.784
7	6.472	6.230	6.002	5.786	5.582	5.389	5.206	5.003	4.868	4.564	4.160
8	7.325	7.020	6.733	6.463	6.210	5.971	5.747	5.535	5.335	4.968	4.487
9	8.162	7.786	7.435	7.108	6.802	6.515	6.247	5.995	5.759	5.328	4.772
10	8.983	8.530	8.111	7.722	7.360	7.024	6.710	6.418	6.145	5.650	5.019
11	9.787	9.253	8.760	8.306	7.887	7.499	7.139	6.805	6.495	5.938	5.234
12	10.575	9.954	9.385	8.863	8.384	7.943	7.536	7.161	6.814	6.194	5.421
13	11.348	10.635	9.986	9.394	8.853	8.358	7.904	7.487	7.103	6.424	5.583
14	12.106	11.296	10.563	9.899	9.295	8.745	8.244	7.786	7.367	6.628	5.724
15	12.849	11.938	11.118	10.380	9.712	9.108	8.559	8.061	7.606	6.811	5.847
16	13.578	12.561	11.652	10.838	10.106	9.447	8.851	8.313	7.824	6.974	5.954
17	14.292	13.166	12.166	11.274	10.477	9.763	9.122	8.544	8.022	7.120	6.047
18	14.992	13.754	12.659	11.690	10.828	10.059	9.372	8.756	8.201	7.250	6.128
19	15.678	14.324	13.134	12.085	11.158	10.336	9.604	8.950	8.365	7.366	6.198
20	16.351	14.877	13.590	12.462	11.470	10.594	9.818	9.129	8.514	7.469	6.259
21	17.011	15.415	14.029	12.821	11.764	10.836	10.017	9.292	8.649	7.562	6.312
22	17.658	15.937	14.451	13.163	12.042	11.061	10.201	9.442	8.772	7.645	6.359
23	18.292	16.444	14.857	13.489	12.303	11.272	10.371	9.580	8.883	7.718	6.399
24	18.914	16.936	15.247	13.799	12.550	11.469	10.529	9.707	8.985	7.784	6.434
25	19.523	17.413	15.622	14.094	12.783	11.654	10.675	9.823	9.077	7.843	6.464

Interest Table C $(1 + i)^n$

INDEX

A

accountant, duties of, 127–28
accounting
    in capital budgeting process, 217–20
    defined, 123
    firms, independent, 40
    funds, types of, 140–43
    Generally Accepted Accounting
    Principles, 39, 40, 123
accounts payable, 126
accounts receivable, 125
activity-based costing (ABC), 72
activity ratios, 197
added value pricing, 64
administrators, financial, 37, 43
advertising, 33
alternative budgets, 149
annuities, 115, 116
arbitrary pricing, 69
assessment measures, economic impact, 22
assessor, duties of, 39
assets, 124–26
auditor, duties of, 40–42
audits, 40, 42

B

balance sheet, 33, 124–26
base reductions, 182
bequests, 114
bids, 157–58
board of directors, 31
    as prospective donors, 109
    role in fundraising, 111
bonds, 211–14, 220
bookkeepers, duties of, 127–28
bookkeeping, 34
Boys and Girls Club, 191
Bradford Woods Outdoor Center, 81–82, 84,
    108
budget
    activity, 158–61
    calendar, 138–40
    cycles, 136–38
    formats, 143, 144–49, 163

    object classification, 163–68
    performance, 172–76
    program, 169–72
    running, 176–78
    zero-based, 178–82
    guidelines, 138–40
    materials, supplies and equipment
    costs, 157–58
    preparation activities, 143, 149–
    56
    preparation for grant proposal, 95
    preparation philosophies, 149–50
    presentation of proposed, 182–83
    project, 132
    review by CEO, 158
    statements, 130–31
budgeting
    defined, 135–36
    purpose of, 163
budgets
    and accounting funds, 140–43
    and contractual services, 156–57
    for fundraising programs, 111–12
    for promotional activities, 192–93
bulk pricing, 65
business plans
    appendices, contents of, 201
    defined, 187–88
    enterprise, describing nature of,
    190
    executive summary, 189–90
    financial profile, 195–201
    front matter, content of, 189
    industry, description of, 190–91
    management team, describing, 194–
    95
    market analysis, 192
    marketing plan, elements of, 192–
    93
    product development, strategies for,
    193
    product/service offering, description

of, 191–92
production/operations, describing, 193–94
title page, content of, 188–89

C
Capital Improvement Programs (CIP) bonds, 211–14, 220
commercial sector budgeting, 217–20
impact and dedication fees, 216
lease purchases and certificates, 214–15
mitigation land bank, 217
public sector budgeting, 203–9
real estate transfer tax, 215
revenue sources, 209–10, 220
revolving loans, 216
Carnegie, Andrew, 103
Carter, Jimmy, 178
cash flow, 218–19
causes, identification with, 31
certificates, 213–15, 220
charitable giving. See philanthropy
charitable lead trust, 115, 116
charitable organizations, 30, 83, 105–6, 108–110
charitable remainder annuity trust, 115, 116
chief executive officer
budget estimate review, 158
duties of, 42
The Chronicle of Philanthropy, 86
codes, object classification, 164–67
collaborations, 59
competition, benefits of, 35
competitive pricing, 69
comptroller. See controller
compulsory income, 47, 48, 53–55
concession operations, 57–58
consumer spending, 33
contract management, 58–59
contractual receipts, 48, 58–59
contractual services, 156–57
controller, 38
duties of, 39
independently elected, 40
cooperation, benefits of, 35
corporate entity, registration as, 30
cost centers, 170–71
cost-recovery pricing, 63, 70, 74
costs, calculating, 70–72

credit, 31
curves, supply and demand, 4–6, 9–10, 12, 13, 76–78

D
debt
ratio analysis, 197
service fund, 142
decision-makers
financial, 37, 39, 43, 97
grant proposals, 97
decision unit, 179–81
declining balance depreciation, 19–20
dedication ordinances and regulations, 53
demand
curves, 5, 76–78
estimating for unit pricing, 70
patterns of, 12
depreciation, 18–20
development projects, 21–24
director of finance, duties of, 39
distribution, influence on differential pricing, 75
distribution of services, 193
donations, 30, 32, 35, 95
duties of, 39–40

E
earned income, 48, 56–58
economic concepts, 3
economic impact assessments, 21–24
effort price, 68
elasticity of demand, 76–78
enterprise activities, 35
enterprise funds, 61
equilibrium point, 6, 8
equipment trust certificates, 220
equity, 125
evaluation surveys, 33
event reports, 132

F
fair market pricing, 61
fair market value, 50
federal government, as revenue source, 54–55
fees, 28, 32, 141–42
entrance and admission, 56
impact/dedication, 216
mandatory activity, 67
membership, 30
for private services, 66–67
program, 57
rental, 56

semester pass, 67
service, 35
single usage, 67
special, 58
user, 30, 57, 66, 72
fiduciary funds, 141, 142–43
financial management, 62
facilitating functions, 38
    organization contrasts, 34
    positions, 39
financial outcomes, 3
forecasting, 34
financial ratios, 33
financial statements, 124, 130–31, 195
fiscal policy, 61–62
fiscal year, 136–37
501(c)(3) charitable organizations, 30, 83, 105
fixed ceiling budget, 149, 164
The Florida Park Service
    Citizen Support Organization Hand
    book, 102
    narrative of charitable activities, 105
    views on support organizations, 117–
    18
    flow, 124
The Foundation Center, 85, 86, 92
Foundation Giving, 82
foundations
    and social service programs, 102
    501(c)(3) charitable organizations, 83
    grantmaking, 82–83
    resource publications, 85
friends groups. See support organizations
fund development
    phases of, 106–8
    role of, 103–4
fundraising, 31, 35, 55–56, 101
    board of directors, 111
    budgets, 111–12
    gifts, 111, 112
    goal setting, 110–12
    importance of, 102–3
    motivations for giving, 104–5
    sources of potential funds, 108–10
    special events, 109, 117
    support organizations, 117–18
    tax-law changes impacting, 103
    types of campaigns, 113–18
    future value, 15–17

G
Generally Accepted Accounting Principles
    (GAAP), 39, 40, 123
gifts
    life income, 115, 116
    outright, 114, 115
Government Finance Officers' Association, 56
governmental funds, 141–42
grantmakers
    categories of, 85
    decision options, 97
    seeking out, 86–87
    selecting, 88
grants, 30, 55
    administration of, 98
    contacting the grantmaker, 88–89
    foundation grantmaking, 82–83
    idea development, grantseeking pro-
    cess, 84–85
    organizations that assist grantseekers,
    85, 86
    overview of grantseeking process, 81
    proposal submission, 97
    proposals, elements of, 90–97
    resource publications, 85–86
    securing grant guidelines, 90
The Grantsmanship Center, 86
gratuitous income, 47–48, 55–56

I
in-kind donations, 95
income statements, 33, 124, 126–27
income, types of, 47–49, 55–58
inflation, 14
insurance policies, 115, 116–17
interest, 14
    tables, 25–26, 222
Internal Revenue Service, 30, 83
investment income, 48, 58
investments, 15, 32, 35
    future value, 15–17
    management of, 34
    present value, 17–18
IRS. See Internal Revenue Service

L
Land and Water Conservation Fund (LWCF),
    55
lease purchases, 214–15
liabilities, 125–26
licenses, 54
life income gifts, 115, 116

line item budget. *See* object classification budget
liquidity ratios, 196
loans
    borrowing money, 29
loan fund, 143
    revolving, 216

M

management, financial, 43
managers
    general, 42
    program, 37
market
    analysis, 192
    pricing strategies, 69–70
    segmentation, 28
marketing, 28
    fund development, 106
    plans, elements of, 192–93
markup, 70
meeting management companies, 32
merit, influence on differential pricing, 75–76
merit services, 66
Mill Rate, 51
mitigation land bank, 217

N

National Guide to Funding in Arts and Culture, 85
National Highway System, 55
The National Park Service, 102, 117
National Recreational Trails Act, 55
net assessed value, 50
net present value (NPV), 217–19
non-monetary resources, 66
nonprofit enterprises, composition of, 30
North American Industrial Classification System (NAICS), 199

O

object classification budget, 163–68
objective price, 78
open-ended budget, 149
operating statement, 124
operation plans, 193–94
opportunity costs, 68
organizational chart, 37, 38
    in business plans, 194
    for local government, 40–41
outright gifts, 114, 115

P

The Parks and Wildlife Foundation of Texas, 110
partnerships, 59–60
    for philanthropy and fundraising, 101
payback period, 219–20
permits, explanation of, 54
petty cash, 129–30
philanthropy
    characteristics of, 102
    by corporations and industry councils, 109
    defined, 101
    individuals as fundraising sources, 108–9
    third sector focus, 102
    See also fundraising
planned giving programs, 114–16
Planning-Program-Budgeting-System (PPBS), 169–70
politics
    corporate, 43
    influence of, 29
present value, 17–18
president, duties of, 42
pricing
    added value, 64
    assessing appropriateness and feasibility, 66–67
    break-even basis, 63
    challenges in establishing, 63
    charging the going rate, 74–76
    cost-recovery, 63, 70, 74
    elasticity of demand, 76–78
    to establish value, 64
    example of varied elements involved, 69
    for-profit basis, 63
    to influence behavior, 64–65
    market, 69–70
    monetary, 80
    monetary influences, 67–68
    non-monetary influences, 68–69
    objective, 78
    to promote efficiency, 65
    to promote equity, 66
    reference, 78, 79–80
    strategies, 33
    subjective, 79, 80

subsidization rate, 70
    unit, 70–74
privatization, 48, 58, 156–57
product levels, effects on pricing, 75
production costs, 63–64
production plans, 193–94
profit, 35
    centers, 60
    motivation and generation, 32
profit and loss statement, 124, 195
profitability ratios, 197
program managers, duties of, 37
project reports, 130, 132
projects, capital improvement program, 217
promotional plans, 193
property
    determining value, 50
    tax rates, 50–53
proposals. See grants
propositions, voter initiated, 48
proprietary funds, 141, 142
psychological price, 68
public services, 66

R
ratio analysis, 196–201
reference price, 78, 79–80
resource allocation, 3
responsibility centers, 171
revenue structure plan, 60–62
reasons to include fundraising, 102–3
revocable charitable trust, 115, 116
The Riley Foundation, 108

S
sales revenue, 57
service allocation, 31
social benefits, 31
special events, fundraising, 109, 117
staff
    budget-related issues, 151–55
    describing in grant proposal, 94
    involvement in budget preparation,
        143, 149
    lack of, 31
    role in fundraising, 110
Standard Industrial Classification (SIC), 189,
    198–99
stock, 4
    as available financial resource, 124
straight line depreciation, 19, 20
strategic planning, 149

subjective price, 79, 80
subsidization rate, 70, 72–73
subsidized services, 63
supply and demand, 3–14
supply curves, 4, 9, 12, 13
support organizations, 117–18

T
tax
    abatement, 50
    base, 50
    collection, 39
    credits, 30
    free status, 30
    law changes affecting fundraising,
        103
    rate expressions, 51
    real estate transfer, 215
    revenues, 32
    subsidies, 28
    user, 52
taxable worth, 50
taxation of public, 28, 30
taxes
    excise, 52
    exemption from, 29
    impact, 53
    income, 52
    local option, 52–53
    property, 39, 50–53, 52
    sales, 52
    special assessment, 53
    state and municipal, 49–53
    support groups, exemption from,
        117–18
Texas Instruments, 178
transfer payments, 54
treasurer, duties of, 38, 39
trusts, 115, 116

U
underwriting, 61
unit pricing, 70–74
The United Way, 137
U.S. Constitution, 28
U.S. Postal Service, 30

V
volunteers, 30, 31, 32, 42, 102, 110

W
work units, 174

Y
YMCA, 180, 191